Praise for *Q*

"Barnett's prose style is brassy and clear-eyed, with echoes of Anne Lamott. . . . Barnett's pluck will appeal to avid memoir readers, who will cheer her hard-won recovery, especially the steadfastness of her best friend, Josh. For those new to recovery and the people who love them, Barnett's story could be a balm. *Quitter* is both a warning and a reminder: If you can stop drinking after one or two beers, you're not better than Barnett and the more than sixty million Americans who binge drink. You're just luckier."

—Beth Macy, *The New York Times Book Review*

"A powerful recovery memoir, in part because Barnett uses her investigative reporting skills to examine how detox centers and treatment rehabs operate." —*The Seattle Times*

"Barnett is . . . candid about her failings, unsparing in the details . . . regarding addiction to alcohol. It can overtake a person's life, debase a person, drag a person into depths of disgraceful behavior; I'm living proof, she tells us." —*The Austin Chronicle*

"As addiction has become more of a national conversation, thanks in part to bestselling books like Leslie Jamison's *The Recovering: Intoxication and Its Aftermath*, women authors have been at the forefront. . . . Erica C. Barnett's memoir continues this important work. . . . By the time Barnett was in her late thirties, she's recovered and relapsed countless times, giving her a unique and eye-opening perspective about the language we use to discuss addiction ('Rock bottom is a lie,' she writes) and how few resources are available to people with addictions who continue to relapse."

—*Bitch Media*'s "17 Books Feminists Should Read in July"

"Journalist Barnett debuts with an intense account of her alcoholism, denial, and, ultimately, redemption. . . . Barnett's snappy prose carries the reader through several rounds of rehab before the final one sticks, pulling no punches as she goes. Barnett doesn't skimp on her life's lows (she goes to an interview drunk, and shoplifts wine) of how her ever-worsening problem caused her to lose her health, her job, and many of her friends, and alienate her family. . . . Emotionally devastating and self-aware, this cautionary tale about substance abuse is a worthy heir to Cat Marnell's *How to Murder Your Life*."

—*Publishers Weekly* (starred review)

"A Seattle-based political reporter recounts her tumultuous, nearly deadly dance with the bottle. . . . Barnett rises to the challenge with a witty, self-deprecating, sometimes snide voice. . . . If you're in the mood for a well-written, relatable, rock-bottom recovery memoir, this will hit the spot."

—*Kirkus Reviews*

"I can't think of another memoir that captures the nightmare of drinking relapse like this one. Erica Barnett's tale is brutal, maddening, and beautiful. *Quitter* will give hope to anyone afraid they can't ever get this thing. Hang in there. You just might."

—Sarah Hepola, *New York Times* bestselling author of *Blackout*

"[Barnett] paints a grotesque portrait of the horror show that is alcoholism with great skill and style. I tore through this book."

—Cat Marnell, *New York Times* bestselling
author of *How to Murder Your Life*

"*Quitter* is all these things: a beautifully told story of one woman's descent into darkness; a rigorously researched exploration of the causes and treatments of alcohol abuse; a furious howl of pain. Erica C. Barnett has written a female story of addiction that moves beyond clichés and accepted truths. I loved this book, in all its raging glory."

—Claire Dederer, author of *Love and Trouble*

"Barnett writes with seismic clarity on the baffling nature of the early morning vodka trip and the anguish and relief it produces in equal measure. This book understands what it is like to fail but have that last bit of hope. Remarkable writing on a disease that effects so many. *Quitter* is the new manual for those seeking a recovered life."
— Erin Lee Carr, author of *All That You Leave Behind*; director of *I Love You, Now Die* and *At the Heart of Gold*

"Erica Barnett's *Quitter* is a harrowing, deeply truthful account of her long journey through alcoholism and repeated relapse—an addiction consequence so common that Barnett calls it 'almost inevitable,' yet one to which most treatment methodologies pay scant attention. Barnett doesn't flinch in showing the impact of her ever-worsening relapses on her health, career, and even her most steadfast relationships, and she holds herself to account while also making it clear how the treatment system failed her. In addition to being a riveting, suspenseful read, *Quitter* will also start important conversations about how addicts can best be helped at all stages of the recovery cycle. An essential addition to the literature of addiction."
— Kristi Coulter, author of *Nothing Good Can Come from This*

"An impeccably researched, long-overdue examination of America's billion-dollar addiction industry and its decidedly mixed record of success. Drawing from her own painful experience in countless hospitals, rehabs and treatment centers, Barnett bravely tackles the limitations and sacred cows of the 12-step movement while also acknowledging the vital role it has played in rescuing thousands of addicts and alcoholics from desperate cycles of despair. In her hard-won quest for sobriety she discovers that it's possible for even the most hopeless addicts to recover if they are willing to give up preconceived notions about what recovery looks like and how to get there."
— Maer Roshan, author of *Courtney Comes Clean*

PENGUIN BOOKS

QUITTER

Erica C. Barnett is an award-winning political reporter. She started her career at *The Texas Observer* and went on to work as a reporter and news editor for the *Austin Chronicle*, *Seattle Weekly*, and *The Stranger*. She now covers addiction, housing, poverty, and drug policy at her website, *PubliCola*. She has written for a variety of local and national publications, including *The Huffington Post*, *Seattle Magazine*, and *Grist*.

Quitter

A Memoir of Drinking,

Relapse, and Recovery

ERICA C. BARNETT

PENGUIN BOOKS

PENGUIN BOOKS
An imprint of Penguin Random House LLC
penguinrandomhouse.com

First published in the United States of America by Viking,
an imprint of Penguin Random House LLC, 2020
Published in Penguin Books 2021

ISBN 9780525522348 (paperback)

THE LIBRARY OF CONGRESS HAS CATALOGED THE
HARDCOVER EDITION AS FOLLOWS:
Names: Barnett, Erica C., author.
Title: Quitter : a memoir of drinking, relapse, and recovery / Erica C. Barnett.
Description: [New York, New York] : Viking, [2020] |
Identifiers: LCCN 2019052898 (print) | LCCN 2019052899 (ebook) |
ISBN 9780525522324 (hardcover) | ISBN 9780525522331 (ebook) |
Subjects: LCSH: Barnett, Erica C. | Women alcoholics—United
States—Biography. | Addicts—Rehabilitation—United States. |
Substance abuse—Treatment—United States. |
Women journalists—United States—Biography
Classification: LCC HV5293.B375 A3 2020 (print) |
LCC HV5293.B375 (ebook) | DDC 362.292092 [B]—dc23
LC record available at https://lccn.loc.gov/2019052898
LC ebook record available at https://lccn.loc.gov/2019052899

Printed in the United States of America
1st Printing

Designed by Amanda Dewey

For Josh
And my parents, Jonee and Paul

Quitter

Rock Bottom

I wake up slowly, like I'm coming out of anesthesia. Something's not right.

This isn't my bed. It isn't even my room. I'm lying on the hardwood floor, just inside the door of my one-bedroom apartment. My bag is a few feet away, wallet, glasses, and makeup spilled across the room; my hot-pink felt jacket is twisted underneath me, and my keys are on the floor by my head.

I notice a red splotch of blood on the floor. What the hell? I sit up sharply, the room careening around me. Clutching the walls, I stagger to the bathroom, stumbling over a pair of boots discarded in the entryway. I rub the mascara out of my eyes and look at my reflection. Is that . . . a black eye? And why is my lower lip split down the middle?

As I peel off my clothes and crawl on top of the bare mattress, I piece the previous day together. At some point in the afternoon, I walked to the Busy Bee convenience store across the street from my apartment and picked up my usual liter of morning wine. (These slim cardboard bottles seem to have emerged in the late 2000s as a gift from the booze merchants to bus drinkers and other sneaky alcoholics; as innocent looking as a box of coconut water, and the perfect size for stashing in a purse.) I waved off the owner's concern about my bandaged hand—an injury from an aborted hike in the Cascade Mountains a few days earlier—and shuffled out into the sunlight as quickly as possible, pushing my huge tortoiseshell sunglasses back over my puffy eyes.

I had planned to walk to the train stop near my house and head downtown to pick up some of the stuff I'd left behind a week earlier at the magazine where I used to work. Instead, I ended up sitting on a bench near the train tracks, drinking the cold, sour wine, and calling everyone I knew—and many I barely knew at all. "Yeah," I sniffled to the former mayor, "things are pretty shitty right now. But maybe this is the wake-up call I needed, y'know?" Struggling not to slur, I told an ex-boyfriend I hadn't contacted in years, "Losing my job is definitely the worst thing that ever happened to me, but I'm going to meetings, I'm doing the things I need to do, and I'm really trying to make the best of this." My friend Sandeep, who was kind enough never to mention the six thousand dollars I still owed him, was uncharacteristically quiet as I went on and on. "What do you think I should do? Go back to rehab? Leave the state? I mean, do you think this might be the kick in the butt I need to get my shit together?" I'm sure he answered. I didn't listen.

Eventually, it started raining, and I was almost out of wine, so I got on the train. I sent a quick text to Emily, the office manager, to let her know I was on my way, then shut my eyes. My phone buzzed angrily in my hand. It was Emily, texting. "You were supposed to be here an hour ago!" *You are on some seriously thin fucking ice with me,* I thought.

Emily was supposed to be my friend. For a while, she and Melissa, one of the top bosses at the magazine, had taken me to AA meetings at lunchtime. In fact, Emily and Melissa were the ones who had driven me to detox a week earlier—dropping me off, sobbing, at Fairfax, a lockdown mental hospital east of Seattle, in a leafy suburb that I had come to think of as the city's rehab annex. I thought they cared about my well-being. But as soon as I had gotten back to work, after a four-day detox that dried me out just enough to start to panic, I was told I no longer had a job.

Melissa had helped make that decision. And now, three days later, Emily was waiting for me to come and clear out my desk.

You knew, I fumed. *You knew when you took me to Fairfax that they couldn't wait to get rid of me.*

I took my time getting to my now former workplace—enough time to buy another bottle at a nearby convenience store and drink most of it, ducking into alleys on my way to the office. Some people carry around an internal map of all the places they've had sex. I can map Seattle by its liquor stores—the basement-level Kress IGA Supermarket by the fancy concert hall where I saw the Monkees play a reunion show in 2013; the corner store and deli just up a flight of steps from my office, where a four-pack of Gallo commanded a steep $9.99; the liquor store on Second and Seneca, where I once pretended not to recognize a government spokesman I knew because I was so embarrassed to be there, buying a plastic bottle of $8.00 vodka from behind the counter.

By the time I called Emily to come and meet me, it was 5:30 and she was in no mood for small talk. Or maybe she smelled the wine on my breath and noticed that I couldn't walk a straight line from the elevators to the door. "Okay, grab your stuff," she barked, standing sentry behind my desk. In my shame-clouded memory, she is tapping her foot impatiently, boring hateful holes in the back of my head.

Just then, I realized that I'd forgotten to bring along anything to transport all my files and memorabilia, accumulated over fifteen years in reporting jobs from Texas to Seattle.

"Where are you planning to put all that stuff?" *Up your ass, bitch.* "I don't know. I need to figure out what's important here." Five more minutes passed as I scrabbled through my papers with one eye closed, struggling to focus. *Photo of me with former Texas governor Ann Richards? I definitely need that. File of documents about a long-dead monorail project, one of the first stories I covered in Seattle? Can't let that go.*

Finally, Emily had had enough. "Okay, you need to leave. If you want your stuff, we can mail it to you later." Indignantly, I grabbed my Rolodex and the Ann Richards photo and crammed them into my bike bag. Hours later, I would recall, with some embarrassment, the empty wine box I had shoved in the back of the file cabinet weeks earlier. Sulking, and somehow drunker than when I arrived, I followed Emily downstairs and stormed back out into the rain.

From here, my memories get patchy, like watching a film with half the scenes cut out. I walked back to the same store I'd visited an hour earlier, going through a different checkout line with a fresh container of Chardonnay. I made it back to the train, swigging away like I was invisible, and managed to stay awake all the way to my stop. I savored this small victory as I disembarked, recalling all the times a bus driver had nudged me awake at the end of the line. I started walking, then running, home, as the rain came down harder. I tripped, catching myself for a split second on my injured hand.

And then I slammed face-first into the concrete.

My memory skips forward. I see a couple with an umbrella, hurrying past the drunk woman sprawled out on the sidewalk, jeans pulled down, underwear exposed. I see myself figuring out which way is up from the direction the raindrops are falling. I see myself a few blocks later, staggering, deciding whether to lie down in the bushes, wondering what the headlines would say if I died. "Promising writer who refused to stop drinking gets what she deserves." Fair enough. It *was* what I deserved.

But I found my legs, and I made it home.

That was rock bottom.

The fourth or fifth one.

I didn't start out good at drinking; like a lot of skills I picked up in my life, I practiced until I got the hang of it. But from the first time I choked down a searing swallow of lukewarm brown liquor, I knew the point of drinking was to get shit-faced.

By the end, nearly a decade into a fall that only looks precipitous in retrospect, I was pulling a bottle from under my bed the second I opened my eyes, buying another on the way to work, and dodging out before the end of the day to pick up a third. By the time I hit rock bottom, it was physical agony to drag myself to my first meeting of Alcoholics Anonymous, where everyone talked about being "happy, joyous, and free." I wanted what they had. I wanted in.

After years of daily drinking, embarrassing scenes I tried to laugh away in the morning, and hangovers so intense I brought a couch from home to my office to sleep them off, I was done.

That's a lie.

That wasn't the end—it was barely the beginning. It took five stints in detox, two inpatient rehabs, two outpatient programs, hundreds of 12-step meetings, years of therapy, and the loss of nearly everyone and everything I cared about to make me stop. By the time I hit bottom, I was barely able to hold it together enough to take a bath (showers were out of the question—they made my head spin). I was hallucinating music and voices no one could hear, and I looked as bloated as an overripe cantaloupe, about to burst. That was when I decided enough was enough. I was sick and tired of being sick and tired.

But that's a lie, too.

The best reasons—getting fired from the company I cofounded, losing the patience and respect of most of my friends, losing partners and money and, very nearly, my home—were never enough to make me quit. Instead, I settled into a wearying pattern—temporary recovery followed by a period of forgetting, followed by a slide into relapse that was so easy it seemed almost like an accident. Once I started drinking again, there was literally nothing you could tell me to make me stop spending my dwindling funds (which, more and more often, came courtesy of high-interest payday loans) on box wine and twelve-dollar fifths of vodka. We've all read it in every recovery story, right? You don't hit rock bottom until you decide to stop digging.

Actually, that's the biggest lie of all.

There's no such thing as rock bottom, even for those who manage to quit, and stay quit, on their very first try. As for the rest of us: We try, we fail, we try again, we fail harder. Eventually, some of us quit for good. But because our treatment system is premised on the other story—the one in which the addict loses everything, comes to her senses, and follows the timeworn path to recovery and redemption—

it isn't serving most of us well, if at all. It certainly didn't serve me well. Instead, it made me feel like a failure. In the messy real world, there are as many routes to recovery as there are people who are addicted, and any person who tells you their solution is the only one that works is lying. Even if they really believe it.

Most recovery narratives follow a familiar, comforting arc—the addict loses control, the addict hits rock bottom, the addict grasps at the nearest available thread, usually AA or another 12-step program, the addict recovers. That narrative, though true to the experience of so many people, isn't my story. Nor is it the story of the countless others who struggle, fail, relapse, abase ourselves, lose everything, lose even more, get better, then worse, then better again. We're told in rehab and in meeting rooms that we never have to drink or use drugs again, even if we want to, and that's absolutely true. But what about those of us who don't "get it" right away—which is to say, the vast majority of us? Do we fail, at first, because we're stubborn, or because of our "character defects," or because we don't really want to get better? Is our problem that we simply haven't "hit bottom" yet?

I don't think so. Nothing I went through during my addiction prepared me for recovery better than so-called failure, and every relapse handed me a few more of the pieces I would need to puzzle together my own solution to an addiction that almost consumed me. I could have lost more things—my apartment, my family, what was left of my health. I could have died.

But I didn't.

For every rock bottom I've hit already, I don't think for one second that there can't be another. But I wouldn't be here—wouldn't, indeed, be alive to write this—if I hadn't learned, slowly, how to cope with life itself, without the warm bubble of a light buzz or the heavy padding of a blackout drunk to insulate me from the world. Each relapse would lead to the same result—a deeper fall, a lower bottom—but along the way, I cobbled together something that looked like recovery.

This book is about how I did it.

One

Up in the Air

I'm sitting at the airport in Seattle, but it's hard to explain exactly how I ended up here, in this black vinyl seat, on this particular afternoon in the fall of 2014. If you walked up and asked me, I'd probably tell you, "I didn't know where else to go," but that isn't the half of it. I didn't know how to *be*.

The plan, if you can call it that, was to move in with my grandparents in Mississippi for a while, long enough to get the booze out of my system and decide what to do next. But when I got to the United Airlines counter, I found out that the ticket I thought was waiting for me wasn't there, and plan A went into the trash along with the big white binder containing my relapse prevention plan from treatment, which I'd tossed in an airport Dumpster on the way to the terminal.

More than a ticket, or money, or a plan, I needed a drink. So I wheeled my suitcase into the nearest bathroom, sat down in a stall, and unzipped the cover. Tucked between the layers of sweaters and dirty T-shirts were two bottles of Svedka vodka. I cracked open the half-empty one and chugged the burning liquid straight from the bottle, thanked God for this small mercy (AA had taught me how to pray), wiped my sweaty face, and depressed the handle.

Flush.

No one was supposed to know I still drank. For the past five years, I had been telling everyone I'd quit, although who knows how many of them still believed me. (In my defense, I *had* quit, again and again and again. The problem wasn't quitting; it was staying quit.) I did my drinking in private, at home or—when I had to go out, which, since I lost my job about a month before, had been less and less—in parks, bus shelters, or public restrooms, gulping as quietly as possible, as quietly as a junkie takes off his belt and twists it around his arm.

Once, I almost got caught in the act. I was sitting in my usual spot near the back of the bus, gulping from a bright-yellow carton of lukewarm Bandit Chardonnay, when a guy across the aisle caught my eye to let me know the driver was coming my way. "Hey, lady, you gotta watch yourself!" he grinned after the danger had passed, pulling a brown-bagged tallboy from his puffy black jacket. "They're checking for that shit now!"

Speak for yourself, I thought. *I'm invisible.* And compared to him, as a still vaguely professional-looking woman in my thirties with a MacBook in her lap, I was.

At the airport, I shoved the bottle, now several fluid ounces lighter, back in my suitcase, rolling it carefully in a sweater to make sure it didn't clank around.

I wandered back into the terminal, thinking, *I can handle this.*

And then, suddenly, I couldn't. That's how I found myself glued to this chair by the United ticket counter, watching the blur of travelers rushing past me to their Very Important Destinations. Things felt unreal. I started to wonder if I was hallucinating, or actually imperceptible. Or maybe I was still stuck in a dream from the night before—the one where security officers had to carry me, flailing and screaming, from the building after I was fired. I should get a taxi home, I thought. Instead, I flagged down two TSA agents and asked them to call me an ambulance.

"What's wrong with you?" one asked. "Acute intoxication," I responded, surprised at my own lucidity. Even when I couldn't force my body to stand, I still wanted people to know that I knew what I was talking about.

The aborted flight was an attempt to trace a familiar path—back home to Meridian, Mississippi, the small town where my family lived until I was seven. I had just been fired from my job at the online news site I cofounded with my best friend, Josh, and I thought that if I could retrace my steps—dry out for a few weeks in a place where I had always been welcomed without judgment, then figure out how to rebuild my life—I would be okay.

Instead, I was en route to the Highline Medical Center in Burien, Washington, twelve miles south of my apartment in Seattle. And if a hospital in the suburbs seems like a weird detour to take at this moment, you don't know what the past five years had been like. You don't know how bad I needed a rest.

Thirty years earlier, I had taken a trip in the opposite direction— the first of many efforts to get away from my Deep South roots. Of course, I was only seven at the time—too young to know that the world wasn't bounded by Louisiana, Alabama, and Tennessee—and I didn't have much say in the matter. Did I take my first trip to Texas by myself, or with Dad and my new stepmother, Jonee, who hadn't yet asked me to call her Mom? Did the Southwest Airlines flight attendant whisk me to my seat, harried but smiling in her orange-and-blue uniform, or did I sit between the two of them, staring out the window in awe as we rose up above the tops of the clouds? I don't remember. But from then on, I would always love the feeling of being between one place and another.

Before I moved away from Mississippi, my family was simple. My dad lived an hour away, in Hattiesburg, where he was finishing school at the University of Southern Mississippi and living in a run-down single-wide trailer with a ratty couch and sloshy brown king-size waterbed. I lived with my grandparents in Meridian—Mama Opal (short for Opaldean), a surgery nurse at Riley Hospital, and Papa Jesse, who managed a Goodyear tire store downtown. On the weekends, we'd drive sixty miles down a two-lane highway to visit my great-grandparents, Grandmother and Granddaddy, in a dot-on-the-map town called Macon (Mississippi, not Georgia), where they lived in a little white house with a backyard and a metal porch swing that always squeaked after it rained. Occasionally, a younger family member would bring their grandkids around (younger being relative—the average age in Macon was probably sixty-five), but the people I remember most vividly were all at least seventy years my senior—"aints" with old-fashioned names like Vernice and Jewel and uncles who could fix a bee sting with spit and a wad of chewing tobacco. In Macon, where Grandmother's backyard garden seemed to stretch for acres, Mama Opal and Papa Jesse let me run around more freely than they did at home, picking beans and shelling them on the screened-in porch, collecting pecans from under the huge tree that shaded the cluttered back patio, and pawing through the boxes of letters and piles of scarves and purses in the guest-room closet, where everything was suffused with the old-lady smell of roses, peppermint, and moldy cardboard.

What my family lacked, I eventually realized, was a mom—mine had taken off to pursue other interests when I was too young to form memories. Growing up, I never thought of being motherless as a deficiency, although I knew it made me a little different. Some kids had two parents and lived in fancy houses with fenced-in yards, some kids were raised by single moms and lived in the trailer park where we visited my uncle Mike and aunt Marilyn, and some kids had long-haired dads who studied biology and were really into *MAD Magazine*, Alice Cooper, and Tron.

Years later, I would develop questions about this woman, Cindy, whom I had glimpsed in photos that my dad kept hidden in a box in our spare bedroom, underneath the ancient copies of *Playboy* and *Oui*. Still later, therapists and boyfriends would inform me that I had been traumatized by this loss, which had led me to seek approval from everyone and fear abandonment like love was something I could earn by memorizing the right combination of words. Later still, I would meet her and look for myself in her eyes, her facial structure, her way of looking at the world.

But back then, I learned that there was no point in asking about Cindy. (Early on, I didn't even know her last name, or whether she was still alive.) Ask, I discovered, and the adults would clam up as fast as if I'd inquired how babies were made, or what happened after you died; so, after a while, I didn't. When I found a clue—my birth certificate, which showed her married and maiden names, or a photo of me as a baby, being cradled on my dad's patchwork quilt by a thin, olive-skinned woman with feathered hair—I filed it away for

Later, when I would be a reporter, or maybe a private detective, and have the skills to find out anything I wanted to know without asking anyone for help.

Much as I loved the company of my elderly relatives, I did have one friend my own age—Mizba, whose parents owned the Valley Motel off Interstate 20. Outcasts at Jeff Davis Elementary School, we spent recess setting up booby traps around the dusty schoolyard for the school bully, Chip Carney, and terrorizing the boy we both had crushes on.

Mostly, though, I spent my time alone, reading my way through the *World Book Encyclopedia* on the maroon shag carpet in my grandparents' formal living room, playing farmer with my toy barn and plastic cows and sheep, and making brownies in my Easy-Bake oven on stormy weekends, while the rain sizzled on the concrete driveway.

On Sundays, we went to services at the Baptist church in town, where Papa Jesse was a deacon and where the very pews seemed like a kind of penance—cherrywood, hard and slick with varnish, too tall for my feet to touch the floor. In between the rapid-fire up-down-up-down of prayer, song, and May-Christ-Be-with-You-and-Also-with-Yous, I sat quietly, swinging my bare, bobby-socked legs and reading picture books from the church library. Afterward, there were ham or pimento-cheese sandwiches, chocolate milkshakes, and Grandmother's vegetable soup, which came out of square white paper boxes in the back of the deep freeze. Afternoons were for MTV, singing along with Michael Jackson on my portable plastic record player, and trips to the mall, where I'd happily spend an afternoon paging through grubby copies of *Dynamite* and *Hot dog!* magazines and trying on ten-cent plastic clip-on earrings at Woolworth's.

If my great-grandparents' house was a museum full of treasure, my grandparents' sprawling brick ranch house in Meridian was an oversized playground: double closets to hide my favorite toys from my cousins (and, decades later, my vodka); hallways where I would build intricate Lincoln Log cities linked by vast, regional train systems; a wood enclosure in the backyard that we filled with pine needles every year until it was deep enough for Papa Jesse to toss me in. Jesse was a karate black belt and weapons enthusiast who taught me, by the time I was seven, how to shoot cans off a fence, why it was important to always look under a car before you approached it (woe betide any wannabe carjacker who tried to slice *my* Achilles tendon), and how to kill a man with a pen (jab it upward through his chin, straight through the Adam's apple to the brain). I thought my grandparents were already ancient, but looking back, I realize that they were only in their early fifties, still spry enough to toss a baseball or stand at attention through a complicated surgery or outrun a mugger if it came to that—which, of course, it never did.

Maybe it was all the talk about kidnapping, or maybe I watched too many *Twilight Zone* episodes at an impressionable age, but even at six or seven, I remember being gripped sometimes by a feeling that things were on the verge of falling apart, and that it was my job, somehow, to hold them together. Sometimes, lying in my big queen bed with the cross-stitched Now I Lay Me Down to Sleep prayer above my head, I would dream that my family had been replaced by shape-shifting demons who meant to do me harm, or that Grandmother's old car was sliding slowly into the lake near her house, the windows closed, going under. On those nights, I would wake up shivering under the quilt Grandmother had sewn from heavy cotton and fabric scraps and wonder if I, or anything, was real. Other times, when I was staying with Dad at his trailer in Hattiesburg, I would imagine that an invisible wall had descended between his room, where I was lying on the waterbed, trying to fall asleep, and the living room, where I could see Dad watching TV on the tattered couch. I stayed as still as I could, praying that whatever was in the room with me wouldn't notice I was there. All I had to do was be quiet and still.

That feeling of anxiety, that nervous energy that marked me as a lifelong insomniac by the time I was six years old, would stay with me. It hung around long after my dad remarried, all the way through Houston and high school and drinking and scholarships and internships and boyfriends and jobs. At that age, it was just a low-level hum—the kind of thing that put me in constant motion, talking, arguing, demanding that everyone pay attention. "Watch me play piano!" I would squeal, plinking out "Mary Had a Little Lamb" on the keys of my grandparents' out-of-tune piano. Or: "Look at this!" followed by an attempt to pole-vault across the room, followed by a visit to the hospital where Mama Opal worked.

Jonee, the woman Dad started dating when I was five or six, was the first of his girlfriends who seemed willing to put up with my constant chatter, and she didn't make me tense the way his previous girlfriend, a swirl of shiny black hair named Jane, always had. Jonee talked to me like I was a person, not a baby, and she listened to what I had to say—about the "Thriller" video, a short story I was writing about elephants, the newspaper Mizba and I were going to publish about our school. (When adults asked six-year-old me what I was going to be when I grew up, that was an easy one: a journalist, like John Stossel on *20/20* and the people who wrote *The Meridian Star*.) Jonee was Jewish, but that wasn't the only thing that made her exotic—her parents, Susan and Barry, drank and sometimes even swore, and had been to faraway places like Dallas and New York

City, and maybe even farther away than that. They belonged to the local country club, hung abstract art on their walls instead of needlepoint, and leased a new Cadillac every year.

Fast-forward through the wedding—held at that very country club—and my departure from Mississippi, an event that I experienced as a total surprise. (Quick pause to see Papa Jesse wiping away tears as he told me to "be careful," his favorite benediction.) Fast-forward all the way to my arrival in Houston, a noisy, unfamiliar place that smelled like exhaust and felt as humid as a wrung-out rag, and to our new home, a two-story apartment in a gated complex that epitomized late-1970s suburban sprawl. Fast-forward, for that matter, past the city of Houston itself—we lived in an apartment in the city for the first half of my third-grade year, long enough for my parents to decide that the city was no place to raise a child. This was the mid-eighties, long before white flight reversed into gentrification, and we fled to Sugar Land, an area a few miles outside the city limits, where planned communities still bumped up against farmland and wildlife preserves. I had never been at the same school for more than a year, and now I was starting over again in the middle of the year—a gawky, gap-toothed beanpole in a school full of strangers.

Two

Sugar Land

Despite its prefab-sounding name, Sugar Land had a story—before it became a "desirable" suburb with a median income of well over a hundred thousand dollars, it was a self-contained company town for the Imperial Sugar factory, which still loomed over a grid of quaint, candy-colored bungalows. But by 1986, when we moved there, Sugar Land had burst past its original boundaries, sprawling across the former prairie in a web of cul-de-sacs, ring roads, and four-lane boulevards separated by big grassy medians that turned brown and crackly in the summer. Our neighborhood, Colony Bend, was the picture of mid-eighties Sun Belt suburbia: crabgrass lawns, crape myrtles, and endless iterations of the same five model homes, all painted the same HOA-approved shades of olive, brown, khaki, and greige.

My parents, still in their mid-twenties, seemed to take their parenting cues from an earlier time and place—Victorian England, maybe, with a bit of post-Depression abstemiousness thrown in for good measure. I exaggerate, a little—I was an only child who had never been acquainted with the concept of "no"—but there were a *lot* of rules, and I was constantly violating at least one of them. No chewing with your mouth open. Don't put your napkin on the table—fold it nicely in your lap. Dinner is for talking, not for reading. (I shudder, sometimes, to think about how they would have dealt with smartphones.) No boys in your room. Smile pleasantly when your face is idle—no wonder everybody thinks you're unfriendly. Lights out by nine. No reading in bed. Write thank-you notes, legibly, on nice stationery. Finish everything on your plate. No TV until your homework's done. No cussing. That includes calling your friends "buttheads," saying "what the hell," and complaining that something "sucks." No taking the Lord's name in vain. "Oh my gosh" is acceptable, but don't push it.

And the cardinal rule: Don't argue.

Violating the rules meant exile—to my room, where I was supposed to sit quietly (no reading!) and "think about what I did," or the guest room, where there was nothing *to* read but a musty unabridged dictionary from the 1960s. If my parents thought I needed to articulate my remorse, I would have to write an essay—explaining, say, why I shouldn't have crossed the street on my bike without looking both ways, or why it was wrong to talk back in class. If I'd been really bad, or tried to whine my way out of being grounded, I'd have to write "sentences"—"I will not cross the street without looking both ways"; "I will not argue"—over and over until the words started looking like random patterns on the page.

I was becoming a jumpy, nervous kid—convinced that there were certain thoughts and feelings I needed to keep secret, and that the worst thing in the world was to be noticed for the wrong reason.

We were the kind of family that kept our blinds shut—not because we had anything to hide, but because nobody needed to know our business. "Close those blinds!" one of my parents would holler. "Why? It's dark in here!" "Because anyone can see right in!" As if anyone was interested in watching a ten-year-old playing with Legos or reading the dictionary.

I started to feel clenched—as if, without even knowing it, I might do the wrong thing and cause my parents' car to drive off the road, or bring so much shame on the family that we'd have to move. I knew that superstitions were silly, but I still thought that if I shut my door too hard when I got up to go to the bathroom in the middle of the night, it might wake up my parents, which might cause them to not get enough sleep, which might make them lose their jobs, which might force us into the poorhouse. So I tried to hold it.

It was around fourth grade—the year I grew six inches, started wearing a bra, and acquired thick, plastic-rimmed glasses that I was sure would doom me to a life of solitude—that my body started refusing to stay asleep at night. No matter how tired I was when I went to bed, my eyes would pop open around 3:00 A.M. and fix on the red digital numbers of my alarm clock. 3:07. 3:45. 4:17. Deep space has nothing on the silence of a house in the Houston suburbs at three in the morning. I became obsessed with getting enough sleep to function—a strange preoccupation for a ten-year-old. Several times a week, I'd ask my dad: "Do you think I have dark circles under my eyes?" And several times a week, he'd say the same thing. "It's genetic." I wasn't convinced. I definitely wasn't allowed to wear makeup, but I started "borrowing" my mom's under-eye concealer.

Thirty years later, during my intake interview at a residential addiction treatment center, the nurse on duty would observe: "[Erica's] trouble sleeping is likely interfering with her life and probably has for so long that she takes it for granted."

On the weekends, Dad was usually busy managing the Goodyear store where he worked, which meant that Jonee, who worked at Texaco, was in charge of keeping me occupied. In elementary school, this was easy enough: I was happy to watch Goose and Mav do victory rolls in *Top Gun* for the hundredth time, or wander around the Galleria looking at Liz Claiborne twinsets and the latest age-reversing miracle cream from Clinique. But as I morphed into an overgrown, cranky preteen with a bad perm and a permanent scowl, it got harder for us to be in the same zip code. Most of what we fought about was trivial mother-daughter stuff—whether I was old enough to wear lip gloss, or if I had scrubbed the plates properly before putting them in the dishwasher—but that was part of the problem. She *wasn't* my mom.

And then, one day, she was. We had been having one of our screaming, door-slamming fights—the kind where I would have shouted "I hate you!" if I didn't know that would only get me in deeper shit. (Instead, I scrawled it in my diary: *I hate her I hate her I hate her.*) I came out of my room to grab a wad of tissues out of the hallway bathroom—my private sanctuary, because unlike my bedroom, it had a lock—just as she was leaving her bedroom down the hall. Out of nowhere, she asked, "Would you think about calling me Mom? You don't have to decide right away. Just think about—"

"Whatever. Sure."

From then on, "Jonee" would be the name I reserved for the times when I really wanted to piss her off.

Dad didn't like to step into a conflict unless he had to, and when he did, it was to play the role of hard-nosed disciplinarian. "You need to grow up and stop crying," he would tell me, or, "You're never going to get anywhere if you just get upset about everything like that." It's funny how parents slip into those roles. I had seen my parents yell at each other—a car-shaking fight outside our temple stands out in my memory—but my dad never yelled at me. To this day, I prefer yelling—any kind of yelling—to the silent treatment.

My parents were always trying to get me to toughen up, and it was true that I was a fraidy-cat—I once stayed indoors for half a day because I was convinced that there was a snake in the middle of our cul-de-sac. (Turned out it was a dribble of tar on the sidewalk.) Mom made me join the Junior Girl Scouts; I went to one sleepover camp, sat in a bed of fire ants, and got sent home for carving my name in the wooden base of a tepee. Mom and Dad decided I might be better off learning to make friendship bracelets and paddle in a canoe at day camp; I fell straight into an algae-choked pond and didn't get into another boat for fifteen years.

The Great Outdoors was a nightmare, filled with things that bit and scratched and burned and stuck to my clothes. All I wanted to do was have sleepovers with my new best friend, Monica, transcribe Monkees lyrics into the special notebook I kept in my denim-covered tape case, and play *Legend of Zelda* until the sun came up. When President Reagan wanted every kid in America to run a mile to prove our worth, I walked all four laps in protest, becoming the only kid in my fourth-grade class to log a twenty-minute mile.

It was around sixth grade—the year that Mom's mother, Susan, told me, "You're starting to get quite the little figure," and that Monica and I discovered the trove of *Playboys* under my dad's side of the bed—that I became aware that my body was a problem to be solved. It bulged and jiggled in all the wrong places, inspiring grown men to stare at my eleven-year-old chest when they talked to me, or holler as they drove by in their mud-splattered work trucks. The women I saw in *Playboy* and *Seventeen* had twenty-four-inch waists, and breasts that seemed to defy gravity; by the time I was twelve, I was a thick-waisted, big-hipped girl with boobs that had to be wrestled into submission with a bra that left marks on my shoulders.

Diet and exercise, it seemed, were the proper remedies for a body that failed to conform to the Jessica Rabbit-meets-Cindy Crawford beauty standard of the late 1980s. The magazines and books my mom brought home promised both "Thin Thighs in One Month!" and "Buns of Steel," and I figured that if I just had enough discipline, the way Mom did, I could get both. I started small, doing Jane Fonda tapes and power walks with Mom, two-pound wrist weights on our arms. When that didn't do the trick, I ate less and less, until, for a brief while, I was eating almost nothing at all. Commercials for Special K and Weight Watchers told me that if I could "pinch an inch," I needed to watch my diet—and I could, so I did. Tuna salad sandwiches dripping with mayonnaise and pickle juice were replaced by iceberg lettuce with lite ranch dressing and steamed artichokes with low-calorie margarine. Novels by Dean Koontz and Stephen King were shelved in favor of my mom's diet books and pocket calorie counters. And ice cream—vanilla Blue Bell, topped with two layers of Magic Shell—was replaced by portion-controlled servings of a watery, crunchy concoction known as ice milk, which promised half the calories and delivered one tenth the joy.

I never lost that much weight—my militant self-discipline tended to vanish at night, when I'd scarf down fistfuls of cereal or nibble away, bite by microscopic bite, at forbidden treats like leftover Halloween candy and Grandmother's chocolate fudge—but it probably wouldn't have helped my self-esteem much if I had managed to sculpt my body into a perfect 34-24-34 hourglass, because I was also taller than every other kid in class. In every photo, I loom over classmates who hadn't hit their growth spurts, hunching to make myself as small and cute as a five-foot-seven twelve-year-old with bad teeth and a crunchy perm can possibly be.

Like many awkward kids, I wrestled with two conflicting desires: I wanted to be the center of attention, and I was paralyzed with fear the second anyone noticed that I existed. The second impulse always seemed to impede the first. I loved singing—so much, for example, that I made my own "audition tapes" on my dual-deck boom box, but when my mom dropped me off for *actual* choir auditions, I ducked into a bathroom stall, tucking my knees up to my chin until the danger of public humiliation had passed. When I did get cast in a play, I forgot my lines, running off stage just as I was supposed to deliver the punch line in our G-rated *Saturday Night Live* send-up.

My career in theater stalled, I decided to reinvent myself, and I found myself gravitating to First Colony Junior High's small crowd of burnouts—scowling kids who smoked in the bathroom, cut classes, and spent school hours drawing skulls, swords, and heavy-metal logos in their notebooks. There was Charles, a dead-eyed, greasy-haired skater who started drinking at nine years old and whose dad let him smoke inside the house; Jennie, an aspiring model whose stepdad, Bob, seemed to be perpetually shirtless, drunk, and yelling; Robert, a laid-back guitarist with bowl-cut blond hair and a repertoire of ironic three-chord Violent Femmes rip-off songs; and Chris, who lived across the street from Jennie, drove a Spree, and had already flunked ninth grade once by the time the rest of us caught up to him.

Robert was dreamy but unattainable—sharp-jawed, aloof, almost feminine in his resolute cool. Chris was the opposite: goofy, approachable, sweet, and always up for whatever anyone suggested.

Robert was the guy I sat next to on the floor of my kitchen, hips touching, cracking jokes at a mile a minute to make it crystal clear that I didn't think there was any chance he'd be into me. Chris was the guy I actually kissed, after getting stoned enough to muster the courage, in a dark corner of the Houston Museum of Natural Science while Robert and Jennie were distracted by the T. rex in the lobby. By thirteen, I was already downgrading my expectations based on what I thought I deserved. Roberts were for the Jennies of the world. Awkward, tongue-tied girls with big feet and bad teeth settled for the Chrises.

When I swallowed my first sip of Southern Comfort or brandy or whiskey, in Jennie's upstairs rec room sometime during that summer between middle and high school, there was no explosion of stars, no feeling that I'd finally found the missing piece that made me feel like myself. In fact, straining my memory more than twenty-five years later, I can't remember my first sip of liquor at all. What I do remember is the woozy backdrop of that summer: the worn brown couch, the faded shag carpet, and the liquor cabinet, a tall glass china case that sat, unlocked, at the top of the stairs.

I used to think that drinking at thirteen made me some kind of badass, but thirteen-year-old me would be disappointed to learn that, in 1991, I was really just a few years ahead of my time. By 2003, nearly a quarter of girls would tell researchers that they had tried booze before they turned thirteen, and by 2015, 45 percent of high school girls would self-identify as drinkers. We know a fair amount about why girls drink, and when, because studies of teenage drinking and drug use tend to be broken down by gender—unlike studies about the consequences of drinking on adults, which have mostly been restricted to men. According to one of the most widely cited studies of girls and substance abuse, by the National Center on Addiction and Substance

Abuse (CASA) at Columbia University, factors that put girls at risk for early drinking and alcohol abuse include low self-esteem, depression, early puberty, anxiety, impulsivity, sensation seeking, eating disorders, insecurity, and rebelliousness—any one of which might make a person likely to try alcohol and drugs, but which, mixed together, make up a potent cocktail of predisposition.* Many of the factors that predict which girls will drink are also the symptoms girls drink to alleviate: We drink to feel more comfortable in our own skins, we drink to relieve anxiety, and we drink to feel less depressed.

Drinking was a magic trick that took me outside myself. I loved that first lightning bolt of pain that tore through my chest when I chugged from a warm bottle of Jim Beam, and I loved that a tall plastic cup filled with ice cubes and Captain Morgan made me feel like I belonged wherever I was. I loved the thrill of getting away with something, and the instant camaraderie that came on when my friends and I got loaded. Sober, I was awkward and shy; tipsy, I could play whatever role I wanted from the limited roster available to teenage girls at the time—from the mean girl making fun of other girls who tried to break into our circle to the flirty vixen who flung her bare legs across boys' laps as we listened to Pearl Jam and the Smashing Pumpkins on Jennie's CD player. Sometimes Chris or Robert would come over and drink with us, or smoke cigarettes and watch us, amused, while we mixed up vodka and Crystal Light, but the times I liked best were when it was just me and Jennie, taking pulls on her stepdad's bottles, "Smells Like Teen Spirit" blaring,

---

* Dieting is another risk factor, one researcher seems strangely keen to emphasize. The CASA study, which is not prone to flights of typographic fancy, italicizes this factoid for emphasis: "Although alcohol is high in calories and contributes to weight gain, only half (56 percent) of the girls surveyed were aware of this; 5.7 percent thought that drinking alcohol helps one lose weight." This tendency to marvel that girls who want to lose weight don't realize alcohol will make them fat—which is by no means confined to the CASA study—made me suspect that researchers don't condemn dieting among young girls quite as much as they should.

and venturing barefoot into the steamy afternoon to smoke our Marlboro Reds brazenly on the sidewalk. Jennie was beautiful, waiflike, and effortlessly cool, and I thought that if she liked me, I might start to be those things myself. I started drinking to feel like I was in Jennie's league; I kept drinking to belong there.

Three

People Make Their Own Problems

Drinking took me out of my body, which was not a territory I especially cared to inhabit. It didn't matter if I was wearing a screaming-pink miniskirt with spangled leggings or a triple-XL T-shirt over jeans I stole from Dad's closet, something about my appearance seemed to impel men in trucks to scream out the window—"Hey, Mami!" or "Lemme see that ass!"—as they drove by. By now, I had developed a thick skin. "Chinga tu madre!" I would yell back, or "Fuck you, I'm thirteen!" With kids I knew from school, though, my bravado evaporated. One afternoon as I walked home from middle school, a small crowd of older boys overtook me on the sidewalk that wound through a playground where I used to swing on the monkey bars. "Ugly skank!" one yelled. "Is your pussy tight like I heard it was?" another demanded. I was supposed to say something clever, but I had forgotten my lines. I stared at the boys wordlessly for several seconds until I regained control of my body, pushed past them, and fled. I still hadn't found my voice.

Jennie—perfect, skinny, confident Jennie—was never at a loss for words. Something about her kept catcallers at their distance. Something about me made me a magnet for guys with smart mouths and wandering hands.

I spent that summer before high school worshipping her, and living in terror that she would turn on me. When she told me she had a crush on the same boy I did, I crumpled his name in a mental ball and tossed it aside. (Roberts were for the Jennies of the world.) When we were walking through the grocery store and she casually said, "Hey, go steal us some cigarettes," I palmed a pack of Reds like it was a deck of cards. When she informed me that my favorite band from childhood was lame, I hid my case of Monkees tapes in the back of my closet next to the Cabbage Patch dolls and Legos.

And when she said, "Let's try acid," I said, "Sure!" It was easy to get your hands on drugs in the suburbs in those days, especially if you were a girl. And none of us were too worried about the consequences. It was the era of Tipper Gore's Parents Music Research Center and "This is your brain on drugs" and Drug Abuse Resistance Education, and ridiculous rules about how we could dress and what we could say and when it was okay to have friends of the opposite sex. We certainly weren't allowed to even talk about "experimenting" with drugs. All the rules seemed equally arbitrary, the product of some capricious council of elders charged with preventing us from having fun. Listening to metal didn't make us worship Satan, and watching *A Clockwork Orange* didn't turn us into violent sociopaths, so why should we believe that drugs would fry our brains like the egg in that stupid commercial?

Everyone in my new circle of friends smoked weed, using bongs made out of Coke cans and ten-dollar screw-apart pipes we bought at head shops and concealed in our cavernous tooled-leather purses. But pot didn't do much for me. I wanted something that would blow my mind wide open.

I bought a few tabs of acid from Jeff, a high-school dealer who sold drugs from his locker. The following weekend, Jennie and I slipped the tiny squares of green blotter paper—such innocent-looking things—onto our tongues, and waited. Half an hour went by, then an hour. And then, as chemicals circulated along pathways and wedged into receptors in my brain, the piece that had been missing during all those drunken afternoons finally clicked into place. *Here* was the explosion of stars, the feeling of connection, the missing ingredient that stole dull time away and imbued every observation with significance. I had started to dabble in painting, and I discovered that acid was amazing for making art—what it took away (verbal acuity, the ability to stifle giggles, a linear sense of time) it more than made up for in visual creativity, and I spent hours sketching, refining, and eventually creating murals of intricate 3-D spirals, bright Pop Art portraits, and vivid abstract patterns in spiral notebooks, and later, on the walls of my bedroom.

Before long, I was dropping acid in the shower before school, slipping it under my tongue in the backseat as my parents drove Jennie and me to see the Butthole Surfers at a Houston amphitheater, taking it at night after my parents went to bed. I knew, from my pile of books about the sixties, all about Woodstock burnouts, hippies who went on a trip and never came down, and the apocryphal story about the guy who freaked out and drove his motorcycle off a cliff on Highway 101. But aside from a few panicky moments—like the time when the giant purple eye I had painted in the corner of my bedroom started blinking messages at me in Morse code, or the time when I was lying on a hotel bed, several years later, and the world lost its vertical hold—I never had a "bad trip." LSD made me feel like I had special access to the secret world behind the visible one, where the connections between events and beliefs and, especially, people were obvious and undeniable. I couldn't articulate the experiences while I was having them, nor remember them clearly afterward, but I never really lost that sense that the perceptible world is only a fraction of what's really going on.

My parents, strict and suspicious as they could be, never seemed to figure out that I soared through much of high school high as a kite. (Maybe I was a better actor than I thought.) While I was marveling at the patterns in my ceiling or stumbling through the Palais Royal department store after an afternoon-long bender at Jennie's house, they were worrying about my reading material, confiscating books like *The Doors of Perception* and the trashy Jim Morrison biography *No One Here Gets Out Alive* because they glamorized the drugs I was already doing. (Dad's hiding place for contraband literature—tall dresser, top drawer—was even easier to find than his *Playboy* stash.) If they suspected anything was out of whack, they never let on (and letting on was kind of their thing). And since, in classic teenage-girl fashion, I was barely talking to Mom anymore, it was easy enough to pass off being drunk or high as status-quo sullenness—just glare, don't giggle, and try to stand up straight. My biggest argument with my parents wasn't about whether I was getting into drugs and alcohol; it was whether my preferred all-black wardrobe (a color still associated, in the late eighties and early nineties, with satanic death cults and ritual abuse) made me "look like death."

Besides, I was a good kid, the kind who made straight As, practiced piano before my lessons, signed up for newspaper and theater club, and never skipped school or snuck out of the house. School came easy to me, and I enjoyed learning. I was a high-school freshman, a total overachiever, and a hard-core drug user.

My friends, on the other hand, were starting to fall off the map. Chris, who was repeating his freshman year and could barely be bothered to show up for class anyway, got kicked out of school for smoking pot in the bathroom and became a full-time bag boy at the local Kroger. Charles, who had a shitty home life and could barely read, started lashing out at everyone around him, including me; I finally cut him off for good after he tried to tear off my bikini top at the end of a long summer afternoon spent chugging Captain Morgan at the bayou behind our houses. Robert stayed in school but eventually developed a taste for heroin—a habit it would take him years to beat. And Jennie didn't make it through freshman year.

In our first two months at sprawling, windowless Clements High School, Jennie's problems at home became more serious, and we started to drift apart as her parents kept her at home more and more. But even when she wasn't allowed out of the house, she told me what was going on by writing notes—stacks of notebook paper, intricately folded and passed from hand to hand across the classroom—and they piled up in shoeboxes under my bed, forming a disjointed autobiography of a life in chaos. To hear Jennie tell it, her mom was constantly calling Child Protective Services on *her* when she ran away, forcing her to come back to the house where her leering stepdad would smack her around for a while before passing out on the couch. I was well into adulthood before I realized that CPS wasn't an Orwellian acronym for an agency whose job was rounding up children and sending them back to abusive homes.

I have no way of knowing how much of what Jennie told me about what went on behind the stained-glass front door of her ordinary suburban house was literally true, and how much was true enough. What I do know is that she was depressed enough to be on Prozac—the most prescribed antidepressant in the country at the time—and to have cycled in and out of a local mental hospital, which she described as a holding pen for the kind of catatonic crazies we had seen in *One Flew Over the Cuckoo's Nest* the previous summer.

Jennie and I kept this last blip in her biography from my parents, because Mom already thought Jennie was a bad influence and had been reluctant to let me invite her to my fourteenth birthday party. (If anything, I was a bad influence on *her*.) The photos from that day, taken a few days after Jennie returned from a stay at the loony bin, show the two of us on the floor, laughing hysterically, identical peroxide-blond streaks in our hair. But it was hard to hide Jennie's troubles. She would call at all hours of the day and night—hysterical over the latest crisis, begging me to come over to her house. I always did. I had no idea how to comfort her, but I could listen.

It was a Tuesday morning in late October, and my Halloween costume was awaiting a few final details. Jennie and I were dressing up that year as the Cycle Sluts from Hell, a silly metal band we had seen on *Beavis and Butthead* a few months earlier. We stole most of the stuff for our outfits from the nearby Target—the black lipstick, the spray cans of hair dye, the garters with little plastic guns. I was putting the finishing touches on a practice run of my makeup—swoop of black up to the brow line, gray on the eyelids—when the phone rang.

I picked up, and it sounded like I was catching Jennie mid-scream.

"Please, you have to come over!" she choked out. "He's hitting me again and I can't take it! Come over as soon as you can!"

I had heard this before, but something in her voice sounded different. I decided to push my luck.

"Please, can we go over to Jennie's really quick?" I asked my dad. "I know we might be late for school, but it sounds really important this time."

"No way, José. Time for school. You're going to miss first period." Dad was worried about getting to his job at Goodyear. Dad couldn't wait until I got my own car and could drive myself to school. Dad was, frankly, sick of Jennie's shit. He had heard this whole routine—the tears, the overwrought claims of child abuse, the hysterical pleas to come over—before. By the time I ran the two blocks to her house, she was always fine—in fact, she would brush off my concern so effectively that even I started to wonder if she just liked the attention. "At some point, you have to just let her deal with her own problems," Dad said—and he was the one behind the wheel. So instead of driving around the block to check on Jennie, we argued in the Volvo all the way to school.

"I'm really worried about Jennie."

"She'll be fine."

"But what if she's not?"

"She always is."

"You don't understand—her parents aren't like you and mom. They're really awful."

"People make their own problems."

"Dad . . . please?"

"No."

Jennie didn't show up at school all day, and she didn't pick up when I rushed home to call her that afternoon. Twisting the phone cord anxiously between my fingers, I called Robert, then Chris, then Jennie again and again and again. Finally, her sister Debbie picked up. It was hard to make out what she was saying through the tears.

"Jennie's." Sob. "Jennie's." Sob. "Jennie's dead! We found her on the bathroom floor this morning. She took a whole bottle of her pills. I have to go!" *Click.*

Death wasn't part of my vocabulary. Almost all my relatives were still alive—even my great-grandmother, by now confined to a nursing home and in the early stages of Alzheimer's. Had Jennie dropped clues, said things like, "If things don't change, I'm going to kill my-self!"? Of course she had. We all had. It wasn't supposed to be literal.

The rest of the afternoon clicked by in fragments. The kitchen clock, stuck on 4:44 for what felt like hours as I slid down the kitchen wall. The sound of someone pounding on the door. A line of ants, crawling aimlessly along the ground. Chris and me, slumped in each other's arms on my front stoop, the weather unseasonably cold for late October in Houston. Slamming my head into the fuzzy blue carpet of my bedroom over and over and over, shouting, "No! No! No!" Crying between two pillows in my twin bed in the dark. My dad coming into my room to tell me—for the first time I could remember—"I love you."

And: "I'm sorry."

I didn't go to Jennie's memorial. I stayed away when they planted the tree in her honor at our school, and glared at the kids who acted like they were her closest friends. I walked out of class and wrote moody poems about death and eternity. I listened to heavy metal and sat sullenly through family therapy, where an earnest young counselor asked me if I was thinking about self-harm while my parents looked on, wet-eyed and worried. I started hanging out in the occult section of the local Half Price Books. I bought a secret ward-robe of black clothes and changed into them at school, and dated a guy with a white stripe through his long black hair, who claimed his legs were so short because he had done too much acid before he hit puberty. (My taste in men would get only marginally better over the coming decades.)

Eventually, things improved. The guy with the skunk hair wouldn't stop offering to relieve me of my virginity—he said it like he'd be doing me a favor—so I dumped him and started dating Mike, a skinny kid with thick, wavy hair and Coke-bottle glasses. As a sophomore and a popular theater kid, he was out of my league, but I wasn't worrying about that so much anymore. Mike was sardonic, smart, and a little bit edgy—the kind of guy my parents wouldn't love, but wouldn't insist I break up with, either. We wrote each other sappy poems and made out in the stairwell after school, and one afternoon when my parents were out of the house, we lost our virginity to each other.

We were both half-formed—him, skinny and smooth-chested, me, still settling into my new teenage body—but I never thought twice about what we were doing, or felt like it wasn't my choice to make. All the lessons I'd learned at church about what happens when a girl loses her virginity—that she becomes like a used-up tissue, or a flower with all the petals plucked off—had long since receded, replaced by a world-weary impatience to skip past the squares on the board marked "adolescence" and head straight into adulthood, where no one would tell me what to do or who to be friends with or what colors I was allowed to wear. Sex? Sex was nothing—something to get over with, so I could say I'd done it.

But I was still a child in the eyes of my parents and the Texas school system, and there was a lot that my parents and the Texas school system hadn't taught me. I knew what sex was, roughly speaking, but the precise mechanics were a mystery I assumed would become obvious when the time came. My formal sex education had consisted of a one-hour lesson in elementary school, when the girls in our class watched a video about periods and pregnancy, and my informal sex education came from movies like *Mermaids*, where Winona Ryder hikes her skirt and clenches her teeth while an older man grunts and thrusts. Mom tried to supplement my education by handing me a pamphlet she got from a rack at the local Walgreens—a little taupe-and-brown number with a title like "What Girls Need to Know"—but the best information I had on the subject came from the copy of *Our Bodies, Ourselves* I had bought at Half Price and hidden away in the back of my closet.

We took it slow—fumbling around under the scratchy sheets on my twin bed until we figured out what went where. No one had warned me that it would feel like my flesh was being ripped apart. Tears spurted from my eyes; the room went dim. "Are you okay?" Mike asked. "Do you want to stop?" "No!" I managed to gasp, my ears roaring. "I want to do this. I'm fine." I had to get it over with *sometime*, I figured. Did I want to be one of those girls who got all the way to college without losing their virginity? I stared at the popcorn ceiling, looking for patterns in the bumps, while he finished. It didn't take long. When it was over, we held each other for a long time, panting. "I love you," he said. "I love you, too."

Safe sex was a given. It was the early 1990s, when HIV was still seen as a death sentence, and if I had ignored the lectures about how drugs would fry your brain, I had somehow absorbed the ones about pregnancy and STDs—especially pregnancy. I knew my mom was on the Pill, because I had seen the pink plastic pill compacts in the drawer next to her bed, but I was about as likely to ask my mom to take me to Planned Parenthood as I was to ask her how her sex life with Dad was going. So we made sure to get together only after school, before my parents got home, and we always used condoms.

I was sitting in my room, on the phone with Mike, when I heard my mom's voice ringing out from down the hallway. She was talking, as she often did, to the dog, but her tone sounded strange—confused, upset, a little panicky. "Ozzy . . . You're not supposed to have that!" later became the punch line to a joke I told at parties, but when our dog trotted up to my mother with a used condom in his mouth, it was the sound of a door slamming shut. I tried every lie I could think of—the condom wasn't ours, we only did it once, what did she expect when she wouldn't even discuss sex with her daughter?—but she wasn't having it. "It's not the having *sex* that I mind," she said. "It's the *dishonesty*." For the record: I'm pretty sure it was both. Before the evening was over, I was banned from seeing Mike ever again, and within two weeks, a woman named Ana started showing up every day when I got home from school and staying until just after my parents walked in the door. Her official title was "house-keeper/cook." Her actual job was "Erica's security guard."

One Saturday afternoon, not long after Ana started, another door closed when I came home to find my dad putting new locks on the liquor cabinet. Although neither of my parents were big drinkers, our house had a large, mirrored wet bar just off the living room, and its glass shelves were always stocked with gleaming bottles of Jack Daniel's, Beefeater gin, and Absolut Vodka, which my friends and I considered the height of sophistication. Beneath those bottles, whose backlit reflections created the illusion of a bar that went on forever, were cabinets filled with more obscure libations, like the sweet Yugoslavian wine from my parents' trip to East Germany in 1989 and the milky crème de menthe that came out during baking season.

For months, my friends and I had been stealing nips here and there while my parents were out of the house, and refilling the bottles of vodka and gin with water. I can't say exactly when they figured it out—like so many things that happened in those years, there was no discussion, only consequences. But I didn't spend long mourning the loss of easy access to liquor, because by sophomore year I had found more interesting things to ingest. Besides LSD and pot, I had discovered Mini Thins—convenience-store speed, now illegal, which made every pore tingle and vibrate with nervous intensity—along with whatever pills my friends stole from their parents' medicine cabinets. Certain drugs remained off-limits—crystal was for dropouts, coke was for the girls whose moms took them to Brazil to get boob jobs over winter break, and heroin was for skinny white guys who lived in New York City. But hand me a pill and say, "This will make you feel awesome," and it'd be down my throat before you could follow up with, "Actually, I'm not sure what those are."

Was I trying to numb myself, to escape from the pain of losing Jennie and the boredom of high school? Probably. Drugs and alcohol may elevate mood and reduce inhibitions, but they also numb some feelings (grief) and intensify others (euphoria). When I was high, I wasn't thinking about whether I would get into the college I wanted, or how hard it was to get close to new people after losing my best friend.

Drugs provided a social buffer that made me feel distant and superior to other people—from my science teacher, Mrs. Robinson, who tried in vain to teach me how to make a functional mousetrap car, to my wannabe druggie friend Meredith, who bought fake construction-paper "acid" and ended up freaking out in the school nurse's office. They also broke up the monotony of public school, which was, let's face it, designed to either bore kids into docile submission or incite an uprising.

Picture it: a flat, uninspiring two-story building flanked by vast parking lots, with a few scrubby trees casting pitiful shade. A student body the size of a small liberal-arts college, organized into the usual caste system of jocks and nerds and weirdos and nobodies, all lorded over by the straight-toothed popular clique. Football the dominant religion (with Christianity coming in a distant second), and even the arty kids, like me, conscripted into participating by painting run-through signs for the players to destroy at every home game. Hundreds of faculty, some attentive, some aloof, and still others a bit too attentive to their female students, offering stress-relieving back rubs during closed-door after-school study sessions. Enough mandatory conformity to inspire rebellion (a senior-year slideshow set to "Chickenshit Conformist" by the Dead Kennedys; dress code-compliant shirts worn braless and half buttoned), but enough academic rigor to keep those same kids on the path to elite scholarships and lucrative careers in finance and technology. In some ways, my high school was engineered for kids like me—left-brained memorizers with strong communication skills who could ace standardized tests through half-closed eyelids. In other ways, it was engineered to *torture* kids like me—easily bored overachievers who tore through the coursework quickly and didn't understand why they had to sit through classes.

It took a while, but eventually I stopped crying every day. Mike and I broke up, but I found a new crush, and started spending Friday nights with him, drinking half sugar, half coffee at the local IHOP. I fooled around, nothing serious, with a couple of other guys—David, a rich kid who introduced me to Monty Python; Chris, a punk rocker from Lake Jackson who I met at AstroWorld when we both chickened out while our friends rode the Zipper. On Saturdays, my new best friend, Sarah, and I would get high and sneak into Houston, where an artsy/gay/hippie district called Montrose beckoned with all-ages punk shows, no-ID foam parties, head shops, and occult bookstores. I started to find my niche at school as an editor and combative columnist for the school's weekly paper, the *Ranger Review*, and decided that the inkling of an ambition I'd had since I was five—the thought that maybe I could be a journalist, like Barbara Walters or Molly Ivins—wasn't just a fantasy, but something I could actually do. The cloud of despair that descended after Jennie died began to lift, and I started to understand the difference between depression and mourning. I had no reason to stop using drugs, until I found one.

His name was Josh.

Four

No One Understands You Like I Do

I met Josh, who was a year younger than me, in journalism class, where we bonded over our mutual antagonism toward Mr. Streich, a former newspaperman who seemed to bear the weight of generations of students' disdain on his sloping shoulders. Mr. Streich had it in for me from the beginning, just because I spent class time painting Wite-Out checks on my black Converse high tops instead of paying attention to his lectures on the inverted pyramid and journalistic objectivity, and he had it in for Josh just because he was always picking fights with the cheerleaders and mouthing off. Although I was a druggie and Josh was a nerd, we had something more important in common: We hated the same people, and isn't that the foundation for many a stable and lasting relationship?

Josh was mordantly witty, moody, and mercurial as the Houston sky. With his creamy, near-translucent white skin and slicked-back swoop of thick black hair, he looked like a hero in a manga comic book, or a character in the Anne Rice novels everyone was carrying around that year. Everything with Josh was always life and death, right from the start: If I ever did drugs or even smoked cigarettes again, he would hate me forever, and he'd kill himself if he caught me flirting with another guy. *Finally*, I thought, *I know what love feels like*. It felt like almost drowning, then coming up for gasps of air.

Josh and I spent as much time as our parents would allow in each other's company, watching *Mystery Science Theater* at his family's oversize brick house in a subdivision called New Territory near the county jail, playing card games at the Just Desserts coffee shop off Highway 59, and breaking into construction sites to make out inside the unfinished houses on the edges of suburbia. Now that I had my own car, a silvery blue 1984 Corolla, I was responsible for getting myself to school after my parents left for work, and Josh would wait around the corner in his green Ford Explorer until he saw my mom's Plymouth, then my dad's Volvo, round the corner of our cul-de-sac. Three minutes later, I'd hear the familiar tap on my window, and I'd give him the thumbs-up and come around to let him in. All clear.

Our fights were volcanic.

Their usual theme was loyalty; specifically, mine.

"How do I know you won't just leave me when you go to college?"

"I won't, I promise." (Hadn't I chosen a college close to home specifically so we could stay together while he finished high school?)

"Would you die for me?"

"Of course I would."

"If I find out you've been dating other people when you go off to college, you know I'll kill myself, right?"

"I would never do that." Somehow, nothing I told him could ever convince him that I wouldn't cheat on him, betray him, or leave him as soon as someone better looking, more popular, or less volatile came along.

No one liked Josh, which made me love him more; they couldn't see his humor, his wit, or his piercing intelligence, but I could. I defended him to my friends when he yelled at me and called me a slut in front of them; I begged my parents to let me keep seeing him even after he kicked the glass out of his bedroom window during one of our epic fights. I made excuses to my old friends when he told me to stop hanging out with them, and told myself that it was for the best: If I did see them, they'd probably just nag me to break up with him. What my friends couldn't see is that it was my fault for wearing an outfit that was too revealing, for refusing to walk out of class with him when he was having a really awful day, for bring-ing up my "wild" past, which sickened him. "I can't believe you fucked that guy," he would tell me, jamming pizza in his mouth. "Why should I believe you aren't still fucking him now?"

When Josh wasn't lecturing me about sex, he was lambasting me about drinking and drugs, which he considered crutches for weak people who couldn't handle real life. "What is wrong with you? Why would you do that to yourself?" I told him the drinking and drugs were in the past, that I didn't need those things now that I had him. (Hadn't I quit drinking and doing drugs for him? How many times had I told him that I only got high because I hadn't found anything meaningful in my life until we met?) We screamed at each other until our voices were ragged, whispered on the phone at night until both of us fell asleep, pulled each other's hair and threw things until we ran out of things to throw.

Days, sometimes weeks, would pass between Josh's meltdowns—which I never quite got over thinking of as "our" meltdowns, as if I were the one kicking out windows and punching walls. But the re-missions were always followed by even worse relapses. I learned not to let myself get too comfortable. One day, after one of us had hung up on the other, Josh showed up at my house uninvited, wheels squealing as he pulled into our cul-de-sac. I watched from behind the blinds in my living room as he parked his Explorer—the bumper dented slightly from the time we were both leaving the school park-ing lot, my car behind his, and he stopped abruptly to get out and yell at me about something—in the middle of the street, got out without closing the door, and held a kitchen knife to his chest, screaming, "I'm going to kill myself and it's all because of you!"

I ran outside, screaming. "Put down the knife! Please! I'm sorry! Just put it down!" Eventually, he dropped the knife in the street and drove away. The knife was small, with a black plastic handle. I picked it up, shaking, and walked back inside. At least my parents weren't home. At least no one saw. At least he didn't actually do it.

Another time, a few months later, we were driving back to Sugar Land from a comic-book store in Houston, with Josh's childhood friend Eli in the backseat, fighting about something I had done wrong. Without warning, Josh took his hands off the wheel. "We're all going to die now, and it's all your fault, you fucking bitch!" he raged, as Eli wedged himself into the backseat floorboards, whim-pering. Instinct, somehow, took over. As Josh pressed the gas pedal into the floorboard, I grabbed the wheel and steered his Explorer one-handed onto the Sam Houston Tollway, merging with traffic at seventy miles an hour. A minute later—it felt like twenty—Josh calmly took the wheel. I shrank back into the passenger seat, closed my eyes, and imagined myself getting smaller and smaller, the size of a basketball, then a marble—too small to hurt. On the way home,

Eli's sobs mixed with the repetitive whomp of tires against pavement. My eyes were dry.

I didn't drink once while I was with Josh. From the moment he told me to quit, and even through most of college, long after he had dumped me for someone else, I stayed away from booze and drugs. But without knowing it, I was already acting like an addict—obsessed with one person, one relationship, to the point that I was willing to put my own health and safety at risk. The highs were always temporary; the comedowns, crushing. Was I an addict even then, doomed to drink myself into near oblivion years in the future, no matter how easy quitting seemed at the time? Or did I only become an alcoholic many years later, after more than a decade during which I drank infrequently, or not at all? Was my addiction caused by emotional trauma I suffered as an infant, or did it swim in my blood courtesy of distant ancestors, unknown to anyone in my teetotaling family? Genetics play a large role in which of us become alcoholic, but they aren't the only factor, and it's possible, maybe even probable, that if I hadn't started to drink heavily many years later, some trigger never would have been tripped.

Who knows. Not me, not anyone.

There's a passage I love in Ruth Reichl's book *Tender at the Bone*, in which she asks her friend, the cookbook author Marion Cunningham, what it felt like to be an alcoholic. Cunningham considers the question for a minute, then responds, "As if there was not enough gin in the world." Reichl, moved, tells Cunningham that her recovery is "amazing." To which Cunningham replies, "Oh, hon. Nobody knows why some of us get better and others don't."

Nobody knows why some people become alcoholics and others don't, or why some of us can drink like normal people—or not drink, also like normal people—for years and years before the switch flips and drinking is no longer a choice but an imperative. And nobody knows why some of us get better—moderate our drinking and drug use, quit for good, replace debilitating vices with seemingly virtuous compulsions—and others don't. It just happens, and one of the tricks to making it stick is not trying too hard to figure out why.

Five

Not Drinking

Leaving home for the University of Texas, two and a half hours away in Austin, cured me of Josh in surprisingly short order, but nothing else about moving out of my parents' house came easy. I wasn't cut out for communal living, even though I had talked my parents into letting me stay in the nicest private dorm at UT—a blue glass tower that looked like it had been airlifted from downtown Houston and dropped on the southwest corner of the dusty campus. For most of my seventeen years, I had slept alone, in a queen-size bed, in a house where silence was a virtue. How was I supposed to survive sharing a 15-x-10-foot cell with a 5-foot-tall Russian named Marsha, who flung herself in and out of our shared space with all the abandon of a hyperactive puppy?

Marsha was tiny and silly—boys adored her—and she squealed with excitement about the smallest things, sending needles into the nerves at the base of my skull. A surprise eighteenth-birthday cake from my mom, or my news that a guy down the hall gave me a flirty look in our dorm elevator, would send her into a paroxysm of giggles. She had grown up poor, sleeping on two chairs pushed together as a makeshift bed, and sharing a room with just one other person seemed to strike her as the height of luxury. A common trope about only children is that we don't like to share anything, and that is partly true—we don't know *how* to share anything, from our food to our shampoo to our living space, until we're forced to learn. Living with Marsha was trial by fire. I never yelled at her—it would be like kicking a Pomeranian—but everything about her filled me with silent, coiled resentment, especially the way guys seemed giddy when she was around, thrilled by her careless, bubbly exuberance.

How can they fall for her stupid act? I wondered. *What is wrong with them?*

What is wrong with me?

The second thing I learned was that college wasn't going to be the amazing, world-expanding experience I'd been sold. I hung on to my journalism major for one semester—long enough to absorb the wise suggestion from an adviser that the way to learn how to be a journalist was to get a job in journalism—before switching to philosophy, because why not. The way I saw it, college was an obligatory stage in my life, a place to hit pause and achieve some milestones before I could go on to the adulthood I'd spent my whole childhood planning. But that didn't mean I had to like living among frat boys and frivolous girls who majored in psychology and didn't understand that life was struggle.

Awkward, shy, and lost among the fifty thousand undergrad students on the massive UT campus, I retreated into exercise, work, and music, spending Friday nights studying or sitting alone in my window seat seventeen stories above the campus and writing moody essays about existentialism while the Cure's "Disintegration" played on the black plastic CD-tape player I'd brought to Austin from my childhood bedroom. I had nothing but disdain for kids whose whole life revolved around Greek life and classes. I wanted to be in the real world, writing stories real people would read, not churning out 50-page treatises on the concept of the Übermensch for professors who had affairs with their students and invited undergrads over for drinks on Friday nights.

Work was the one place I felt at home. Two places, actually—I had a paying gig at a large chain bookstore that was in the process of conquering exurban America with its crappy coffee and comfy chairs, and an unpaid internship at a scrappy, liberal weekly magazine called *The Texas Observer*.

At the bookstore, I could judge people all day long, and my co-workers would be right there beside me, judging, too.

"Ugh, can you fucking believe the brides tonight? How many of those books are they going to make us clean up?"

"Seriously. We should go over there and start clearing them away right as they put them down on the table."

"They're so entitled they think we're their cleaning service."

"They're so dumb they think we're a library that sells coffee."

"I dare you to start picking up their shit right in front of them."

"I will if you do."

"Oh, shit, here comes Randy."

Randy was one of our bosses, a skinny gay guy with thinning hair who went around with a fake $3 bill in his front blazer pocket and was way cooler than the other managers who said things like, "If you'd apply yourself, you could have real management potential." Randy knew the most important thing about working in a dead-end retail job: The customer was always an idiot, and it was our job to make him feel like one. If someone approached the counter and said, "Hi, I'm looking for that book Oprah liked—the one about the woman? I think it was blue?" the proper response wasn't "Let me help you find that." It was: "I think the blue books are in the back," accompanied by a wide, open smile and a vacant stare. If a guy tried to hide his *Penthouse* under a stack of *Architectural Digest*s, we'd accidentally-on-purpose knock the dirty mag on the floor in front of the counter, forcing the guy to pick it up and maybe exchange an awkward glance with the blonde standing behind him with a stack of bridal books. (Just kidding: The brides never bought anything.)

Matt, who was sort of in between things when he washed up at the bookstore, was twenty-three, handsome in a heavy-browed, darkly Germanic way, and smarter than anyone who worked for minimum wage in a big-box bookstore had a right to be. Immediately, I got Randy to assign me to the section next to his—Philosophy through New Age, with Religion in the middle. (Matt was History, World and American.) I learned that, like me, he didn't drink or eat meat or dairy; that he was studying for the LSATs and wanted to work to end the death penalty in Texas; and that he considered himself a feminist. *Hot.* I insinuated myself into his life. He introduced me to Howard Zinn and Noam Chomsky and Fugazi, a band I've never liked, and I feigned interest in all of it because I wanted him to think I was the kind of girl who *got it. I'm probably just too dense to understand why this is good*, I thought to myself as I fidgeted on his scratchy polyester couch through the three-hour running time of *Manufacturing Consent*, the film based on Chomsky's book of the same name. "That was great, but have you read *The Media Monopoly* by Bagdikian?" I asked when it was finally over. It worked. He fell in love.

Being pursued was a welcome reversal of fortune, but I didn't want to ruin a good thing by reciprocating. Young women who think this whole "affirmative consent" thing is a recent development, hear this: In the mid-1990s, at least in the crowd I ran with, it was rare for a straight man to make a move on a woman without a lengthy, mood-killing conversation about everybody's feelings and wishes and long-term intentions. I managed to keep Matt at bay for months, feigning ignorance while he doted on me like a courtesan, until one day when I was laid up inside my apartment with a running injury during a rare Austin ice storm. Matt—always sweet, selfless, eager to please—had walked four miles across town and up an ice-slicked hill to bring me coffee, and as I thanked him and started to close the door, he went in for a kiss. I gave him my cheek, which was awkward enough—we weren't the cheek-kissing kind of friends—but then he turned bright red and ran away, muttering "I'm sorry" as he tried not to slip on the icy stairs.

I felt terrible about what I'd done to Matt—who was, after all, such a nice guy—and so, after some thinking, I relented. Maybe I *was* being too picky. Maybe I really *did* like him in that way. Maybe I *didn't* know what I wanted. Within a month, I had invited him back to my apartment, where I put a stop to his lecture about the evolution of punk rock into New Wave by climbing on top of him.

Matt had a lot of reasons for being the way he was—delicate, soft-spoken, *super* uncomfortable around people who drank—but the main one was that his dad killed himself when Matt was fourteen, ending his long battle with alcoholism. As a result, Matt had vowed that he'd never touch the stuff, and that was fine with me; my main preoccupations in those days were making enough money that I didn't have to move in with my parents over the summer, getting through college before my scholarship ran out, and getting a job in journalism, which had become an all-consuming goal, far ahead of making good grades or saving money or seeing the world. By the time I graduated, I had managed to do all three.

The last thing I had time to do was drink.

Six

My People

Back in the 1990s, when there were still enough jobs in journalism for anyone with talent and a taste for twenty-five-cent ramen to get their name in print, the traditional path for kids straight out of college was to move to a small town like Killeen or Lampasas, cover church suppers or Little League for a year or two, then take a job at whatever midsize or big-city newspaper would have them. For some, this meant joining the general-assignment desk at the local daily; for others, particularly those inclined to editorialize and swear, it meant covering cops or neighborhoods for their city's free alternative weekly, or taking an entry-level position at a liberal rag like *The Progressive* or *The Nation*.

If I'd ever had any doubt about which route I wanted to take, it dissolved as soon as I walked into the offices of *The Texas Observer*, which occupied two rooms on the ground floor of a crumbling Masonic Lodge building in downtown Austin. Stuffed to bursting with old papers, magazines, and yellowing reporter's notebooks, overrun with old desk chairs that had long ago lost their stuffing, the *Observer* was my Platonic ideal of a scrappy newspaper office. The two editors, Michael and Lou, were as different as two middle-aged white guys could be: Mike, the hangdog naysayer, was forever predicting that this next issue could be our last and breaking the bad news that there might not be enough money to pay the freelancers this month. Lou, the dashing, twinkly eyed optimist, was always bolstering Michael's spirits by rushing in with a scoop, a last-minute donation, or a pep talk. Both men terrified me, in different ways. Lou was hard to keep up with, and seemed like the kind of guy who would hide his disappointment in you with quiet forbearance, all the while thinking, "I thought she had it in her, but I guess I misjudged." Michael struck me as dour and critical—qualities common to many great editors— and I did everything I could to stay out of his crosshairs. In my months at the *Observer*, I tried to make myself indispensable— checking facts, running down documents, and copyediting columns by Jim Hightower and Molly Ivins, two pillars of progressive journalism in Texas.

After a while, they trusted me enough to let me write a few column inches, though it was far from clear their faith was justified. In those early days, nineteen and faking confidence I didn't have, I had to force myself to pick up the phone. The first time I had to call a Republican lawmaker, a good ole boy from Lake Jackson named Buster Brown, my voice was shaking so hard I had to close my eyes and clench my jaw just to scare up the courage to ask him about his involvement in promoting dioxin production in Texas's Gulf Coast "cancer belt." Michael handed back that story, my first feature-length piece for the magazine, covered in a forest of red marks so thick I could barely make out what I had written. I was used to getting school papers back with a big "A" at the top, followed by margin notes like "Excellent!" and "Perceptive"—not "confusing," "over-written," and "unclear." I considered turning in my key to the office, moving across town, and changing my major to something more suitable for someone who couldn't communicate in the English language—geology, perhaps, or visual art. But in the end, I decided that if I was ever going to make it in journalism, I'd just have to work harder than everybody else.

So I did.

Still in college and working two low-wage jobs, at a gift shop and the box office of a downtown theater, to pay my rent, I started logging long summer hours in freezing committee rooms at the Texas State Capitol. I thumbed through piles of documents at the public records division of the state election office, and I wrote up stories longhand in a yellow notepad in the ticket booth of the Paramount Theatre a few blocks down Congress Avenue from the Capitol. Like more than a few reporters I've known over the years, I was painfully shy, and few things terrified me more than talking to a possibly hostile stranger.

Or a friendly one: Nervous and distracted on my way to an interview with a famous death penalty opponent, I lost control of the pump at the filling station and showed up at her office reeking of gasoline. Another time, I was interviewing a prominent civil rights attorney when I started to panic that my questions weren't making sense, and I finished the interview in a dissociative state before rushing to the restroom to vomit. And if the stress of playing reporter wasn't bad enough, I was also working against a self-imposed deadline: Get a real job, in a real city, by graduation, or all the work—the unpaid internships, the dead-end retail jobs, the rush to finish in four years—will have been for nothing.

After my yearlong stint at the *Observer* ended, I took a second unpaid internship at *The Austin Chronicle*, the city's alternative weekly paper, and put my shoulder into the job like a straight-A student cramming for an English midterm (which, when I wasn't at the *Chronicle* office, I still was). I shoehorned myself in wherever I sensed opportunity, commandeering reporters' desks before office hours, volunteering to take notes at meetings the full-time reporters didn't want to attend, and refusing to go home until everyone had run out of things for me to do.

The truth was, I didn't know what I would do if I failed—I didn't have a plan B. I wanted everyone to think I was a grown-up so badly that I added a few years to my age whenever anyone asked, but I was still basically a teenager—impulsive, thousands of dollars in debt thanks to the credit cards they handed out like ADHD meds on college campuses in the nineties, and clueless about the basics of adulthood. I didn't know the first thing about paying my bills on time, talking through a disagreement without storming out the door, or which color of wine was the one you drank cold. I had a job as an editor before I knew how to tap a keg, or stick to a budget, or say no to sex I didn't want.

I didn't even know when guys were into me. Matt and I were on-again, off-again, and I was flirting with guys at work like—well, like an insecure twenty-year-old who wants everyone to like her and hasn't learned about things like "boundaries" or "mixed signals." On my first night out with Kevin, a 31-year-old copy editor at the *Chronicle*, it didn't dawn on me that we were on a date until he invited me to his place, a tiny garage apartment near the UT campus, and offered me a glass of wine. "Um, I'm okay," I said. His face fell. "Do you not drink wine?" he asked. "Oh, I do, of course," I lied, "but you know what? I actually think I might be getting sick. I'd better go. Sorry!" But then, a few months later, while we were both taking a break from the *Chronicle* to campaign for the Democratic candidate for state attorney general, Kevin asked me out again, and this time I said yes.

I avoided drinking during those late-teenage, early-adulthood years, turning down glasses of wine at parties or nursing a half pint of beer until it got warm in the glass. *I just don't like to drink,* I thought. But there was another reason: Something about it scared me. Years of dating boys and men who chose, for personal reasons, to be sober as Mormons had had their effect, but I also worried about losing control. I saw the way people got at parties—sloppy and unfocused, telling the same stories again and again—and I knew I didn't want to be like them. I wanted to keep my edge.

By the time I graduated the following year, my relentless usefulness had paid off. At twenty (twenty-three as far as anybody at the *Chronicle*, including Kevin, knew), I was an editor, hired to help edit the news section and cover the statehouse and city hall for the unfathomably generous sum of twenty-four thousand dollars a year. I hadn't had to go to Killeen or Lampasas. I had jumped the line.

I t wasn't long, though, before I started to see the drawbacks of working in a place without clear boundaries or schedules.

Wednesday nights at the *Chronicle* went like this:

"Jesus, when will they finish up at the tree?"

"I don't know—maybe if it ever gets dark?"

"Geez Louise, man, I want to get out of here!"

"Not gonna happen—looks like they're getting ready to play volleyball again."

My boss, Amy, and I—she's the one who said things like "Geez Louise"—had formed a rhythm over the year or so I'd been working at the *Chronicle*, and part of that rhythm was bitching about the tree.

The tree was where all the guys who worked at the paper, including our ostensible bosses, Nick and Louis, got high on production nights—also known as the nights when we were supposed to be putting out the paper. To get to the tree, you had to walk across the volleyball court (located where, at a normal office, the parking lot might be) and into a secluded area behind the construction trailer that housed South by Southwest, a scrappy but ambitious music festival the guys at the *Chronicle* had started as a side project back in the late eighties. Visits to the tree often segued into long, boys-only volleyball matches or mass excursions to the HEB grocery store across the street, and inevitably slowed production to a crawl. Even today, it makes me clench my jaw just a little to think about all the nights Amy and I sat in that overrefrigerated office, waiting for the publisher, Nick, to sign off on a piece of clip art ("Hmmm. I'm not sure which of these windmills really communicates 'wind power' "), or for the editor, Louis, to put the finishing touches on his crotchety stream-of-consciousness column, "Page Two."

If you're sensing a pattern here—men in the top jobs, making the decisions, women doing the grunt work at the bottom of the pyramid—so was I. Most of the newsrooms I've worked in have been led by men, with women in subordinate and administrative roles—section editors at best, junior reporters in charge of picking up public records at worst. In a dozen years in the alt-weekly business, I worked under just one female editor-in-chief, and she was pushed out after less than a year on the job, to be replaced by—you guessed it—an older white guy.

Back then, though, I still thought it was possible to be one of the guys—or, failing that, a cool girl, the kind who could match the boys round for round and didn't bitch about getting stuck at work because work itself was one constant party. I didn't know much about office politics, but I could tell that being a guy in journalism beat being a woman: No one ever made Hunter S. Thompson ride herd on a bunch of deadbeat production staffers or rewrite a higher-ranking male reporter's slapdash piece about police accountability. I couldn't play volleyball with the guys, but I could drink with them, and so, shortly after I turned twenty-one, I did—tagging along, practically unnoticed, whenever I heard the vaguest intimation of an after-work get-together, like a kid sister pleading, "Can I come with you?" to her teenage brother and his friends. For a while, I was the kind of drinker who would literally pour the rest of her glass of wine into a potted plant when no one was looking—that's how much I disliked the way drinking made me feel—but it wasn't long before I realized the power that alcohol had to untie the tongue, to blur social boundaries between successful, sexy, well-adjusted adults and awkward imposters, which is what I considered myself to be.

It didn't occur to me that the last time I drank with any regularity was in high school, and that my goal then was to get obliterated. It didn't even occur to me that people like me could *have* drinking problems. Why would it? Everyone drank, and if everyone drank, it must be normal.

The grown-up world replicates high school in ways we don't always recognize or acknowledge. I wanted to fit in with my older, sophisticated coworkers (most of them all of twenty-five), and drinking seemed to help. A few Mexican martinis (Patron, Cointreau, and lime juice, shaken and strained) brought out a sparklier version of my regular self—more gregarious, less judgmental, more flirtatious. Experts say that one of the warning signs of alcoholism is the ability to "hold" your liquor better than other people—to drink more, and faster, while acting less drunk—and by that standard, I was a textbook case. Maybe that should have given me pause, but no one had ever told me to worry about drinking; it was normal, something adults did as a reward for having hard, stressful lives. Alcoholics were middle-aged men with red, gin-blossom noses and three-day stubble, not pretty young women doing shots with the boys and calling out cheerfully for another round. Drinking offered a provisional entry into the boys' club, and I considered the fact that I could drink most guys under the table a point of pride. Tequila, sangria, vodka martinis—all were self-confidence, distilled. Two drinks in, I could turn off the critical voice in my head that insisted, *These people are way cooler than you*, or, *Everybody here thinks you're an incompetent child*. Four drinks in, I could silence the one that nagged, *These people are trite and annoying*. And six drinks in? Good-bye to the voice that said, *You have a boyfriend*, or, *Come on, this guy is beneath your standards*.

Guys seemed to like me better drunk than sober, and who could blame them? Sober me was impatient and critical and never talked to strangers; drunk me was brassy and confident, flirting with guys I wasn't attracted to and tottering off just before they could try to invite me home. There was always some reason to go out for a drink—it was a long production night, or an unexpectedly short one, or someone's getting married, or we're all about to go on a three-day weekend, let's get it started early! Dos Equis for everybody, bottoms up, shots all around.

Finally, I'd found my people.

The night I had my first blackout started much like any other—a quick bottle of wine over dinner with Kevin at Mother's Café, one of those college-town places that serve veggie burgers and tofu enchiladas in a glassed-in "garden" with a waterfall and hanging plants. After dinner, we drove over to Trudy's, a fajitas-and-margaritas place with a comfy back patio, where we met up with some friends from the paper and settled in for the night. The Mexican martinis at Trudy's came in chilled glasses, with the "extra" served in an ice-cold shaker on the side. One turned into two turned into tequila shots and closing-time beers. My final memories of that night are oddly vivid: a quick walk to the car, parked a block away on the wide street facing Hemphill Park. Kevin unlocking the door of his old blue 280ZX. The heavy coffin-lid sound of the door slamming shut.

And then, darkness.

My memory wasn't erased. It never existed.

Blackouts, if you've never experienced one, are profoundly disorienting; they can obliterate entire afternoons, convert whole conversations into static, by short-circuiting the brain's ability to record short-term memories. When you talk to someone who's in a blackout, they may seem almost normal, if a little loopy—until they start repeating the same stories over and over, or start the same argument again and again, because they can't remember what they said five minutes ago. Talking to a person in a blackout can be like talking to someone with dementia. There's no reasoning with them, because they've forgotten what you said before, and they're going to forget what you're saying right now, and so on, until time clicks back into place.

When time blinked on again for me, it was the following morning, and I was naked, sprawled sideways on my bed with Kevin snoring quietly at my side. I never let Kevin, or anyone, sleep over—insomnia, my old friend, made it next to impossible for me to share my bed—and yet, indisputably, here he was. So what the hell had happened last night?

I nudged him awake. "What did we do last night after we left Trudy's?" I asked.

He looked sheepish, and a little confused. "Um . . . I think we were fooling around, and then I think we both kind of . . . passed out." I had no earthly idea what he was talking about. Driving home, unlocking the door, getting naked, passing out on top of the sheets—none of it tracked. I didn't doubt that I had done all those things. I just couldn't remember a single minute of it. "Are you sure? We were making out? I don't remember that *at all*," I said. "I'm almost positive," Kevin responded, "but we were both pretty wasted."

I stayed home from work that day with my first real hangover, grateful for seltzer water and the *Chronicle*'s liberal sick-day policy. (Compared to the music guy who sometimes stayed out for days on a bender, my one-day absence was too minor to register.) By afternoon, I was feeling better, and I decided to put those missing hours out of my mind. *It happens*, I told myself. *Just be more careful next time.*

And I was. I kept on saying yes to drinks, kept matching the guys shot for shot, but I usually left before things got too blurry and headed home to basic cable and bed. I made sure to eat before I drank, and dialed back on nights out—top-shelf tequila was expensive anyway, and it was cozier to drink wine over dinner with Kevin in his new apartment, which occupied the upper half of a building designed to look exactly like a barn. It would be years before I had another blackout, years before I had trouble saying no, years before my "off" switch—the one that says, "You've had enough, it's time to stop drinking"—broke for good.

In the meantime, Austin was starting to make me itch. Two years earlier, writing for the alt-weekly in my college town had seemed like a chance to be big woman on campus—like going back to your high school as an adult, only now *you're* the principal—but increasingly, Austin felt like a festival wristband I couldn't take off. Living there, in the years before the tech boom brought high housing prices and deadlocked traffic, was just so easy; if I stayed, I would never have to build up a new circle of friends, learn the rhythm and politics of a different city, or think twice about what I was doing for the holidays. (Thanksgiving: Sugar Land, two and a half hours down Highway 71; Christmas: Meridian, another nine hours east on I-20 in Dad's old Volvo.) It didn't help that the summer of 2001 was *hot*—not the tolerable heat of a Mississippi scorcher, where you could get some relief by sitting in the shade with a sheet of stiff paper folded into a fan, but hot like a Russian steam room, the kind that sucks the breath from your lungs. The bank signs displayed numbers I'd never seen before—109 degrees, 111, 116.

Maybe it was the heat, maybe it was just that we were ill-suited for each other from the beginning, but Kevin and I had been fighting—not in the normal, bickering way that long-term couples do, but screaming, chair-throwing fights, the kind that make you wonder if maybe you just aren't built for relationships. I felt threatened by how much time he was spending with his roommate, and the fact that they went out all the time without me. He thought my politics were naïve and that I would see things differently once I'd grown up a little. I was insecure about my age and inexperience. He was insecure about his career, which seemed to be stalling just as mine took off. And both of us were ill-prepared to deal with conflict. My tactic was to fight until I wore out, then run away; his was to hold his breath until he exploded, which sometimes meant grabbing the nearest serving dish or lamp or folding chair and flinging it at the nearest wall.

Without asking Kevin what he thought of moving across the country, I started applying for jobs out of state, anywhere that would get me far enough away from Texas that I wouldn't be tempted to drive right back. Baltimore seemed like a promising option until I flew out for an interview, which included a drive through some of the city's toughest neighborhoods, whole blocks boarded up and abandoned to junkies and squatters. The problem wasn't the city or the job, it was me—I had only imagined I was fearless. "I guess I really am a sheltered suburban kid at heart," I told my mom from the airport on the way back to Austin, shivering at the memory of all those windowless, dead-eyed houses.

A few weeks later, I landed an interview with *Seattle Weekly*—a paper I knew little about, in a city so remote it might as well be in Canada. Two days before I flew across the country, after another interminable editors' meeting in the *Chronicle*'s dank, practically subterranean conference room, I traced the path from Texas to Washington with my fingers on the big map on the wall, marveling at the prospect of living somewhere so foreign. Seattle was perched on the edge of the country, three thousand miles away from any home I had ever known.

Summer had started unseasonably early when I landed in Seattle in late June, and the sky was the kind of blue you see in travel magazines, or cartoons—three shades darker than the washed-out sky that hung over Austin that year, without a single cloud to ruin the postcard effect. The air was warm enough to go sleeveless but not so hot you'd want to run for the nearest air-conditioned space, and the day stretched on forever, light still streaming through the curtains in my downtown hotel room at 9:30 that night. My interviews had gone smoothly—so smoothly, in fact, that they'd offered me the job that morning and taken me out for a celebratory lunch at a café overlooking Elliott Bay and the Olympic Mountains—and I was sitting on my king-size bed, savoring a bottle of red wine and an enormous slice of chocolate cake from room service, when I decided to call Kevin with the news.

"We're moving to Seattle!" I announced excitedly. The line was silent, so I tried again. "*I'm* moving, and you can come with me if you want."

"Well . . . Um . . . Seattle, huh?"

"I'm getting back tomorrow. Talk to you about it then?"

"Sure. Well, congratulations, I guess!"

Giddy with excitement, I polished off the bottle and fell into the soundest sleep I'd had in months.

Seven

Jumping Ship

As much as I liked to pretend that I was impulsive and carefree, moving to Seattle threw me for a loop. In the South, people practically go out of their way to interact with each other on the street—my mom, famously, will say hello to a homeless person passed out on the sidewalk until she gets an affirmative greeting back—but in Seattle, it's just the opposite. Strangers would cross the street midblock to avoid eye contact, and even in the middle of the summer, they pulled the hoods of their sweatshirts tight to create a physical shield between themselves and the world. Even my coworkers, most of them a decade or more older than me, seemed to vanish after 5:00 P.M., whisked off by express bus to one of the many picket-fence neighborhoods in this oddly suburban city. The closest the *Weekly* crowd ever came to socializing was at the Friday wine tastings, which is what the drinkers did before it was time to go out drinking. I was desperate for something to do after work besides hitting the gym, so I was usually one of the last to leave, which meant that I got to hang out with the paper's hard-core lushes—brassy broads who impressed me with their ability to put away a whole bottle of wine at a sitting. Years later, I would see one of these women in the checkout line at the grocery store, and avoid eye contact while we paid for our identical bottles of cheap 1.5-liter Chardonnay.

If Seattle's social cues were weird, its political scene was ass backward from anything I'd ever seen. In Austin, liberals dominated the city council and not much else; the state legislature was the bastion of right-wing Republicans, and developers were cartoon villains that wanted to pave over the aquifers that supplied the region's drinking water. But in Seattle, it seemed, the "conservatives" were actually all liberals, and the "liberals" were actually socialists. (The right-wingers were all across the mountains in Eastern Washington, and nobody paid much attention to them.) The notion of a one-party city was hard to wrap my mind around, and I was confused by how much the city's left seemed to hate certain local leaders, just because they supported one form of transit over another or had a different view on how to house the city's working poor. In Austin, where everyone had a car, riding a bike on the street—as I did—was a political statement, and drivers were as likely to nudge you off the road as give you an inch to maneuver between the windows of their F-150s and the curb.

In Seattle, owning a car was a political act, a subtle fuck you by the NIMBY ("Not in My Back Yard") reactionaries who ran the city to the wave of density-loving newcomers who were just moving in. I blew in to the city, knowing none of this, and immediately wrote a cover story about how much I loved my car (the unsubtle cover image: a license plate emblazoned "BUS SUX"), followed by a series of pieces lambasting the city's transit agencies. I wanted to be a smart out-of-towner with a fresh perspective, but my first acts as a writer in what turned out to be a very small town pegged me as a clueless, entitled jerk.

Worst of all, Kevin was still back in Austin, working up the nerve to quit the *Chronicle* and saving up money to make the move out west. I was lonely, and scared of the silence in my big basement apartment, and I took it out on him, leaving increasingly hysterical voice mails when he didn't pick up the phone, berating him when he finally did. I had kept a diary, off and on, for years, and now I wrote and wrote and wrote. July 26: "Victories today: Went for walk instead of crying." November 17: "I can't do anything right anymore and all I do is cry." December 2: "I'm too socially awkward and insufferably inarticulate to ever warm up to anyone." April 22: "Tonight went well. I didn't say a single stupid thing."

Reading those pages now, I wish I could go back and tell that scared twenty-three-year-old that it all turned out okay in the end, more or less. *Ease up on yourself*, I would say. *This wasn't even the hard part.*

Back in high school, when things were going really badly, I started having what I called out-of-body experiences. One moment, I would be in a bookstore with Josh, whisper-fighting over my outfit or why I was taking so long or what we were doing next, and the next, I'd be outside myself, listening to my heart pound from a great distance as I watched my body hustle toward the nearest exit. These spells were often triggered by some innocuous sound—rustling paper, or the bell on a cash register, or the jingle of coins in someone's pocket— and they were unpredictable, sometimes going on for hours. They drove me further inside myself. I never knew when an attack would strike, so I never ventured too far outside my comfort zone: School, my part-time job at a Hallmark store six blocks from home, my room, and Josh. Over time, I came to recognize these "spells" as panic attacks, but it would be years before I learned to manage them, and more than a decade before I learned to do anything other than run away.

The attacks had come on less and less frequently after college, thanks in large part to my therapist, Miriam, who taught me how to "talk back" to the thoughts that were making me leave my body. But as soon as I moved to Seattle, they returned with vertiginous urgency. A panic attack is like a fire whipping through a forest turned to kindling by drought: Even as it starts to die down, the slightest gust of worry (*Is my heart still pounding? Can everyone tell I'm freaking out?*) can whip it back into an inferno. Worry piled upon worry piled upon worry (the clinical term for this is catastrophizing), and even though I knew obsessing over my state of mind wasn't doing any good, I just couldn't stop. (Addicts, it turns out, are a bit prone to obsessive behavior.) I started writing long instructional notes to myself in a jittery hand, things like: "Just <u>stop</u> focusing so much on how you're feeling physically. It doesn't do any good and only makes you panic & feel worse. If you just decide to stay in bed again, focusing on how much fun you're not having, then you shouldn't be surprised when you feel worse.") My self-directed lectures did nothing, and before long, I was downing a quarter milligram of Xanax every morning, with a Prozac chaser, courtesy of the free clinic near my office. (I had health insurance, but for some reason, getting a real doctor seemed beyond my capability.) The Xanax mitigated the attacks, but only as long as I kept taking it, and the Prozac made me feel like I was walking under water, choking for air. *Nothing will ever feel different or better*, my brain told me. *You'll eventually be so paralyzed with fear that you'll lose your job and have to move back in with Mom and Dad. And then they'll get sick of you and you'll end up living on the street. And what will you do then?*

One thing did seem to help. I noticed that if I had a drink in the evening after work, the attacks would subside for a while and I could get through the night without climbing the walls, feeling like my body belonged to someone else. Before long, I started keeping a bottle of vodka in my freezer—a frosted fifth of Absolut, the ultimate symbol of glamour in my eighties childhood. (Jennie, always two steps edgier than I would ever be, plastered the wall above her bed with those Absolut ads that were ubiquitous throughout the nineties—the ones where the bottle was turned into a skyscraper or a pile of presents or a reflection on water. When she died, I couldn't help picturing her mom tearing down all those liquor ads from her wall.)

Buying liquor in Seattle in those days was a bit of a hassle—hard alcohol was only sold at state-run liquor stores, and the closest one was a couple of miles away—so I tried to make a bottle last several weeks, indulging in a weak vodka soda after I had eaten my spartan dinner of canned vegetable soup and Wheat Thins. Drinking alone felt subversive, the kind of thing I found noteworthy enough to joke about with Kevin: just two weeks in Seattle, and already the place was turning me into an alcoholic. Sometimes, if I was feeling especially sorry for myself, I would pour a second drink—just vodka this time, over ice—and settle in to watch *Terms of Endearment*, which was always on rotation on AMC. Kevin would know it had been a two-drink night if I called him, sobbing, to accuse him of abandoning me in Seattle and trying to meet someone better in Austin. But those were also the nights when I slept the best; when the jitters didn't overtake me, and when the silence in my quiet neighborhood in a sleepy corner of Seattle didn't feel as overwhelming as it did when my nerves were running at full voltage.

Kevin did make it out to Seattle, and I fixed him up in an apartment a couple of miles away from me, a top-floor unit in an old building with awful brown shag carpet and a glassed-in balcony that always left the place with a bitter chill. I felt more grounded with him around, but I still missed the easy human connections I had made in Austin.

For months, the only people who passed for friends were my middle-aged coworker Jim and a few city council aides who were still more like sources than confidants. As my social life shrunk and stalled, I started to wonder: *What does it take to make friends in this town?*

Less than a year after I took the job, the *Weekly*'s new owners fired all three of the women at the top of its masthead—the editor, managing editor, and publisher—and replaced them with three middle-aged guys who were supposed to revive the paper's flagging readership. To accomplish that, they hired more white guys, until the only women on the editorial side of the office were me, a half-time education reporter, and a music writer who spent her days shopping for clothes on eBay. The paper became a mirror of its new management. Detached Gen-X irony was out; indignant baby boomer outrage was in. Dishy columns poking fun at city council members were replaced by dour ruminations on the state of the local peace movement, or opinion pieces bemoaning the impact of urban development on a local creek. The house style became reflexive contrarianism with a libertarian bent. Stories that poked at "conventional wisdom" ("The Excesses of Affirmative Action") made it on the cover, even if that wisdom was conventional because it was true.

Weekly staffers under forty started talking about jumping ship to *The Stranger*, our younger, cooler competitor, and details of our editorial meetings started to leak into its pages, making us look prissy and out of touch. Furious, the new management team vowed to find and fire the culprit. (Punishment for disloyalty was a bit of a company tradition; a few months after I started, someone broke into my boss George's office after hours and plastered every surface with signs for Grant Cogswell, a city council candidate George despised. I thought it was hilarious, but my bosses disagreed, and the next day, HR tracked down and fired the ad rep who'd let the pranksters into the building.) *The Stranger* wasn't just our crosstown rival—it was our enemy, run by enfants terribles like Onion cofounder Tim Keck and sex columnist Dan Savage, who hadn't so much paid their dues in the journalism world as plowed through it in a party bus. My counterpart/nemesis over there was a guy named Josh who showed up at city council hearings in a basketball jersey and helped orchestrate a "dance-in" at council chambers to protest a city law called the Teen Dance Ordinance prohibiting all-ages clubs.

The guy who was behind the leaks, a skinny former intern named Tristan who hadn't stopped sulking since our old bosses got fired, wasn't hard to catch. He sat and scribbled openly throughout our editorial meetings, and then his notes, translated into gossipy news items, would appear in *The Stranger* a week later. Shortly after he was fired, Tristan's byline started showing up in *The Stranger*. And while I didn't condone his ingratiating tactics I was desperate to follow him, so I let Josh know I was looking to make a move.

Within a few weeks, after a warm-up interview at which I don't recall saying a single word, I found myself walking nervously into a bar across the street from *The Stranger*'s office. For an hour, the guys—Dan, Tim, and Josh—drank and joked and pummeled me with questions. The *Weekly* sucks. Why did you go to work for them? (Tim.) How do we know you aren't a spy? (Dan.) "Why should we hire you when you're an apostate on the monorail?" (Dan again, referring to a story I had written criticizing a plan to build a citywide monorail system that was, believe it or not, the hottest issue in Seattle in 2003.) I nursed a half glass of red wine with sweaty hands. By the end of the interview, the guys were tipsy, I was terrified, and Dan and I were yelling at each other about transportation policy. I got the job.

The following week, after I handed in my notice at the *Weekly*, I went to Friday staff drinks at Bill's Off Broadway, a grungy pizza place with pies so buttery they practically slithered off the plate. Years later, Bill's would be the place where I would burn a hole in the collar of my favorite red wool coat by draping it drunkenly across a candle; the place where an eighteen-year-old intern would pour himself into my lap, begging me to buy him a beer; and the place where I would make awkward small talk with the wife of the co-worker with whom I was having an affair. But tonight, I was the new girl making small talk at a party full of strangers, clinging to a beer I didn't want just so I'd have something to do with my hands. I was two nervous pints in when Dan showed up, sauntered over to my side, called everyone to attention, and said, "Welcome to the team!" Then he slid his hand onto my back and undid my bra.

"Um . . . what?" I giggled, feeling a dozen pair of eyes on my chest. "Ha, ha, nice welcome." Grabbing at the clasp through the back of my sleeveless top, I fled for the restroom, face ablaze. *What did I do to make him do that?* I wondered. *Is this some weird kind of hazing? Does he do that to everyone?* By the time I got back, bra securely clasped, everyone had moved on to talking about other stuff, so I pulled Dan aside. "Why did you do that?" I asked. "I used to be a drag queen!" he responded, laughing. *Oh. That explains it.* I smiled nervously, said, "Oh, I didn't know that!" and poured myself another pint.

Big changes happened in rapid succession. I moved from the basement apartment to a place six blocks from work, within stumbling distance of a few dozen bars. As I got more enmeshed with the people I was meeting through my job—artists, politicians, people who knew where the after-party was—I started to pull away from Kevin, and he noticed; there was always an argument brewing beneath the surface of our Saturday-morning farmers market trips, and more and more I spent weekend nights in the company of my friends from work, drinking and laughing and drinking and drinking and drinking. I was embarrassed, I think, by Kevin's Oklahoman sincerity, his slow way of talking that people sometimes misinterpreted as being just plain slow. "Why don't you break up with him?" my new friend Tiffany, *The Stranger*'s food critic, would ask me, raising one quizzical, perfectly contoured eyebrow. "I mean, I couldn't date anyone that short, but you are shorter than me, so . . ." I shuddered to think of the two of them in the same room together. So I compartmentalized. I kept my two worlds—Kevin world and *Stranger* world—apart. I tried to be two different versions of myself—the Erica who loved cooking and dad jokes and bad TV, and the one who did shots and took dares and made fun of posers—until I didn't know which was real, which was a false front. Until it didn't matter.

That's when I started sleeping with Josh.

Kevin and I had broken up—that is, he had stormed out of my house, saying it was over, and I had decided to take him literally—and it was the end of a six-drink night when I offered to drive Josh home on my scooter and ended up hanging around for six months. Josh was one of the smartest, weirdest people I had ever met, and we had an uncanny connection, right from the beginning. I had always found it hard to be fully myself around anyone, but Josh and I were so similar that it was impossible to be dishonest with him, or pretend to be anyone other than I was—a messy, insecure, emotional young woman with outsize ambition and a lot of things I wanted to talk about. When I tried to keep things from him—like the existence of my birth mom, Cindy—they would come pouring out anyway, until I felt that there was nothing I couldn't tell him. What incredible luck to find someone I never get tired of talking to, I thought. I told myself—not for the first time about a guy I had just started dating—I think I'm in love.

And then—you knew this part was coming, right?—he dumped me. Too emotional, too young, too literally-his-employee. I was devastated. Our coworkers were vindicated. I didn't know how I would ever get over him while seeing him every single day, but I was determined not to quit. We fought at work for a year—screaming fights, superficially about work—and I frequently stormed out, slamming his office door so hard the whole floor shuddered. And the weirdest part about the whole thing is that it all worked out. Josh—who has airlifted me out of bad situations and picked rocks out of my back after a bad bike accident and saved my life more times than I can count—became the brother I never had: a brother who stays up too late, like I do, and shares some of my idiosyncratic obsessions, but also spends his time doing things I admire but can't understand, like reading his own poetry to people out loud and striking up conversations with strangers on crowded trains. He's my rock, and I haven't always deserved him. In fact, long after we got whatever *that* was out of our systems, I spent a good five years doing my best to drive him away.

Eight

I Can't Say It, But
You Know I Do

D oes anybody really love being in their twenties? I sure didn't. I spent most of this supposedly happy, carefree decade trying on personas—embarking on a series of unsatisfying relationships, investing in friendships that made me feel worse about myself, feeling profoundly uneasy in my own skin. The idea of "happiness" itself seemed like something dreamed up in a marketing lab, like "zen" or "bliss." Who the hell is happy? Not me, not my friends. Instead of happiness, we had each other, a bunch of deeply discontented people, sitting around and drinking and making fun of the world.

I spent my mid-twenties waiting to feel comfortable, and drinking to fake it. I didn't get shit-faced every time I drank—that came later—but I came to appreciate the power of alcohol as a social lubricant. Soon enough, a midday beer started to feel like an earned indulgence, and if I got drunk on both Friday and Saturday nights, who cared? So did everybody else, and besides, that's why God invented Sunday. I didn't want to be the outsider who worked until eight and then went home alone to soup and crackers. I wanted to belong.

And eventually, I sort of did.

By now, it was 2004, and my group of friends included Tiffany, an archivist named Sarah, Tristan (the former *Weekly* spy turned *Stranger* rising star), and a tall, curly-haired musician named John, who wrote film reviews and fronted a band that had had a big hit when I was in college. I had a parallel group of friends from the political world, including Lisa, a flame-haired, opinionated city council aide who defied every convention associated with the term *public servant*, and Stephanie, another council aide who talked a mile a minute and somehow knew everyone, from gray-haired ex-governors to the band that was playing at Chop Suey on Friday night. Lisa was the friend I went to bars with, one-on-one, on weekends when I wasn't busy tagging along with the *Stranger* crew; with her red hair and flamboyant outfits that accentuated her va-voom figure, she inevitably ended up waving off guys' numbers by the end of the night.

I liked to keep my friend groups separate—city hall people after work on weekdays, *Stranger* friends on weekends, when a night might last until five in the morning, long past the bars closed at 2:00 A.M. The city hall people found the *Stranger* crew shallow and snobbish, and the *Stranger* group found the city hall crowd boring and square. It was high school all over again.

On Saturday nights, five of us—me, Tristan, Sarah, Tiffany, and John—would often end up at Tiffany's elegant apartment, which was perfect for languid late-night drinking and complaining. Everything was just so, from the pristine cloud of white linens on her bed (visible through the French doors that opened onto the living room) to the elegant monochromatic glassware displayed in the cabinets that lined her perfectly put-together kitchen. Even the toiletries were all carefully covered with blank white labels, like an art project about the concept of bodily functions. After taking off our shoes and filling up our champagne flutes, we'd flop down on the couches and gossip lazily about who was trying to sleep with whom, who were no longer sleeping together, and who was secretly sleeping together and didn't want anyone to know.

But guess what? Some of us were better at keeping secrets than others.

John was married but was infamous for pushing boundaries— Tiffany told me he once grabbed her by the waist and said, "If we had met at a different time and place, I would kiss you right now"— and when he sent me an initial, testing-the-waters text on my 2003 Nokia candybar phone ("This is more than a test"), I figured it wouldn't go much farther than that. Married guy, used to be semi-famous, starts feeling insecure and seeks some validation from pretty women to prove he's still got it, and that's as far as it goes. Right?

As if that's ever where it ends. Within months, we were texting each other from across the room at Tiffany's house—*what if we left together, right now?*—and then one night he was standing at my door, acting nervous, bottle of red wine in hand.

I had always assumed infidelity would involve more pretense—a tortured conversation, maybe, some self-justifying explanation about how his marriage was a sham—but there was nothing to it. We sat, we drank, and he opened his arms. And then, after a while, I took his hand and led him into my bedroom.

Sneaking around had always come naturally to me, and I slipped into the role of secret girlfriend like it was the part I had been born to play. It was thrilling, like a shot of tequila—a little hit of dopamine every time my phone buzzed and the little pixilated envelope indicating a new message flashed on my screen. If I had qualms, I just reminded myself that I wasn't the one who was cheating—and what business did I have worrying about the state of his marriage? Before long, John and I were stealing away for midday "lunches" at my apartment, and I was sitting up waiting for him to come over after band practice, which often lasted until eleven or twelve. Occasionally, he would spring for a hotel room—once out by the airport, when he was flying somewhere for work, and once on a whim, when I was out drinking with Lisa at a bar downtown. "I'm at the Ace downtown," he texted. "Can you get here?" I told Lisa I had to take an emergency phone call and ran down the street, leaving her alone at the bar.

It was all worth it, though, when he played me a new song that he said was about me, and when he finally told me that he loved me. Well, not exactly. What he actually said was, "I can't say it, but you know I do." Close enough. A comment like that was like a drink of water at the end of a long, grueling hike: It replenished me in a way that the predictable generosity of a regular relationship just couldn't. I could live for a week on "I'm so happy I got to see you tonight," or a T-shirt he thought to buy me at the airport on a trip to see his family back East. "Somebody in Nashville loves you." Hey, he's talking about *me*!

Eventually, when gifts and late-night texts were no longer enough to assuage me, "I love you" became an all-purpose balm. It smoothed over all the times he disappeared for days without texting, or the times when my phone buzzed with some vague excuse—"I've been held up by circumstances, but I'll be there as soon as I can," meaning one in the morning, or never. "I love you," he would tell me when we finally saw each other. "I *need* you." And all the despair and anguish I'd been feeling would disappear, the way a hangover vanishes when the first drink kicks in.

Everybody knows that cheating men don't leave their wives. And everybody who gets "chosen" by a cheating man thinks they're the exception, even if they tell themselves they know better, as I did. Eventually, though, I did start to wonder: Was I just like all the rest of them? Because, as I quickly discovered, I wasn't the first—or the fourth, or the tenth. I started to resent his wife, and, increasingly, him. I did little things, then bigger ones, to make him jealous, thinking maybe if he knew how easily he could lose me, he would try a little harder to keep me around. Meeting guys at bars, it turned out, was the easiest thing in the world—if someone had told me all it took to start a conversation was a few drinks for bravery and an ability to act interested in a guy's screenplay or band or alma mater, I would have started doing it a whole lot earlier. I had never thought of myself as the kind of person who had one-night stands, but now, weeklong or monthlong flings became a point of pride—proof that I didn't give a fuck, a way to avoid giving someone time to disappoint me.

Not that every guy I met was a dud—I liked some of them quite a bit, but, you know, I was taken. So I always came up with some excuse to dump them or drive them away. One guy wanted me to throw a football with him in the park like I was his kid or something. Another couldn't name the mayor. Still another once referred to my breasts as "titties." Gone, gone, gone. Eventually, an act of rebellion— going home from a bar with one of John's old friends—led to something that could have turned into a real relationship, but it came with a built-in kill switch. What was I going to do—dump the guy who said he loved me, or come up with some excuse to end a relationship that John said was "killing" him?

Still, I told myself that I was under no illusions—John would stay with his wife, and I would move on. Just not yet. It wasn't even like John was the kind of guy I'd want as a partner (he was a cheater *and* a musician). What drew me to him was the feeling of being chosen, as if no married man would cheat on his wife unless he felt compelled by an attraction too strong to resist. If John, whose stories about one-night stands and backstage hookups had me convinced he could have anyone he wanted, would risk everything to see *me*, then I must be something really special.

By Christmas, it had become harder to maintain the façade. I was drinking almost every night, and every show of affection from John felt like a referendum on my value. When he showed up at my apartment loaded down with a ridiculous number of gifts—an expensive stainless-steel Cuisinart food processor, cookbooks, a red rhinestone brooch—I wasn't grateful; I knew, from his text telling me he'd be late, that he'd been shopping at Tiffany, and I didn't see any blue boxes on my floor. When he got us a hotel one evening shortly before he left for the holidays, bolting after just a few hours with a paper-thin excuse about a last-minute band practice, I sulked: I just knew he would never treat *her* that way, inviting her out for a special occasion and then leaving in the middle. I started getting my revenge wherever I could—making out with a friend of his at a party while he waited for me in his car back at my apartment, or talking about my latest boyfriend while we were all at Tiffany's, knowing he had to sit there and take it—but I always felt that he had the upper hand. Compared to just . . . *being married*, dating was so much work, and going out for conveyer-belt sushi with a nice guy you met through a friend of a friend is never going to provide the same thrill as having midday makeup sex in the office bathroom with your married lover.

Things went on like this for two years. They might have continued for years longer, if we hadn't decided to take a trip to California—a significant step, I thought, because it meant being out in the real world together, not confined to the 600 square feet of my apartment or some anonymous hotel room. Surely, it *meant* something. Maybe he was ready to leave his wife and be my boyfriend, but for real.

In reality, it was a swan song. We landed in San Jose, picked up the red convertible John had reserved at the airport, and drove down to Monterey—an adorably romantic coastal town with a beach called Lovers Point. In theory, we were free. But outside the familiar privacy of my darkened bedroom, John and I were like strangers, people who had never seen each other in daylight and were suddenly getting a look at each other's flaws. What do you talk about when you suddenly have not a couple of stolen hours, but all the time in the world? I had no idea, and I babbled about anything to fill the silence—the aquarium we'd just visited, books I'd read, the wonderful food at the famous restaurant we went to in Big Sur, and on and on and on and on. I was just so terrified that I would turn out to be a disappointment, and he would stay with his wife after all, and then what in the world would I do?

Finally, it was the last day of our trip. In an attempt to be close to the airport for our flight in the morning, I had booked us a room in Mountain View—home of Google, LinkedIn, and ten thousand office parks—and the place was a dump: Burger King in the lobby, cracked plastic Jacuzzi tub in the bathroom, and scratchy polyester bedding that looked like it hadn't been laundered since the nineties. We were sitting in bed, under a pink thermal blanket, when he said it.

"I can't do this anymore."

"This? You mean—this trip?"

I knew perfectly well that he wasn't talking about the trip.

"No. This. All of this. This trip was a bad idea. But the whole thing has gotten out of control."

"No. No, you don't mean that." If I could stall him, just for a minute, maybe I could figure out what I'd done wrong. Was he saying this now because I had acted so needy for the last few days? I could be less needy. Was it because I mentioned that it was Valentine's Day when we were at the restaurant? I didn't even care about Valentine's Day—surely he knew that! Did I act like I cared? Did I pry too much into his long disappearances, when he wandered off to call his wife, or—who knows—some other girlfriend? I didn't mean to be nosy; I could learn to be less insecure.

When I came out of my reverie, he was still talking. But now he was talking about his wife.

"When we get back, I'm going to tell her everything. All of it. Fuck it. I'm going to write her a letter and just confess. I can't do all this lying anymore. It's killing me. This was a bad idea." He was spiraling. Crying, like he wanted me to sympathize with him when it was *my* life he was ruining. "I don't want to throw away my marriage. I'm just going to tell her everything and let her decide what she wants to do," he said.

Did I take this news graciously, recognizing with equanimity that all affairs must come to an end? Reader, I did not. Instead, I bawled, begged, screamed, accused—"Why the fuck did you bring me all the way to California if your plan all along was to just break up with me?"—until John threatened to leave me alone at the motel and drive back to San Jose by himself. "Oh, so you're just going to abandon me out here in Mountain View without a car? You fucking asshole!" I screamed.

Then I begged him not to go.

We flew back to Seattle the next day in bruised, exhausted silence. I had finally stopped arguing. The following weekend, John kept his word, writing his wife a long letter confessing everything, or at least the part of "everything" that had to do with me. Unmoved by his honesty, she kicked him out, keeping the cat and the apartment and the couch on which I had once sat, scrolling furtively through the images on his phone. I visited John a few times at his new apartment—a tiny studio above a four-lane highway, with a cramped sleeping alcove and a view of nothing—but there was a chill about the place. John had never wanted to date me; he had wanted to feel wanted, the same way I had. Within a few years, he would be married again, and I would still be drinking with the same old crowd or, more and more often, alone.

Nine

You'll Never Guess
Who I Went Home
with Last Night

I don't want to romanticize the relationship between writing and
drinking—sober, my mind can follow a thread through to the end
in a way that I couldn't in the days when the longest thing I had to
write was a 500-word column about city hall. But there is also this
truth: Every writer I know drinks, or did until they couldn't anymore. Some of the most brilliant writers I have known have been
what are euphemistically called "high-functioning" alcoholics—
guys who head to the grocery store at noon for a bottle of red wine
to tide them over at their desks until they can hit the bar at four,
women whose lunchtime martini orders are seen as a sign of joie de
vivre, not medicine to forestall the shakes. Alcohol can fuel creativity, and it can shake loose the cobwebs that form when you're staring

down a blank screen and a deadline. But drinking can also make for muddled writing, and mistakes—and as I started to drink more heavily while I wrote, my work got sloppier, and I found myself filling in gaps and fixing errors the morning after. Even worse were the times when I was ready to turn in a column or story I'd thought was full of clever turns and insight, only to read it in the light of day and realize: *Fuck. This makes no sense.*

Tiffany and I still spent a lot of time together, but I was starting to wonder just how much she really enjoyed my company. It wasn't that she said anything explicit, like "You're lame. Leave me alone." It was just the way she talked to me, like I was constantly fucking up—buying my own shots at the end of the night instead of waiting expectantly for a guy to pay for them, or borrowing her lipstick without asking. And I had seen how she talked about our friend Sarah, like she couldn't do anything right. Like one time, Sarah brought a mixed five-pack of beers to Tiffany's, and as she took them to the kitchen, Tiffany looked at me and mouthed: "Five mixed beers? Why bother?" Sometimes, it even seemed like she was testing me to see how much I'd put up with. For my thirtieth birthday, I cooked a massive southern dinner for twenty friends from both my friend groups in my tiny, no-smoking apartment, and near the end of the meal, Tiffany pulled out a pack of Camels and lit up right at the table. Stephanie still talks about it.

But I needed someone to hang out with on the weekends, and Tiffany always knew where "everyone" would be. The thought of spending a weekend night alone paralyzed me, and whenever it happened, I just had no idea what to do with myself. Go to a bar and read? Pathetic. Stay home and drink alone? Even worse. Go to the gym? What, like someone with an eating disorder?

I started to realize that I felt more comfortable around my two best friends when I'd had a little to drink before I went to meet them, and since we might not start drinking right away, it made all the sense in the world to just buy a pint of vodka at the liquor store and keep it in my purse. I even justified it as a money-saving move: If I snuck off to the bathroom occasionally for a few quick swigs, I would only need to buy half as many drinks. It's funny the things you can talk yourself into. Before long, I was getting drunk more nights than not, and sleeping with guys I had known for a couple of hours, or whom I'd known for years and never thought about that way, until I was six drinks in and not thinking about much of anything. *You'll never guess who I went home with last night. . . .*

One night, I decided to go home with an acquaintance of mine, another one-hit wonder musician notorious for trying to sleep with any woman who was conscious, and probably some who weren't. (Tiffany told me he had once cornered her in a bathtub, where she had gone to escape during a coke-fueled party, and tried to force her to give him a blow job. If that happened, it was the kind of thing we laughed off in those days—just another "can you believe that guy" story to roll our eyes about over Bloody Marys in the morning.) I don't recall exactly how or where we started talking—drunk memories can be blurry like that—so let's just say it was after my fifth or seventh or ninth vodka-soda of the night, and he asked if I wanted to come to his apartment, and I shrugged, smiled coyly, and said, "Okay!"

Here, my memories go black. I don't remember how we got to his place. I don't remember where he lived or what we talked about on the way there. When my memory clicks back on, I'm climbing the stairs into an ultramodern townhouse: three stories, one and a half baths, and a kitchen that, while bachelor-small, is stocked with a full bar's worth of liquor and Le Creuset cookware that had probably never touched a burner. The room is starting to list sideways and I make a hasty detour to the nearest restroom. As I'm kneeling on his bathroom floor, trying to puke as quietly as possible while he rustles around in the kitchen for more champagne, I can't stop myself from thinking, *Damn. Are these heated floors?* Even as I'm kneeling there, wanting to go home, I'm also writing tomorrow's story: *You won't believe who I went home with last night. And—you're not gonna believe this—his bathroom has heated floors!*

Did I enjoy it? You'd have to ask someone who was there. My brain clocked out again sometime between the first sip of champagne and the bedroom upstairs, and it didn't click back on until later that night, when I stole back down to the bathroom to hack up whatever was left in my stomach and steal a swig of something from the shelf of liquor to forestall the inevitable reckoning. In the morning, I made a quick inventory, stealing a glance around my side of the bed before he heard me rustling. My clothes were in a tangle on the floor by the bed—taken off, by the looks of it, by someone who couldn't wait to get out of them. It was late-morning bright outside—maybe eleven. And there was a condom wrapper—several, actually—on the table by the bed. *Phew.*

One hour later, licking the salt from the rim of a cold Bloody Mary in the dark cocoon of Linda's Tavern—our favorite bar for picking up guys at closing time and nursing our hangovers the following afternoon—I told Tiffany and Sarah about my adventure. "You'll never guess what happened last night." And they couldn't.

The problem was, more and more, I couldn't either.

I didn't think a lot about consent in those days, at least as it applied to myself. I was moonlighting as a writer for a national feminist blog, covering issues like sexual harassment and rape culture, but the idea that I, personally, could ever be too drunk to say yes to sex just never occurred to me. I was in control of my own body, and if I wanted to get shit-faced and have sex I didn't remember, that was my choice, right? I had *chosen* to get wasted, right? I *liked* sex, didn't I? And besides, wasn't I usually the instigator, the one who said, "My place is just a couple of blocks away"?

Even in sobriety, I don't have easy answers to any of these questions. Yes, there were plenty of nights when I should have said, "This is a bad idea. I'm going home." Yes, I had sex with guys who would be beneath my standards if I'd been sober, like the one-hit wonder with the fancy bathroom floors. Yes, I took risks that I don't take now. I know that an impartial observer, watching me from the outside, might conclude that I was a victim of men who took advantage of me when I couldn't give meaningful consent, or that I should feel bad that I had sex I didn't fully choose and can't fully remember.

I get that—intellectually, I get it. If it wasn't me we were talking about, I'd probably say all those things, too. But it isn't how I feel. What I regret now isn't the sex itself, or the things I don't remember. It's the fact that I spent so many years thinking that if I got drunk and had sex with a guy, my own value would increase, just by getting his stamp of approval. I knew better than this—knew, for example, that my true value was my own self-worth and the work and good I could do in the world. But I didn't really know it, not at the gut, boundary-setting level of self-respect. From the moment I became aware that the two options for women were be desired or be invisible, I wanted to be desired. I wanted it when I was a teenager envying my beautiful best friend, as a young person who felt special for being "chosen" by a married man, and as a woman just entering her thirties, watching the options at the bar dwindle as 2:00 A.M. approached.

Ten

All Will Be Well

I liked working at a place where you could roll in, shoeless and in someone else's clothes, at eleven or show up so hungover you spent half the day on the couch. But there were some downsides. Not only was dating your boss perfectly acceptable, so was using the paper's unpaid internship program as a dating pool, or buying booze for a minor, or dropping your pants in the middle of an argument about rape culture. (Whatever question you have about that, the answer is yes.) Upside: I could slip off in the middle of the day for three hours and not have to explain where I was. Downside: When a colleague did a story about a local guy who got in trouble for making vomit porn, guess what played in the background all day in our open office? Upside: If someone heard you puking in the bathroom, you could tell the truth—"hangover"—with no repercussions. They might even offer you a hair-of-the-dog shot from the bottle in their desk. Downside: When someone made a rape joke that crossed the (invisible) line, or said, "Hey, we're all watching the

Paris Hilton sex tape, come join us!" it was hard to know what to do. I know *The Stranger* had an HR policy of some sort, but the HR *practice* was to ignore all kinds of gross or questionable behavior until someone complained. This left the definition of "work-appropriate behavior" in the hands of individual staffers. One incident, of many, stands out: I was stretched out on the dirty couch in the paper's second-floor office, reading over a pile of notes for a story, when Tristan leaped on top of me, grinding his pelvis hard into my crotch until I managed to push him off. "What? It was a joke!" he said in protest. "I'm gay!" I told Josh what had happened, but I never filed any kind of official complaint. I figured, why bother? It happened in full view of plenty of people, and no one said a word.

I stayed for more than six years, because as much as I sometimes hated my dysfunctional work family, I loved the work. Dan was a temperamental typo machine with a blind spot for his own prejudices (fat people; trans people; women who, like me, dressed in ways he considered provocative), but he was also a deft, incisive editor who could pinpoint the heart of a story, often in some throwaway paragraph, and slash and burn around it until the true theme emerged. And Josh and I had become a team—a somewhat dysfunctional, bickering, brother-sister-style team, but one that turned the paper's news section and editorial board into a force for change in the city. We made endorsements, broke news, built influence, and threw our weight around.

But around 2007, the balance of power started to shift. Tristan had been promoted to editor—a meteoric rise from his days as a sulking intern taking notes in the *Weekly*'s editorial meetings—and he, along with Tiffany, became my fourth and fifth bosses, after Josh, Dan, and Tim. (If you're keeping track, that's one woman and four men.) Suddenly, the two of them were making decisions that impacted the news section, which had always been Josh's and my personal fiefdom, and delivering unparsable edicts like "Make it more like *The New Republic*" and "News is boring; I want more reported opinions" from on high. Josh and I gritted our teeth at each new indignity and plotted a way out.

None of my colleagues ever suggested I stop drinking—if they had, I would have assumed *they* were the ones who had a problem. It was only when I stopped to actually compare myself to everyone else around me that the ready excuses—*it's a stressful job; everybody drinks; I'm just more creative after a few glasses of wine*—started to break down. So I tried not to think about it too often. It's a feature of alcoholism that the more you drink, the more you have to drink to get to the point where you don't worry so much about your drinking. By 2007, I wasn't giving myself many opportunities to worry. So stressed that I was popping Advil like jelly beans, I started keeping a liter of box wine in my bottom desk drawer, just in case. (In case what? In case I had to fire the intern for screwing up the endorsement interview schedule. In case Dan added one more goddamn typo to my copy. In case Tiffany floated past my desk again and wanted to know what I was working on and whether I was going to get everything in on time, as if it were any of her business. You know. *In case.*) I zeroed out the equation every day by spending a furious hour at the gym (conveniently located above the grocery store where I bought my wine), texting a coworker, "Best cure for a hangover: 2 SmartWaters + 1 hour on elliptical."

Oh, and I got an alcoholic boyfriend, too.

You often hear that alcoholics just find each other, and it's easy to see why—when your weekend routine revolves around flirting with guys in bars, the odds are good you'll run into a kindred spirit. Alcohol is like a magical potion that turns introverts into extroverts.

Sober me would never have met Nick, because I wouldn't have had the guts to go up to the big, bearded stranger holding court at the Hideout (the darkest bar in town, and therefore my favorite) in the first place, much less plant myself in his way just as he was heading out the door for a smoke. Sober, I was terrified of striking up a conversation. Drunk, I was the kind of girl who'd leap into a stranger's lap on a dare.

"Hi," I said. "I'm Erica. Can I bum a smoke?" I didn't smoke, but he didn't know that.

"No problem. I'm Nick. I was just—"

"You heading outside? I'll go with you."

I followed in his huge shadow out the back door.

Nick was tall—about six foot six—but seemed even bigger, with blue eyes that looked at whoever he was speaking to like they were the only person in the world. He gestured toward his friend, who was just lighting up a bowl.

"You want a hit?"

"Obviously."

Nick was a "planetary futurist" who ran an environmental website and gave lectures—or something. I was always a little hazy on the details, even after he'd shown me a video of his TED Talk and his book's introduction by Al Gore and his calendar crowded with speaking engagements around the world. That very first night, though, I was struck by his magnetism—he was one of those charismatic people who create their own gravity. I didn't understand much of what he was talking about—something about systems thinking, and heroic optimism, and the need for insistent urgency on climate change—but I knew I needed to see him again. I came back inside and joined Tiffany and Sarah at the bar, but I kept my eye on Nick, and as soon as I saw him putting on his jacket, I rushed over and hugged him good-bye. He smelled like fuzzy wool and old smoke. "Call me," I said, and pressed my number into his hand.

And he did.

And guess what? He drank more than I did! *Score.* Pretty soon, we were staying out until 2:00 A.M.; arguing in taxis; stumbling, hungover, to the grocery store for dinner from the deli and a curative bottle of wine; and fucking on the hoods of other people's cars. I couldn't believe my luck. I traded my old drinking routine for a new, higher-intensity program. After work, I'd head down to one of the two bars near his house—a brightly lit alehouse that closed at ten and only served wine and beer—his favorite—and a dark, sticky-floored place that poured stiff five-dollar cocktails and never seemed to close, which was mine. Moving my Monday night office hours to Nick's quiet residential neighborhood felt like a step up the adulthood ladder. I wasn't a kid looking for a party anymore—I was a young urban sophisticate, sipping Chardonnay (which just happened to be the highest-ABV wine they offered) while I wrote my column for the best alt-weekly paper in the country. And if I was routinely getting wasted trying to keep up with a beer drinker twice my size, at least I wasn't doing it at home alone, like some kind of alcoholic.

I could tell you that Nick and I had a whirlwind romance—long, carefree trips to Berlin and Barcelona, nights spent discussing the books we would write together, extravagant plans for the self-sufficient home we'd build—and that is one version of the story. Nick was the kind of guy who spent a lot of time working through big ideas out loud, and around him, I thought big, too—about what life would be like as soon as I started drinking a little less, quit my job, planted a garden, wrote a book. We did get serious very fast. We did go on those trips. If you squinted, you could probably look at Nick and me and see what looked like a happy couple.

But there's another, truer version of the story: When I was with Nick, I was the worst version of myself—angrier, pettier, smaller, drunker.

Nick and I were one of those couples that started fighting pretty much as soon as we got together, and about the littlest stuff—the fact that he didn't always call me when he was out of town, or the way I acted around his friends, who were well adjusted in ways that made me nervous, with carefully curated lives filled with long-haired, gender-fluid children, camping trips, and backyard chicken coops. Nick was running a business, which he said made him too busy to do adult things like putting his clothes in the closet or exercising or doing the dishes; and I had a stressful job ("insanely stressful," I told anyone who would listen) and needed to drink to relax. I held my tongue (until I didn't) about his lax housekeeping, and he held his tongue (until he didn't) about the amount of time I spent with friends he didn't like. We were a positive feedback loop of negativity: He would complain about how the board of the nonprofit he had founded was hounding him to come up with money, and I would complain about how *The Stranger* was a soul-sucking pit of vipers, and we'd drink and drink and drink and drink.

I didn't exactly plan to move in with him. At the time, 2008, I had a pretty sweet apartment, a spacious corner unit in a renovated 1920s building with a view of the Space Needle, downtown Seattle, and the Olympic Mountains. Like a lot of rash calls I'd made over the years, moving in with Nick seemed like a fix—in this case, for the fights that came more and more frequently, and the nagging sense that even he was starting to think I was out of control. We had been dating for about a year when I informed him, after six or seven glasses of wine at "our" bar, that I had given notice to my landlord and would be moving into his place at the end of the month. He didn't act quite as overjoyed as I had expected. In fact, he asked me to go back and tell my landlord I had made a mistake. I told him that it was too late for that now, and that I thought this was what he wanted, and we fought, made up, and had another drink. Play, pause, rewind, repeat.

Three weeks later, I was standing in Nick's front yard, arguing with the movers, who were demanding an extra five hundred dollars to move my shiny black upright piano, which had followed me all the way from my parents' living room in Houston, from their truck. "You pay, or we go to California," they said. I stood in the doorway, hysterical. "DO something!" Nick pulled his phone out of his pocket and loomed over them, bellowing as he punched at the numbers. "Nine! One!" That did the trick. They dumped the piano on the sidewalk and peeled away. Moments later, it started to rain. I ducked back into the bedroom, where no one could see, and took a long pull off the bottle of vodka I just happened to have tucked away inside my backpack.

Glassy-eyed but calmer, I wandered back out into the yard. Like a miracle, two drunk guys wandered by and offered to help, and between the four of us, we hauled the thing up the four steps to the house and into the living room. "Wow! It all worked out!" I told Nick when they left. "Sure," he said, and looked at me doubtfully—this strange woman, whom he'd known barely a year, already bringing chaos into his house.

Nick decided to make the best of it. He even threw me a house-warming party—Barcelona themed, to commemorate our recent trip—and I had such a great time, I passed out on my old bed in the spare bedroom before all the guests had left. I had decided to bring most of my furniture to his house, which made it feel like we were always just about to have a garage sale—tables next to tables and kitchen furniture on the patio and half-empty boxes of books stashed in bedrooms. My stuff got shoved into the empty places in his house, like the basement and the sunken living room that looked out onto Nick's little-used wooden deck, where my ultramodern brown folding couch—the first piece of "real" furniture I'd ever bought—sat, unused, the whole time I lived there.

Nick hadn't done much to make the place feel like home before I moved in, and he didn't do much after I got there. He had plenty of shelving units, but all his books were scattered in the front bedroom, and he had plenty of money, but as long as I lived with him, he never bought a real bed. Instead, we slept on a full-size futon mattress, tossed on the floor next to a heap of clothes and a completely empty closet. I nagged him about the pile, which he had given the infuriating nickname Piley, and that became one of the things we fought about—along with the dishes, his flirtations with other women, whether he even wanted me there, why he hated all my friends, and, oh yeah, my drinking.

Not since Josh, in high school, had I had a more volatile sparring partner. We became the couple you'd cross the street to avoid—the crazy lady screaming, "You fucking asshole!" in the middle of the street and the giant, barrel-chested guy grabbing her arm and bellowing, "Calm the fuck down!" Few nights went by without some kind of conflict. Nick told me to get off his back about cleaning the dishes, since he paid for a maid to do "his" part of the housework. I was convinced he was sleeping with someone else, so I went through his emails when he wasn't in the room. He banished me to the guest room one night and I retaliated by tossing a glass of water on his computer before passing out on the floor. He thought I was drinking too much; well, I thought he was a hypocrite. Anyone who drank as much as Nick did—sometimes nine or ten drinks a night, one pint following another—had no business telling me not to order another round, or snooping through my stuff to see if I had a bottle stashed somewhere, which—not that it was any of his business—I usually did. You would hide your drinking, too, if you lived with someone who was up your ass about it all the time. That's what I thought.

Increasingly, we slept apart—him on the futon on the floor, me on my old bed in the guest bedroom, a bottle of wine or vodka secreted away between my folded T-shirts a few feet away. I still wasn't sleeping well—alcohol, no surprise, is great for falling asleep but tends to wake you up after a couple of hours, a phenomenon known as rebound alertness—so I compensated by always keeping a bottle within reach. Just knowing there was a plastic bottle of Smirnoff in the closet by my bed was a comfort, like sleeping on a mattress filled with money. If I miss anything about drinking, it's the feeling of security I discovered back then, when I knew I'd never have to stay up all night if I didn't want to. Whatever else fell apart, there was always one thing that wouldn't fail me.

I kept a diary during this period, too. It's hard to read because the writing jitters drunkenly across the pages, but here's a sample: "I'm tired of being shouted down, tired of being called a bitch, tired of being told 'fuck you.' I deserve better than that. I feel stuck, like I can't get out of some horrible predicament I've put myself in." All this was true, to a point. I wrote about what Nick did to piss me off. I didn't write about my part—the shouting, the *fuck you*'s and accusations I hurled right back at him, or the drinking, much of it now done in secret. I'm not trying to make excuses for Nick—we were both our worst selves around each other—but when drug or alcohol abuse is part of the mix, a toxic relationship can turn into something much uglier, and it becomes harder and harder to do the obvious thing and just get out.

I had always kept lists of goals—*Don't respond when John texts. Sign up for class in music theory*—but I wasn't doing that anymore. Goals seemed too . . . goal oriented. Most days, it was all I could do to scrawl out a few indignant words before I passed out in the guest bedroom at the end of the day. But if I had, it would have read something like this: *1. Get out of this relationship. 2. Get therapist. 3. Stop drinking.*

Plenty of people had been suggesting number 3. Girlfriends—not Sarah or Tiffany, of course, but the friends I was avoiding, like my old pals Lisa and Stephanie from city hall—were starting to ask if I was okay. (They surely noticed, but didn't comment on, my sallow skin, puffy face, and bulging waistline.) And a few weeks before I moved into Nick's place, I had shown up late to Josh's birthday party, then babbled at his friends Tom and Lee for an hour or so before passing out on the floor in his living room. That night, Josh had written me a tense, angry letter about my behavior. "I'm worried about you," it began. "What do we need to do to get you some help?" We were still at the point when my drinking was a "we" problem. We were still at the point where "just quit drinking" seemed like a viable option. The problem was that I drank; the solution was that I had to quit. Not an easy task, maybe, but simple. Right?

Even Nick said he'd had enough, and for once, I didn't blame him. A long weekend in San Francisco had recently ended in disaster. The evening started as most of our evenings did—with drinks, which were supposed to be followed by dinner—and ended with us sloppily shutting down the bar, a dim, candlelit trattoria near my aunt and uncle's house, where we were crashing for a couple of nights before heading back to Seattle at the tail end of a trip down the coast. Somehow, we started fighting on the street, and carried the fight right back into the house, where my aunt Lisa and uncle Alex and their four-year-old son were sleeping.

What happened next? Well, I remember yelling. I remember Nick telling me to shush. I remember that "shush" making me madder than it felt like I'd ever been. ("Drunk people tell the truth," goes one recovery maxim. I guess the truth is that I'm an angry drunk.) I don't remember puking all over my little cousin's bedroom. I don't remember passing out on the guest bedroom floor. I remember my uncle cracking the door open a few merciless hours later and telling Nick, "You have to leave." I remember thinking that if I just kept my eyes closed, he would change his mind. And I remember him adding, "Now."

I scrambled from my spot on the floor, pulled on my clothes from the night before, and staggered out into the early-morning sunlight, Nick trailing behind me, suitcase in hand. Slowly, the enormity of what I had done started to sink in. Lisa and Alex would never invite me to stay at their house again, obviously, and my parents would find out, and everyone would gossip, and they'd talk behind my back about "Erica's problem," and I'd have to avoid family events from now on, and my parents would probably be ostracized, too, and it wouldn't be long before none of them would even talk to me, and, and . . .

These self-flagellation sessions typically ended with me dying alone, in the gutter, a plastic bottle of Burnett's Vodka dangling from my hand. But there was no time for the usual denouement, because I had a very angry, very concerned, very *imposing* boyfriend to contend with. And he was standing right in front of me, waiting for some kind of acknowledgment. I looked up at him, the thin California sunlight stabbing my eyes, and started to wail.

"What am I going to do?"

He took a long pause, assessed me, and said, "You need to quit drinking."

"I know. But I don't know how."

I knew that I needed to quit—we both needed to, although my own drinking had eclipsed his some time ago. But inside, I was already thinking about where my next drink would come from.

"Shh." Nick folded me up in his big arms. My mascara stained his crisp, untucked white button-down. "All will be well."

In fact, it got much, much worse.

Eleven

Wake-up Call

I don't remember why I stopped going in to work; I only know that Nick and I had hosted a party the previous weekend and something had gone terribly wrong. Blackouts are merciful in one respect—you can't remember exactly *how* you offended everybody, you just know that you probably shouldn't call them for a while.

What I do recall is what happened later: a screaming, dish-throwing fight with Nick. Accusations—something about me hiding the booze from the party and drinking it in secret—and denials. ("Why would I do that? There's alcohol all over this house. Someone must have stolen it from the party!") My decision, if you can call it that, to start drinking and just keep drinking, day after day after day. The phone ringing on Monday morning, then Tuesday, then Wednesday—Josh, calling from work, wondering where I was. Increasingly implausible excuses. Climbing up onto the counter to reach the spot above the highest cabinet, up where the stagnant summer air was hottest, where Nick had hidden a gallon bottle of gin. The taste of that gin as I guzzled it straight from the bottle—like rubbing alcohol filtered through a Christmas tree. Light turning into dark into light through the drawn red-velvet curtains, as I lay in bed and ignored Nick's footsteps outside the door. Occasional trips out of the room to swallow a handful of nuts, or a piece of pizza, remembering in my more lucid moments that a person must eat food to survive. A haze that wouldn't lift. And sleep. Fitful, but near constant sleep.

Nick was about to leave for a long business trip, and I avoided him as much as I could avoid someone who lived in the same house—waiting until he had closed his bedroom door before venturing out to the bathroom, or rifling through the cupboard to see if I'd missed a dusty bottle. He worked just as hard to avoid me, and who could blame him? I was a sinkhole in the middle of his house, and all he could do was tiptoe around me, waiting for me to collapse.

When I finally called for help, I didn't ask Nick; that would have meant admitting he was right—about me, about my drinking, about everything I had ever claimed he was wrong about. Instead, while Nick was out at work, I called Josh. I didn't explain where I'd been; I didn't apologize. I just told him I needed to quit drinking. "Can you come over?" I asked weakly. He hesitated. "Sure."

While I waited, I drank, and while I drank, I called detox facilities, which I understood to be places people go when they want to get sober without the embarrassment and disruption of rehab. As I later learned, medically supervised detox is critical for full-time alcoholics like I was—people who detox alone put themselves at risk of delirium tremens, severe dehydration, and seizures, any of which can lead to death. Detox programs provide medication, hydration, vitamins, and twenty-four-hour supervision.

Rehab, also known as treatment, is a longer program, usually a month or more, designed to take you out of regular life for a while and teach you the skills you'll need to stay sober and cope with your problems in the real world. I knew a little about rehab from the many addiction memoirs I'd read over the years, usually with a bottle in my hand, but at this point, that kind of long-term treatment wasn't remotely on the menu. As far as I was concerned, I was still super-human, the person who had torn through every obstacle in front of her through willpower alone. The only reason I needed detox, I thought, was that my mind was temporarily clouded, which made it hard to quit on my own. I even had a term for what I was after: A *hard reset.* I didn't know yet, nor did Josh, that addiction isn't like a button you can unpush.

The first thing I discovered when I called around looking for a detox bed is that it's not like booking a hotel. Most of the places told me to call back the next day, or put my name on a waiting list for a bed that might open up in a week or more. (Forget the hotel analogy—imagine calling the hospital with a broken leg and having them tell you to call back in a week.) Finally, one place—the detox unit at a high-end Catholic hospital in northwest Seattle—said they had an opening the next day. They just had to ask a few questions. Number one: "How much do you drink?"

For the first time since I had started drinking in secret, back when I was hitting the bars with a bottle in my purse, I told the truth. "About . . . eight or ten drinks a day? But in the past few days, a lot more. Maybe twelve or fifteen." It didn't feel good to tell the truth. But it did feel like cracking a door.

The doorbell rang, and I quickly swallowed the last inch of Gordon's and shoved the bottle into a suitcase with a dozen other empties. Josh walked in, assessed the situation, and told me we were going out. "Hode on, I need to gerready," I slurred. Then I disappeared into the bathroom.

"Are you drinking in there?"

"No! I'm just brushing my teeth." Indignant, because I was telling the truth: I had stopped drinking right before he got there.

When I finally unlocked the door, Josh stormed through the bathroom, zeroing in on a bottle of mouthwash.

"Have you been drinking that?" he demanded.

"No!" I said, looking repulsed. "I would never drink mouthwash!" Jesus. I wasn't some *wino*.

"Besides," I added after several beats, "it's *non*ackoholic."

My detox appointment was the following afternoon, so all I had to do was get through the next sixteen hours. Josh and I headed up to my old neighborhood, Capitol Hill, to a screening of *Man on Wire*, a documentary about the French tightrope walker who walked between the Twin Towers in 1974. It's a strange, beautiful film about someone who risked his life for reasons that would strike most reasonable people as absurd.

I didn't even have reasons, really.

Why did I start drinking in the first place?

Why hadn't I just quit on my own?

Why had I let it come to this?

I didn't know. It had just turned out that way.

After the movie ended, Josh put me in a cab. His brow furrowed. "Don't drink, okay?" I had sobered up quite a bit. "I feel like I'm going to die," I said. "But I don't know how to stop." Josh held my hand fiercely, told me it was going to be okay, and said he'd see me in the morning. Later, he told me that he thought this was the first step in the straightforward process of recovery, the kind we've all learned about from watching movies like *28 Days* or reading inspiring stories by alcoholics who got better: Quit drinking, go to AA, live soberly ever after. I really thought it would be like that. All I had to do was make this one difficult decision and the rest would fall into place.

By the time Josh picked me up the next day, Nick had gotten rid of all the booze in the house. He was heading to New Zealand for a speaking gig the following afternoon, and although he had offered a half-hearted expression of regret for going, there was never any question of my asking him to stay so he could be home when I got out.

By now, sixteen hours after my last drink, I was a mess of nerves. Sweat poured from my forehead and darkened my collar as Josh and I walked slowly through the mild summer morning, killing time in the neighborhood while we waited for my afternoon check-in time. It was late August—a few weeks before my thirty-first birthday—and far too bright. "How are we going to get you through the next hour?" Josh asked.

"How about a drink?"

In lieu of a crisp, cold glass of white wine—which would be *totally normal* at this hour, by the way—we wandered around, looking in the windows of gift stores and froyo shops. All the people seemed so aggressively normal, and I tried to reassure myself that one day soon, I would be, too. "This is just a bump," I said, my voice shaky with exertion. "All I need to do is get through this, and get off the booze for at least right now, and I'll be fine. I think maybe I'll even be able to have a glass of wine with dinner eventually. I mean, not right away. But someday. Don't you think?" Josh started to say something, thought better of it, and led me through the doors to the hospital bed that I thought would be my wake-up call.

The physical part of withdrawal is no joke—estimates of the death rate for people with delirium tremens, a severe withdrawal symptom, range from 5 to 25 percent—but the psychological aspect is what hits you like a hammer. *Existential dread* is such an inadequate term. What you feel is the certainty that you've fucked everything up so bad that it can never be unfucked again. Every step felt like I was walking on broken limbs, every ray of sunlight was an arrow through my corneas, but the physical pain was at least a distraction from the despair. What I realized then, well past the point of turning back, was that I would never feel better again. I knew, in some bone-deep way, that nothing in that cold, ammonia-scented building would ever make me well.

There's a scientific explanation for this feeling, having to do with chemicals called neurotransmitters, which keep your mood in balance. Alcohol, like heroin and Valium, is a depressant, and if you drink a lot of it on a regular basis, like I did, your brain starts to think you're in a permanent depressive state. To compensate (in technical terms, to return itself to a stable state called homeostasis), the brain pumps out fewer of the "downer" chemicals that produce feelings of well-being and calm, and more of the ones that produce feelings of alertness and arousal—sort of like drinking coffee to counteract the effects of a night of drinking. Take alcohol out of that equation, and you're left with an excess of stimulating chemicals, combined with a shortage of sedating chemicals to balance them out. The effect is a bit like eating a ton of sugar on an empty stomach—your brain kicks into overdrive and you get an extreme form of the jitters. The effects of this overstimulation can be mild—shakiness, an elevated heart rate, high blood pressure, and sweating—or severe—delirium, hallucinations, convulsions, and seizures. If you've ever abruptly stopped taking antidepressants, or quit drinking coffee or cigarettes, you may have experienced a mild version of this—a chemical imbalance that leaves you feeling overstimulated or sluggish.

Kicking caffeine is a drag—I've done it. Kicking heroin will make you feel like you're going to die. But the most dangerous drug to quit suddenly isn't heroin, or cocaine, or any other illegal substance— it's alcohol. When your body is used to high doses of booze, quitting cold turkey can kill you, and the danger can last a week or more. That's why detox (and access to detox) is so important for alcoholics. Without it, many of us won't get help; without it, many of those who try to quit on their own will die.

Of course, I didn't know any of this back then. All I knew was that I had tried to quit on my own, and found, inexplicably, that I couldn't.

Detox wasn't at all what I'd expected. Movies like *Clean and Sober* and *Trainspotting* gave me the impression that quitting would involve a lot of dramatic sweating, scratching, and puking in buckets, but it was actually a lot like staying in a regular hospital, at least once my first dose of Librium—a powerful benzo known in the sixties as mother's little helper—kicked in. After the nurses had searched my bag and clothes for drugs, booze, or anything containing alcohol, like perfume or Purell, they hooked me up to an IV bag filled with fluids and electrolytes, watched as I swallowed a handful of pills, and left me to chill out in my private hospital room, comfy rubber-soled socks on my feet, remote control at my side.

If you ignored the IV, beeping machines, and orderlies filing in and out every couple of hours, the place wasn't so bad. I had a little desk and a door that closed, and access to cable TV whenever I wanted. I could even call down to the front desk to order room service—cheeseburgers, mac and cheese, fettucine Alfredo—at any hour of the day or night. I ate a lot of fettucine in the first couple of days, and drank prodigious amounts of water; even so, I was so dehydrated that a full day passed before I rose to pee, my IV stand clanging beside me as I trundled over to my private bathroom.

The days went by in a Librium haze. The other patients were scarcely more real than the politicians giving speeches at the Democratic National Convention on the TV in the corner—muffled voices through the walls and hollow-eyed wraiths who looked sicker than I did, trudging around the hallway in robes that hung from their skeletal frames. The care was kind but utilitarian—the nurses and occasional doctor were there to make sure I stabilized and didn't die, not to put me on the path to lasting sobriety. Fine by me. I knew that once I got out, I would never want to go through anything like the last few weeks again. I didn't need some well-meaning psychologist or social worker to tell me not to drink.

One afternoon, I heard a commotion outside in the hall—a man's voice, screaming, "LET ME GO! I DON'T BELONG HERE! LET ME OUT!"—and I asked a nurse, as calmly as I could, what was going on. "Oh, he's just in here for benzos," she said serenely. "They'll give him something to calm him down." Just then, on cue, the screaming stopped. An image—Nurse Ratched plunging a syringe the size of a turkey baster into the arm of a man twice her size—popped into my head, but after a few minutes of silence, I turned back to my book about 9/11 and let the walls of the room fall away.

The ward I was on, I learned, was primarily reserved for pregnant women addicted to drugs and alcohol; only a handful of the beds were for people there for short-term detox, like me. After a couple of days, when I started feeling well enough to leave my room, I started stepping out into the hall to watch them walking around the ward, past a sign that read: 64x=1 MILE. I often wondered how they got to the point that their addiction was more important than the life of another human being.

How could someone use drugs while they're pregnant? I thought. *It's one thing to harm yourself, but what kind of monster would hurt an innocent baby?*

And if the next thought was *That's why I'm on birth control*, and the next one, *I mean, I'd obviously just have an abortion*, that didn't make me judge the women waddling around the ward any less harshly.

If I was going to have a baby, I thought, *I would figure out a way to quit.*

Never mind that if I could figure out a way to quit, I would be sleeping in my bed at home, not hooked up to IV fluids in a hospital. And never mind that I had driven drunk more times than I could count, putting not just my own life but those of everyone on the road at risk. *I* was careful. *I* knew what I was doing. *I* drove just as well dead drunk as most people do stone sober. Didn't I?

After a few days on this regimen, I felt well enough to start feeling guilty. I called my parents, but played down the seriousness of the situation—which, come to think of it, wasn't really *that* serious, now that I was feeling so much better. "I'm detoxifying from alcohol in a facility," I said to Mom, as if all those extra syllables would distract her from the fact that her daughter had checked into a detox ward—a term that evoked images of nineteenth-century flophouses and moldy-walled loony bins. Besides my parents, I didn't call anyone other than my closest friends—Tiffany, Sarah, and steadfast Kevin. At some point, Nick had dashed off a quick, semiapologetic email—hope everything's okay, sorry about the timing of this trip but it sounds like I couldn't do much anyway if I was there—but I didn't respond. I wasn't ready to deal with Nick yet. I was happy that I'd be coming home to an empty house.

Five days later, when I was ready to be discharged, a nurse summoned me to the office of the detox director, a stern but kind-faced man who proffered a sheaf of papers and asked me what I planned to do after my release. "This may seem like the hard part to you now," he said, "but it isn't. This was the easy part. The hard part is staying sober once you get out of here." *How can that be the hard part?* I thought. *I'm sober now, and I feel better than I have in years. Why would I want to throw that all away on a drink?*

"So, what is your plan?"

"Ummm . . . Not to drink?"

Wrong answer.

"You can't just say that you aren't going to drink again. You need to be in a program for recovery," he told me. "For most people, that means going to AA meetings at least once a day at first, staying away from the people, places, and things that might trigger you to drink, and finding new activities to substitute for drinking. Think about the things in your life you gave up when you were drinking. What are some of those things you'd like to do again? How would you like to live the rest of your life, starting the moment you walk out of here?"

What kind of question was that? It was like this guy didn't realize that, for me, coming to detox had been a huge, humiliating step. I pretended to think for a long time, then responded. "I think I'd like to just go back to the way things were before I started drinking all the time."

"Okay, but it isn't that simple. We really recommend that you try to do 'ninety in ninety'—that's ninety AA meetings in ninety days."

I looked at him like he was suggesting that I give up my apartment, quit my job, and take a vow of celibacy.

"I think I've got a pretty good handle on this—don't go to bars, don't drink, and have a good support system. I have a lot of friends who know I'm here, and they've promised to keep me accountable." Plus, I said, I had just started seeing a therapist who knew I was trying to quit drinking, or at least cut back, and I would definitely make an appointment with her the moment I got home.

Of course there was no therapist. There hadn't been for months. I had started going to someone, Janine, the previous year, but our visits were sporadic, because I would usually cancel. When we did meet, I talked about my relationship problems, issues at work, my past. I don't think she even knew I drank.

The detox director wasn't buying it.

"People in your situation often don't get a second chance." He meant people who show up to detox voluntarily, before they've suffered any serious losses. "You should take this one."

Then he pressed a list of AA meetings into my hand.

I arrived home—Nick's home—to a house overflowing with flowers and cards from friends. "Let me know if there is ANYTHING I can do. I am HERE for you!!" said one from Stephanie. Another, from Sarah, read, "Congratulations on taking this huge first step. Welcome to the rest of your life!!" Strangely, none of my work friends had bothered to write.

I didn't want to sleep in an empty house, so I asked Stephanie to stay with me for my first few nights back home. Actually, I had asked Tiffany first—she was my best friend, after all—but she didn't have the time. "Ugh, just so busy with the paper—let me know if no one else can do it! So proud of you," she texted. I stared at the screen. *Huh. That seems kind of rude.*

Well, it didn't matter that much—having a chaperone around the house was just my way of demonstrating an abundance of caution. I didn't feel the slightest bit tempted to drink.

My five days in detox had made me realize how much I had let myself go, and I craved physical activity in a way that I hadn't since college. I invited friends I hadn't seen in months along for strenuous hikes in the Cascade Mountains, rode my bike seven miles to work and back, and started lifting weights again. At work, I filed copy at a furious pace, like I was making up for all the times I'd come in at eleven, so hungover I had to take a nap on Josh's couch at three just to get through the rest of the day. Or the times I'd failed to show up at all.

"I feel like I've gotten a new chance at life," I told Josh.

"I'm really glad to have you back," he said. And I was, too.

Twelve

Anything but AA

I knew I was supposed to have some kind of ongoing support. I also knew, after reading up on the 12 steps and talking to a few people who were "in the program," that it couldn't be AA. The deal breaker—dependency on "a power greater than ourselves"—was right there in step 2. I didn't want to trade dependency on alcohol for dependency on a God I could barely convince myself to believe in. I needed a way to reclaim my own power.

It wasn't as if I were alone in my dim view of 12-step programs. Everywhere I looked, there were stories debunking the "myths" of AA. "Sorry, AA doesn't work," *The Huffington Post* declared. *Slate* promised shocking details about "the pseudo-science of Alcoholics Anonymous." *Psychology Today* decried "the dogma of 12 steps."

But it didn't take a searing exposé in *The Atlantic* ("The Irrationality of Alcoholics Anonymous") to convince me that AA didn't work. All I needed to know about "the program," as its adherents reverently call it, was right there when I walked through the door for my first meeting, about two months after I got out of detox. I could tell right away that I had nothing in common with the earnest, bright-eyed women who greeted me that first day at the Capitol Hill Alano Club. They were "happy"—insistently so—and therefore delusional, because no one was happy. Certainly no one I had ever met.

I stayed anyway—not because I wanted to, but because I was out of ideas. Everyone said I needed to try something new, and sitting around listening to a roomful of lesbians babble on about how they feel "happy, joyous, and free" certainly qualified. (And why were there so many lesbians in AA, anyway? As I learned much later, my first "home group" was a women-only meeting marked "LGBT" in the meeting book, not that I bothered to check before plopping my butt resentfully in a seat.) For ninety minutes, I struggled to stay awake as the women talked about problems that struck me as so mundane they had no right to complain about them. How was I supposed to care that someone's ex-girlfriend might be using again, or about a "rough patch" another lady was going through at five years sober, when I wasn't even sure I wanted to go another five days? Some of the women sounded like they'd been through a lot—one talked about how she only started coming to meetings to get her license back after her third DUI; another said her last relationship ended when her ex got drunk and burned her with a cigarette—but here they were, declaring themselves "grateful" to be alcoholics. What the fuck could that even mean? It was like saying "I'm so grateful to have cancer." And yet everybody nodded in sympathetic recognition when the lady with the cigarette burns delivered this week's tale of woe. "When I first got sober, I was on, like, this pink cloud," she said. "But lately, it's like nothing ever seems to go my way. I know drinking only makes problems worse, never better, and it's not that I'm tempted, but it sometimes just seems like God is testing me: 'You said you wouldn't drink, no matter what. How about now? How about now?' Anyway, I'm grateful to be here. Thanks for letting me share."

I listened to the women's words, rolling them over in my mind like a new language I couldn't figure out how to translate. *Grateful* to be here in this room, with its glittery rainbow-flag banner and fluorescent lights, instead of—well, literally anywhere else? *Grateful* to be an alcoholic instead of a normal person, who can go out for a couple of drinks and not have to shut down the bar? And "God" who? I grew up around plenty of religious nuts—Sandy, the girl in Sunday school who was convinced God told her she was going to be an angel; Leticia, who started the flagpole prayers at my middle school—and I didn't come all the way to Seattle to meet more of them.

Suddenly, someone "tagged" me and it was my turn to speak. My voice caught in my throat. "Hi, um, I'm Erica," I stammered. They stared expectantly. "And I'm an alcoholic." "Hi, Erica," they responded in unison. *Shit.* This was harder than it looked. "This is my first meeting, and, um, I don't want to be here. I'm not sure I belong here. You all keep talking about how you're 'grateful alcoholics,' and that doesn't make any sense to me. I'm not grateful. I'm pissed. This sucks." I found myself choking back unexpected tears, and paused until the silence ached.

"Uh. That's it." Pause. *How did the other women make this stop? Oh yeah.* "Thanks for letting me share."

"Thanks, Erica."

I felt like I had accidentally said "I love you" to a total stranger, or posted my diary online for everyone to see. I wiped my tears and fumed, fumed and tried to shrink all the way down into my fuzzy wool jacket. What kind of organization manipulates people into sharing their deepest secrets, then forces them to hold hands and say a prayer, followed by a ridiculous chant?

"Keep coming back, it works if you work it, and we're allllllll . . . worth it!"

As I headed for the door, chin tucked in my collar, my anger was replaced by embarrassment—not for myself, but for the women in the room. If joining AA meant turning into a cliché-spouting zombie—"Don't give up five minutes before the miracle happens!" "Meeting makers make it!"—I wanted nothing to do with it. After accepting unwanted hugs from several strangers, who all chirped, "Keep coming back," I backed out the door and down the stairs, determined never to return.

That shit might work for people with no sense of irony, but not for me.

No thanks. I'll find another way.

For the next few years, I would show my face in "the rooms" another ten or twenty times, usually when I was trying to convince my worried friends that I was doing everything humanly possible to get sober or stay that way. (Sometimes, I'd even bring them with me: *See what I put myself through? Now do you believe that I'm willing to go to any length?*) I figured it must have been pretty convincing: No one would willingly spend an hour trading platitudes with a roomful of strangers unless she was really trying.

Looking back, I would remember the years when I was first

trying to get sober as a relatively stable time, but that's only in a rearview mirror distorted by everything that came later. At the time, I felt like I was losing the trail back to the life I had planned out since well before college, the breadcrumbs disappearing behind me as I moved further and further off the map.

Thirteen

Just Don't Drink

My friends—Josh, to whom I'd said I would die if I kept drinking, foremost among them—couldn't understand why I wouldn't just go to AA. I needed an endorsement—a real-life drunk or junkie who had gotten clean on his own and would sign off on my choice to forge my own path. So I wrote to Chris, a friend of Josh's who had gotten sober a few years back, asking for advice. "The AA programs around here really turn me off. It's not just the God stuff—it's the idea of permanently embracing powerlessness, if that makes sense," I wrote.

"Anyway: There's an all-woman outpatient program in Seattle, A Positive Alternative, that has a good track record. It's based on healthy choices and self-empowerment (plus meditation, naturopathy, and nutrition—did Josh mention I'm a bit of a hippie about that stuff?), which appeals to me, but if I wasn't convinced it was a successful program, I would just go to AA."

Chris responded right away. "That makes a lot of sense. There is a great deal about AA that I found baffling and irritating at first. Particularly this notion of letting go in order to maintain control. Say what? I think what I've learned since is that I very much have agency in my life, but I've kept sober with the help of others, especially folks in AA." Then he told me I should go to ninety meetings in ninety days.

Ugh. *This* again. As if I had two extra hours in my day just waiting to be filled by a new obligation.

Chris continued: "Meditation, nutrition—all good things! Perhaps you can check out the program *and* AA meetings. I have met many people, from all walks of life, who have all gotten great things out of AA. It's very hard to explain. You will not become a Moonie."

Which, of course, is *exactly* what a Moonie would say.

A Positive Alternative seemed like a good fit for other reasons, chief among them the fact that they didn't let just anybody in. Unlike AA, which is open to literally anyone—street drunks, Bible-thumpers, joiners who think their only option is to "surrender" and come to meetings for the rest of their lives—this group was aimed at critical thinkers who wanted to reclaim control, not relinquish it. The program bragged that almost none of its clients were court referred—the "slip signers" who tended to sit in the back of the room at AA meetings and leave as soon as they could get their court slips signed—and all the counselors were professionals with an MA degree or higher, which meant they knew a lot more than your typical AA member about the scientific, hard reality of addiction.

Perhaps most important, A Positive Alternative didn't allow men, whose stories I couldn't bear to listen to anymore. Besides the Friday women's AA meeting, I had been to a couple of coed meetings, and it was pretty clear to me that guys had just two reasons for showing up: to hear themselves talk, and to keep women in their place. Guys who were going through a bad divorce, guys who were under re-straining orders because they beat the shit out of their girlfriends, guys who were there because their wives were threatening to take the kids, all told the same story: "Things were going along fine until a woman came along and screwed things up." At one meeting, a man who had just gotten out of prison complained that his real problem was the woman who had put him there, by reporting him to the police when he smacked her around. (The rules against "crosstalk"—responding to or addressing other members directly—prohibited anyone from telling him that he was the one who was being an asshole.)

Men dominated AA meetings the way they dominated board-rooms, gym equipment, and the seats on public transportation: They shouted over women who tried to talk (in many meetings, the person who shouts the loudest—"I'M BRAD, AND I'M AN ALCO-HOLIC!"—gets to share), and they got away with ignoring the time limits that were supposed to give everyone a chance to talk. As they did in every other venue on the planet, guys at AA meetings seemed to think it was their birthright to take up more than their share of space, and bully women into silence by complaining about the "bitches" who were making their lives miserable.

I was unusually tender—still fuming at John and Nick and all the other men who had disappointed me, by leaving in the morning or failing to call or being less than what I needed to fix myself—and I needed a safe haven where men wouldn't interrupt or judge me.

I signed up.

But I only lasted for a couple of meetings. I had a million differ-ent reasons. I didn't like the counselor, a heavyset woman who wore her gray hair in a messy braid and tried to strong-arm me into disclosure with nosy questions. How much do you drink? *Why do you drink? Why do you want to quit? At least AA lets you sit in the back and just listen*, I thought. Also, the cost of the program—about a thousand dollars a month, all out of pocket—was tough to swallow, especially after I'd gone without drinking for a few weeks and started thinking of better ways to spend my money. It wasn't exactly convenient, either. Unlike AA meetings, which at least were everywhere (and free), A Positive Alternative was in a neighborhood across town from my job and apartment, and making the meetings meant missing other stuff—important things integral to my work, like city council meetings and campaign events. Worst of all, the women in the meetings—middle aged, sturdy, well-to-do—were nothing like me at all. Their idea of problem drinking was probably finishing a whole bottle of Chardonnay before their husbands got home and hiding the bottle under the *Reader's Digest*s in the recycling bin. They would never understand how hard-core I'd been, how many times I'd headed out for an after-work drink with friends only to end up passed out in some stranger's bedroom, then sneaking out the door in the morning with my shoes in my hand, hoping he didn't have my number.

Fucking lightweights.

Not drinking was easier than I had expected. All I had to do, it turned out, was not drink! Weeks went by, then months, without much of a problem. I didn't crave alcohol, nor really miss it, except when I tagged along with coworkers to the bar across the street—the same bar where I had nervously nursed a glass of wine during my job interview for *The Stranger*—and tried to match their mood as they drank their real drinks and I clutched a sweating glass of soda water, hoping nobody asked why.

It was the life stuff that tripped me up. Contrary to what I'd expected would happen, things didn't magically get better at home; if anything, they seemed to be getting worse. The stuff I used to ignore or save up for the next drunken rage—the dirty dishes piled a foot high in the sink, the pile of clothes, the dying garden that I had spent dozens of hours building, alone, over the previous summer—was all still there, only now I had no way to push it off to the periphery of my awareness. Nick was still Nick, I was still me, and the things that bothered me about my life were all still there, more present than ever. I needed to move out, or fix the relationship, or quit my job. I needed to fix my credit and start saving money and go on vacation and buy a car. I needed to repair absolutely everything about myself.

Who could deal with all that? Maybe my real problem wasn't drinking, it was the stuff I drank to avoid. Maybe it would be okay to drink, just a little. I had shown that I could quit; maybe that was a sign that this was the one place where I actually *was* in control. Maybe I didn't really have a problem.

I decided to test my theory on a crisp late-fall afternoon. Crunching through the leaves, toward the liquor store I had spent the last three months crossing the street to avoid, I felt almost giddy, like I was meeting a long-distance boyfriend I hadn't seen in months. Walking through the familiar doors, I scanned the place for acquaintances who might know I'd quit—worst case, I could always grab a lime and a bottle of seltzer and say I didn't have time to go by the grocery store—and when I saw the coast was clear, I grabbed two airplane bottles of tequila from the plastic spinner and plunked six dollars in the cashier's hand.

Outside, almost giggling with anticipation, I ducked into an alley.

Click click click, went the tiny cap as its metal teeth ripped apart. *Glug glug glug,* went the amber liquid down my thirsty throat. Within thirty seconds, I had downed both bottles. The warm clarity of a pleasant buzz hit my blood before my brain had time to process what I was doing. *Oh, hi, old friend,* I thought. *I've missed you.*

Fourteen

Self-Delusion

Nick and I had been trying, tensely, to make it work. He had quit drinking around the same time I did, partly from fear that he might be an alcoholic and partly from concern that I probably shouldn't be living with a bad example. Our relationship mellowed into a kind of détente—a strained accord between two people who had never really gotten to know each other without drinks in our hands. It was working, sort of—we weren't fighting as much anymore—but we seemed to be on a treadmill, biding time to see who would fall off first.

When I met up with Nick the evening I drank those two minis of tequila, he could sense right away that something was off. "Please tell me that isn't liquor I smell," he said. "Of course not!" I responded a little too loudly, linking my arm through his. "It's probably just my hair spray or something. You know I don't drink!" It didn't feel like a lie. I had quit drinking. Except this once.

A few days later, I decided that since nothing terrible had

happened, it would be okay to drink again. Why should I deny myself, now that I had proved I could have a couple without going on a bender? I knew I could handle it. I also knew that my friends wouldn't understand—not after I alarmed everybody with that rash trip to detox—so I would have to drink in secret, and carefully. White wine and vodka, never anything brown. Always have plenty of gum on hand. If gum is unavailable, eat something with a strong aroma, like baba ghanoush or garlic bread, to mask the smell. Look people straight in the eye when you talk to them; don't be shifty. Don't talk too much, or too little. Wait a while before drinking more to see how you feel. Don't forget to eat.

I didn't consider this return to drinking a "relapse." For one thing, there were so many rules! Drinking a pint of vodka over eight hours, or a bottle of wine over the course of a full day of hiking in the woods, seemed so insignificant compared to the days when I was missing work and passing out at people's birthday parties. Besides, I wasn't doing it all the time the way I had been, back when I had a drinking problem. Weeks would pass at a stretch before I crossed the threshold of the liquor store, or paused to browse the aisles in the vast wine section at the supermarket before casually dropping a bottle in my shopping cart.

That I drank in secret was everybody else's fault, not mine— everyone had overreacted to my weird behavior a few months back, and now I had to do penance for that by hiding bottles in my bag at work, or in the back of the closet in the spare bedroom, where I knew Nick would never look. Sure, I got "busted" a couple of times, when I drank too much, but those were isolated incidents. Nick caught me passed out in the dining room, a plate full of uneaten mac and cheese congealing on the table. Josh held my gaze a little too long, and asked point-blank, "Are you sure you haven't been drinking?" Mom held her tongue when I called her, sobbing, at odd hours, lamenting that I'd never have any money or that Nick was off at another conference, doing god knows what. If those were the worst things that ever happened, was it really fair to say I had a drinking problem? If I held it together most of the time, then who was I hurting?

Drinking alone, in the secrecy of my separate bedroom, relieved me of the need to pretend I was normal. There, I could try "controlled" drinking without anyone else watching and judging—bringing home only enough wine to get me buzzed, or the smallest bottle of vodka on the shelf. But drinking makes you forget that you have a drinking problem. The first sip settled in my stomach like a warm welcome; the second whispered, "Just one more won't hurt"; and by the third, there was so little left in the bottle I might as well finish it off—and then, of course, I would need to go out and get another, *just in case.* Motivation slipped away almost unnoticed when I was drinking—the ledger in which I'd planned to track my drinks the way I'd once tracked how many cups of unbuttered popcorn I had eaten stayed empty as a sheet of paper in the printer tray.

I decided again that I needed to stop drinking—this time, on my own. Searching online, I discovered a booming subculture of relapse prevention counselors, people who promised to give me the tools I needed to get through life without alcohol, or even to drink like a normal person. I settled on Ken—an open-faced guy with wispy blond hair and a curio cabinet full of five-hundred-dollar eyeglass frames—because he didn't use labels like "addict" or "alcoholic," and because I found something reassuring in his soft, lilting voice. Also, he took my insurance.

Ken specialized in cognitive behavioral therapy (CBT), which teaches you how to identify the thoughts that lead to negative actions, then talk back to those thoughts before they turn into destructive behaviors. CBT is thought to be especially useful in dealing with addiction and relapse prevention, because it's a way of trapping dysfunctional thoughts (I can't deal with this bullshit without a drink) and modifying them (I *have* dealt with bullshit without a drink, and I don't need one to get through this bullshit now) before you act on them (I don't have to have a drink). CBT is common in rehab, but it's also useful in all sorts of regular life situations—think about all the times you've been angry that a partner or friend "made" you angry, then consider all the assumptions, beliefs, and judgments that went into the conclusion that the other person caused your anger. Ken taught me to work on that stuff, too. After a year with Ken, I was an expert on CBT and how it worked; even if I decided to drink anyway, at least I knew why, and that it was a choice that no one else was forcing me to make.

The best thing about Ken was that he was forgiving. If I had told Ken, "I went on a binge last night, had sex with a stranger without a condom, and crashed my car into the front of my apartment building," he would have looked at me over the top of his blue-rimmed glasses, raised an eyebrow, and said, "Well, that was yesterday. How are we going to get you back on track today?"

The worst thing about Ken was that he trusted me not to lie to him. I could come into his office after downing half a bottle of wine, bullshit for an hour, then leave with a packet of homework and a plan for staying sober another week. Based on what I told him about my drinking—a fantasy I spun in which I had quit drinking for good when I went into detox, wanted to make sure I didn't relapse, and needed help figuring out what to do with all the free time I had now that I wasn't drinking—we wrote up a treatment plan, which summarized the issues I needed to address within the next year. The plan included "problem statements" and "methods" for addressing them. "Problem: Erica's stress in the past year spiraled into heavy drinking with associated problems. Connected with this, Erica reports a history of a 'racing mind' and a related 'drive' to avoid boredom. Having gotten sober, she wonders, 'Do I want to quit, or control it?' Method: Commit clearly to a period of abstinence (a year?) and clarify what you want to learn (e.g., dealing calmly with others) before deliberately exploring appropriate boundaries with drinking."

It should have said: "Problem: Erica drinks too much and lies about it, even to her therapist. Method: Stop drinking. Not for a year. Forever."

Of course, I wouldn't have accepted that prescription either, any more than I truly believed I couldn't control my drinking like everybody else did. (*Tiffany drank every night, but did she puke in the bushes or pass out in the other room in the middle of a party? Of course not. She held her liquor like a lady.*) CBT is great for people who suffer from negative thoughts—I know I did—but it doesn't work for relapse prevention if you can't even relapse because you're still drinking. And it requires that you get honest with yourself.

That was a problem. Even when everyone close to me was telling me I was out of control, I still thought I could find an "out." What if I drank only on weekends, or only outside the house? What if I set a drinking budget and kept close track of how much I was spending? What if I *only* drank when I was alone? What if I got really into something other than drinking, like yoga, gardening, or meditation? Controlled drinking didn't work, drinking alone just got me wasted faster, and I discovered that it's possible to garden and do yoga drunk, too. By midsummer, my garden was overrun with vegetables

I'd planted in meandering, tipsy rows and I was known in class as that lady who always fell down during Tree Pose.

Nonetheless, I thought I'd figured out my problem. It wasn't drinking—it was self-control. All I needed to do was reclaim the kind of willpower I'd had in high school and college, when I quit drugs and drinking altogether, or in my twenties, when I could have a couple and call it a (boring, drama-free) night. Such is the human capacity for self-delusion.

Fifteen

Eighty Miles an Hour

E very blackout ends with an assessment: *Where am I? How did I get here? Did I hurt anyone/pee my pants/embarrass myself?*

Similarly, every blackout begins with a decision: *I'll only have one more. Eating will just dilute the effect of the alcohol. Fuck it, I deserve this.*

This story starts during a trip to Texas, the same year I went to detox, when I had plenty of vacation time but nowhere to go. I was traveling alone. I tried to avoid bringing guys back home, because I didn't want my parents thinking I was going to settle down, and because I didn't want the guys I dated to get in fights with Mom and Dad over their conservative political beliefs, a fact that perhaps says more about the kind of guys I dated than it does about my parents. It was hot in Houston, and I was sitting in my mom's home office in the old guest bedroom, chattering away about how terrible *The Stranger* was, and how much I wanted to leave. Familiar territory. But this time, instead of delivering the usual lines about how they didn't deserve me (Mom's go-to: "Dan is such a sexist!") and I could do so much better, she swiveled around in her chair, put a hand on my knee, and demanded: "When did you start drinking again?"

I tried to look incredulous. "I didn't! I don't know why you would say such a thing!" Faking indignation, I actually became indignant— how dare she suggest that I had a problem, that I couldn't handle my liquor like everybody else on the planet? Why did she always have to treat me like such a child? Why wouldn't she just leave me alone and stop hassling me with all her nosy questions?

Why, indeed. Maybe because I'd been acting off-kilter ever since I landed, ducking into the airport restroom with my luggage to swig from the vodka I had taken to carrying with me every time I traveled. Maybe because I had spent half the trip sleeping, passed out in a vodka coma in my childhood bedroom. Or maybe because my breath smelled like the floor of a bar, strong enough to make my mom scooch her office chair a few feet away during my monologue.

I was fine. Why wouldn't my mom believe I was fine? "I'm going out for a run," I huffed, and headed out the door.

I made it all the way to the new liquor superstore that had just opened in their neighborhood. Reeling from the heat, I plunked two items on the counter: an ice-cold bottle of water, and a fifth of Absolut. Back outside, I wandered across the street, to the parking lot of the day-care center I had attended as a kid. Stooping behind a low wall with a sign that read LA PETITE ACADEMY, I gulped a bit of the water and poured the rest in the grass, then poured the vodka in the water bottle, careful not to spill a drop. I took a swig from the bottle, retched quietly as my stomach ejected the liquor into the water-soaked dirt, then tried again. The liquor stayed down. Fuck my parents. This was normal. I was normal.

There was not a single thing wrong with me.

I left Houston two days early, pulling out of the driveway in a rage. *Jesus, why does Mom have to be so* suffocating? On the way to the airport, just before the entrance to the freeway, I stopped at another liquor store and grabbed two more bottles of vodka, tossing one in the backseat of my rented PT Cruiser like a Coke I was saving for later. The other bottle went straight into the cupholder. *Fuck this.* I was off.

Four hours later, I opened my eyes. My hair, my clothes, and the car seat were soaked in sweat, and it was immediately obvious why: The midday sun had turned the car into an oven, and my seat—reclined and pushed back as far as it would go—was in what you might call the "broil" position.

Every blackout ends with an assessment. Easing myself up, I unfastened my seat belt, rolled the seat back into the upright position, and looked around, blinking hard. To my right, across a vast asphalt emptiness, was a Home Depot. To my left, a freeway. By my knees, the bottle of vodka, still in its cupholder. I lifted the bottle by its base, saw an inch or so of precious liquid left, and finished it off, tossing the empty in the back. *Okay, so I drove here*, I thought. *But where is* here?

How did I manage to park?

How have I not been arrested?

I pieced it together using a road map and freeway signs. I had driven, all right—but I hadn't gotten very far. Currently, I was parked just south of the East Freeway, the main road that leads from Houston to Louisiana, about thirty-five miles from my parents' house. I was still about twenty-five miles from the airport, and had missed my flight, but I was safe. No one had called, no one had seen me, no one would ever know. People who believe in miracles point to stories like this as proof that God is benevolent and concerned with human affairs. Miraculously, I drove 80 miles an hour in a blackout without hitting anybody. Miraculously, I did not get pulled over. Miraculously, I had the presence of mind to leave the freeway and find a safe place to park. Miraculously, I did not get caught.

But it didn't feel like a miracle. All it felt like was an accident. People die in drunk driving crashes every day, as victims and as perpetrators. People with less alcohol in their system than I had get arrested every day. Nothing about my own survival made me special. All it made me was lucky—and ashamed.

The shame is what kept me from thinking too hard about the implications of my actions—what it said about me that I kept ending up in situations like that. I would contort myself into a pretzel trying to explain away the crazy stuff that just seemed to happen to me—I must have forgotten to eat that morning, or my wallet must have fallen out of my pocket, or I must have conked out at my desk because I had insomnia the night before. When the truth was, I drank too much. All my problems stemmed from that. But I wasn't even close to ready to face that yet, so instead of thinking, I hit "erase." I opened the second bottle, took a swig, and headed to the airport. I bought a new ticket for a flight that afternoon, and thought, *Thank God no one will ever know any of this happened.* I sat down for a Bloody Mary and gumbo in an airport restaurant and told myself, *I'm safe.* I crouched in a stall at the airport, and thought, *I have to drink less.* Never *I have to stop drinking.* Even when you're losing your lunch in an airport bathroom, denial can be more powerful than the plain reality of the situation. "Are you okay in there?" someone asked from outside the stall. "Just a nervous flier," I choked. *All will be well all will be well all will be well.*

On the flight back to Seattle, the guy seated next to me said I smelled "like a homeless person." "Do you have any other clothes you could change into?" the flight attendant asked. She looked sheepish, and I wanted to help, but all my clothes were in my checked luggage, along with the leftover vodka. They found the man another seat. I could feel his contempt for me—I smelled like vomit and alcohol sweats—but I just didn't care. All I wanted was to make it home, to collapse in the spare bedroom, fully clothed. Addiction has a way of shrinking the size of your ambitions. I made it home. I didn't die. I felt like I had finished a marathon.

I told no one what had happened.

Sixteen

The Incident

After Houston, I spent a few months on my best behavior—not because I wanted to "get better," as people like Josh and Nick insisted on saying, but because I needed to prove to them that I could. The time between drinking binges stretched out to weeks, and the longer those stretches lasted, the more Josh started to think that maybe I had really turned a corner. Throughout 2008, during walks through an Olmstead park that we called the forest, we had started to plot our escape from *The Stranger*. We talked and talked about what we would do when we got out until the fantasy started feeling real. Our plan was to start our own local news and politics website—one that would combine the legitimacy of "straight" reporting with the perspective both of us had earned from years of covering our respective beats (his: the state legislature; mine: city hall). The site would be called PubliCola—Josh's idea—after the nom de plume used by authors of the Federalist Papers. ("The first bloggers," Josh insisted.)

Josh left first, and I took over as news editor, a position in which I now had four bosses, three staffers, and no authority. I wasn't the best pick for a job that involved babysitting writers—I refused to spend hours debating every edit and cut—but it didn't help that I was always finding out about things that were happening in my own section from people outside the news department. *Oh, so Eli's moving his desk across the office and no longer coming to news meetings? When was someone planning to tell me?* Some editors can make up for a lack of authority with a soothing bedside manner, but not me— my style was more "bitch boss" than indulgent den mother, and I was always more than happy to rewrite the damn thing myself, a practice writers tend to hate. Management, I told people later, just didn't suit me; I didn't have the patience, I said, to sit around coddling writers in love with their own preciousness. But I was also spinning out of control again—drinking, yelling at writers, and fighting with Nick over everything and nothing. He had stayed out too late again. He was monitoring me too closely. He invited a beautiful younger woman to stay with him during a conference and here she was, sleeping in our bedroom like a guest of honor.

The next time I hit rock bottom, I didn't have the option of keeping it to myself. I was sick, broke, and lying to everyone, and one day I got caught shoplifting a bottle of wine from a grocery store. The thing is, it wasn't the first time I had shoplifted. As a teenager, I was practically a professional at slipping a beaded bracelet around my wrist at the mall, or dropping a lipstick to the bottom of my big, floppy purse, and as an adult, I had gotten back into the habit. During my last couple of years at *The Stranger*, I stole stuff like it was a joke—walking out of a store with a giant, worthless cardboard display on a dare; slipping an expensive jar of saffron in my shopping bag in the self-checkout line. I'm not proud of this. But it happened, and the fact that it went on for so long—several years, mostly in my early thirties—is a testament both to my shaky moral compass and to the social contract that says busy young women in yoga pants don't shoplift, they just sometimes forget to pay.

The night I got caught, I was on my way to Josh's, where I was going to work for a few hours before catching the bus back to Nick's house. It was less than six months after I graduated from detox, and a month or two after my casual return to drinking. But it wasn't so casual anymore. Since that first thrilling nip of tequila in the alley near the liquor store, I had slipped back into my old routine, drinking nearly every day and feeling off-kilter when I managed to make it a day without buying a bottle. I was living paycheck to paycheck. Booze costs money, and even a ten-dollar-a-day habit makes a big dent in a journalist's salary. My bank account would be overdrawn until the end of the week, which left me with just the few dollars I had in my wallet. I decided to go grocery shopping before heading to Josh's apartment for "Trad Monday"—our traditional Monday-night writing party. I grabbed a couple of items—Cajun snack mix, a box of energy bars—and a liter box of Chardonnay, which I slipped in my bag while making eye contact with the bins of granola in the bulk aisle.

I walked up to the self-checkout line—casual, same as I had a million times before. Paid. And stuffed the paid-for snacks in my bag on top of the stolen wine.

One foot past the security gate, I felt two strong sets of arms on my shoulders. A voice from behind me yelled, "Don't try to run!"

I wasn't indignant. But I didn't feel like a criminal, either. My mind shut off for a minute, like it was powering down to get me through whatever came next. I followed the guard back into the store, trying to will myself invisible.

Please take me out of sight please take me out of sight please take me out of sight.

The voice turned out to belong to one of two young-looking guys in rumpled white dress shirts and black slacks. "I'm so sorry," I babbled under my breath. "I just want you to know that I am going to totally cooperate with whatever you tell me to do. What happens now? Do I get arrested? Where would you like me to put my bike?" I tried to make myself helpful, get on their good side. *We're on the same team, right? Right?*

The skinnier of the two security guys, who was pale with large, unfashionable wire-framed glasses and thinning mouse-brown hair, gestured blandly toward the back of the store. "No one is going to arrest you. Just come with us." He had a vacant, clock-watching demeanor. "We just have to file a police report and have you fill out some paperwork, and then you'll be on your way." His tone of voice was much more "I can take the next customer over here" than "You're in big trouble, young lady."

A lot of thoughts went through my head in the next few moments. Thoughts like: *Will I have to tell Nick about this?* And: *What lie can I tell Josh to explain why I'm late?* And: *What if anyone finds out?*

And, most pressing: *Where am I going to get a bottle of wine now?*

By the time I sat down in the security office, the neck of my T-shirt was dark with sweat. They had questions, so many questions: What was my name? Where did I work? Why did I steal a bottle of booze? I tried to be the picture of compliance. Erica Barnett. *The Stranger.* I didn't have any money to pay for it. And that's basically what ended up on the police report. Charge: first-degree misdemeanor theft. Reason for theft: broke.

The second security guard—older, bored, matter of fact—asked me if this was my first charge. *What do I look like, some kind of criminal?* I nodded. "Okay. Here's what happens next. This will take a while to process. When it does, you'll go to the judge and ask for prefiling diversion. They'll make you do some community service and the charges will be dismissed. Oh, and you won't be able to come back in here for a year. Just do everything right and make sure you never do this again, Okay?" I nodded again, grateful that they had been so easy on me. "Here's your license back. You're free to go."

Back outside, I headed—where else?—to the liquor store, where I peeled seven sweaty dollars from my wallet and plucked the cheapest plastic bottle of vodka from the bottom shelf.

Months went by. I told no one. Not Josh, who asked what took me so long when I showed up to his house later that evening, disheveled and probably stinking of vodka and flop sweat. Not Nick, who was already *this close* to kicking me out over my drinking, which I was doing a bad job of hiding. And certainly not my parents, to whom I had barely spoken since leaving Houston in a huff.

Surely, I told myself, this was more than a close call. This was my wake-up call.

I drank less for a while after that, and for days, sometimes weeks, I didn't drink at all. I showed up dutifully for court, and got reprimanded by a bailiff for plugging in my laptop to work on a story while I waited for my name to be called. And just as the security guard had promised, my case was diverted without charges, and all I had to do in exchange was twenty hours of community service. I spent a couple of hungover weekends pulling poison hemlock and nettles from a greenbelt alongside other petty thieves, and over months, I started to forget "the incident" ever happened. Another lucky draw.

Then one day, the phone rang at my office.

"Hello, it's Erica."

"Hi, this is Linda Edwards at *Seattle Weekly*."

"Yes?" I assumed she was calling to get a phone number for a source—reporter to reporter—so I slid my Rolodex across the desk.

"I'm calling because I'm about to run an item on a shoplifting charge that was filed against you for trying to steal a bottle of wine at the Broadway QFC last year, and I just wanted to know if you care to comment before I hit publish."

This couldn't be happening. "I'm sorry, what are you talking about?"

"The shoplifting charge." Smug—like someone who had scored a huge scoop and was just springing the trap. "Against you? At the QFC. Just seeking comment."

"Hang on." I got up and closed the office door, phone still clutched in my shaking hand. *Breathe.* "This is completely off the record." *Breathe.* "Please, consider what you're doing. I'm a real person. Is ruining another reporter's life worth it to you, just to burn *The Stranger*?" At the time, *The Stranger* and the *Weekly*, which has since stopped publishing its print edition, were bitter rivals. "This is my reputation—my *life*. I could lose my job. I'm asking you, not reporter to reporter, but human being to human being, not to do this. Think of how you would feel if you were on my end of this call. Please, I am begging you, do not do this."

"No, we're going to run with it," the voice on the other end said coolly. "Care to comment?"

"What the fuck. No!" I slammed down the phone.

Seattle Weekly posted the story moments later, with a perfunctory "Barnett declined to comment" and a quote from a Seattle Police Department spokesperson who confirmed that "SPD records indicate she wasn't arrested at the scene."

Within five minutes, *The Stranger*'s publisher, Tim, was in my office. I'm sure Tim had known I went to detox the previous summer, but it might not have made much of an impression. After all, I was hardly the first person at his paper to have dealt, publicly, with a drinking problem; another writer had written a moving feature about her recovery at just four months sober, then relapsed.

But I knew he hadn't wanted to hire me, and I thought he might use the fact that I had embarrassed his paper as a pretext to correct Dan and Josh's mistake. I couldn't have been more wrong. "Jesus, Erica, are you okay? This is so awful. What a shitty situation. If there's anything I can do to help, let me know." I turned beet red with shame and gratitude. I had no idea how to respond.

"No, I guess we'll just have to see what happens," I finally squeaked.

The next thing that happened is that I told my friends, and Nick, and my parents that I had been caught stealing wine, and listened (forbearingly, I thought) as they told me they were concerned about me, that things would only get worse if I kept drinking like I was. "I knew something weird was going on when you showed up so late," Josh told me, "but I can't believe you just acted like nothing was going on! We've got to get you back to meetings." Hadn't I already told him that I didn't like going to meetings, that I got nothing out of them? "You aren't taking this seriously," he responded. Nick, who had to live with me, was more succinct. "Jesus, Erica." He had quit; why couldn't I?

The second thing that happened is that everyone at the office rallied to my side. They published stories on *The Stranger*'s blog about occasions when they had walked out of stores without paying for things, and defended me in the comments section, where anonymous readers were gleefully ripping me to shreds. I prayed that my parents weren't reading the site, and I especially prayed that they weren't reading the comments, where total strangers were calling me a "sanctimonious hypocritical cunt," a "shrill, humorless scold," a "smug, smarmy bitch," and hundreds of other variations on that theme. The commenters dug up my financial records and parking tickets and speculated on what my parents must be like to have raised such a worthless piece of trash. They reveled in the certainty that I would lose my job and end up on the street. They let me know that they couldn't wait for that to happen.

Back in the real world, the *Weekly* wasn't through hassling me. Two of their editors—guys I knew, including one I'd worked with—ordered a bouquet of flowers for me from the grocery store they knew I was not allowed to enter, to be picked up inside the store. The floral department left me messages for days, until I finally picked up, had the clerk read the card out loud (something along the lines of, "Hope you enjoyed the wine!"), and told her to throw them in the trash.

All of it—the online hate, the comments about my worth, the prank with the flowers—worked as intended. The more strangers (apparently) hated me, the more I hated myself. The more I hated myself, the angrier I was at everyone around me; the angrier I was, the more I wanted to crawl inside a bottle and never come out. Worse, I had to reassure Josh and Nick and everyone I knew that I would stop drinking—was, in fact, actively trying to stop for good—right as I was starting to really doubt that would ever happen.

What I needed, I thought, was a change of pace. Within six months of my promotion, I had turned in my resignation letter—a melodramatic flounce that instantly ended my friendships with Tiffany, Tristan, and, by extension, Sarah—and PubliCola officially became a two-person operation. I decided to stop drinking—for real this time. I had a reason now: I wanted to make PubliCola succeed. I never thought to do it for myself. Me? I was fine.

Josh trusted me enough to start a business with me, and, although I would ultimately let him down, we worked our asses off in those first few years, and broke a lot of great stories, too. Going to work every day was like heading to the treehouse where my best friend was waiting. We dubbed our first office—a windowless room in the corner of a huge video production studio that a friend let us use rent-free—the Playpen, because whenever we had the place to ourselves, we sprawled on the floor, notes and documents and laptops littering every surface. On Josh's birthday in 2009, one year after I had laid down on his living room floor during his birthday party and passed out in front of all his friends, he sent me a text: "For the record: One year ago today was your disaster. And look at you now. It's so great to see. Love you. Josh."

After a couple of months in the Playpen, we moved—to another borrowed office, then another, and eventually to our own space, a carpeted, 12-x-12-foot box with a wall of windows that looked out onto Elliott Bay. Finally, things were looking up.

Seventeen

White-knuckling It

Relapse, according to one popular theory, is a process, not an event. It starts long before you pick up the first drink, when you begin to slip back into old ways of feeling, thinking, and behaving that marked your active addiction. Some behaviors that might constitute the beginning of a relapse include: Continuing to keep alcohol in the house. Feeling sorry for yourself because your life hasn't improved dramatically since you got sober, and not talking to anyone about it. Blaming others for your problems. Failing to deal appropriately with triggers—which, if you're an alcoholic, are probably everywhere. (A crushed beer can on the street. An ad for vodka. A recipe for brandied pears in a cooking magazine.) Without a support system to keep you thinking rationally, small problems can start to seem like crises, and setbacks can make you feel as if nothing is going your way. Depression sets in, then immobilization, and from there, drinking is inevitable; the only question is when.

I used to think this was total bullshit. But looking back, I realize that every time I picked up a bottle, it was after I had neglected the boring work of staying sober—all the stuff that Ken and even AA had taught me about staying connected and developing new habits to replace the old ones and getting outside myself. And before I knew it, I'd be on another run. People who aren't alcoholics often say things like, "Nobody forced you to pour that liquor down your throat." What they don't realize is how little it feels like a choice. Life without alcohol can feel like walking and walking toward a horizon that never gets any closer. Eventually, your feet get tired and you sit down to rest. That's what drinking feels like, after all that trying. A rest.

Nick, more than anyone, had a front-row seat for the uglier aspects of my drinking. He was the one who was there when I ran to the bathroom to throw up at eight in the morning or eight at night, the one who would shake his head at me as I emerged, sweaty, red-faced, and shaking, making some excuse about how I shouldn't have had coffee on an empty stomach. He was the primary victim of my rages, which could be set off by anything—jealousy, insecurity, a fight over the dishes—and the witness to my worst behavior, whether it was starting arguments to divert attention from his suspicions or burning dinner to cinders when I passed out with the oven on. Nick drew from his own menu of bad behaviors—staying out too late without calling, raging at me in that booming voice that bellowed from a body twice my size—but if you isolated just my part in our problems, it was enough.

Enough was staying out late and refusing to tell him where I'd been. Enough was passing out in my bedroom when we were supposed to go out, forcing him to make up excuses that became less and less convincing to our (his) friends. Enough was drinking a bottle of port at Thanksgiving, long after I had supposedly quit drinking, and blaming him for letting me pick a recipe for cranberry sauce that included wine.

Enough was the time when Nick mistook my suitcase for his while getting ready for a trip, and unzipped the bag to find a dozen empty vodka bottles, stored away in plain sight the way a cheating spouse keeps text messages from his girlfriend, practically begging to be caught.

Enough was showing up at home early one morning, grass in my hair and clothes soaking wet, after accidentally spending the night in a park across town, where I'd passed out in the grass, empty Smirnoff bottle at my feet, after storming out of the house and heading to the park "to read." My book, one of many I never finished in those days: *The Night of the Gun*, an indelible memoir about addiction by David Carr.

Enough, finally, was enough for Nick. We were walking back from the natural-foods store one Saturday morning when I decided to test him with a question about the future.

"What do you think about getting chickens?" I asked.

"I think you should move out," he responded.

I did everything I could to talk him out of it. I begged, I promised to quit drinking, I told him I would go to AA and get control of my anger and change everything about my life. I didn't ask him to do anything different—I felt far too guilty for that, after all I'd put him through—but it didn't matter. He had reached his breaking point a long time ago—after the time I passed out at the dinner table, but long before he had to start making excuses for me to his friends. This was just when he chose to tell me. There was no bargaining: I had to go.

But I didn't go far. In the end, after half-heartedly looking for places in a more convenient neighborhood near downtown, I settled on an apartment just a few blocks away from Nick, in a motel-style 1960s complex that had been cheaply updated with stainless-steel appliances and landscaping so half-assed that many of the bottom-floor units had black plastic sheets covering their tiny fenced-in "yards" instead of mulch. The toilet wasn't caulked or sealed when I moved in, and painter's tape still covered the patchy, unfinished bathroom walls. Even the stacked washer and dryer, a big selling point for the agent who showed me the place, weren't working properly—the dryer vent opened directly into the closet, sending torrents of lint onto the ceiling.

I didn't care. If Nick was going to kick me out, did it really matter where I lived, or if my apartment had mold on the walls? I was damaged goods, a hopeless alcoholic, unlovable whether I got sober or not. If self-pity had a shape and color, it would have been the 10-x-10-foot cube of my bedroom for that year, and for several years afterward, blinds drawn to create a box of permanent twilight, bottles stashed behind sinks and in suitcases and under the bed.

There's a famous quote that AA detractors use to illustrate how histrionic people in "the program" can be: "We are people in the grip of a progressive illness whose ends are always the same: jails, institution, and death." (The quote actually comes from Narcotics Anonymous.) I thought it was histrionic, too, until I didn't. I never ended up in jail, but I sure came close, and there were plenty of times I could have died. And by 2010, I had already begun what the AA book refers to as "the weary round of sanitariums and hospitals," a phrase that came to mind every time I checked myself into a new emergency room.

The first time I ended up in the ER for withdrawal, a few months before I moved out of Nick's house, I was slow to catch on to what was happening. I took the bus to the hospital and walked up to the triage desk in a state of near delirium, convinced I had come down with some kind of terrible flu. The symptoms all fit the bill—heart palpitations, excessive sweating, dehydration—until a nurse asked me how much I drank. "Six drinks a day? Sometimes eight?" I didn't even know when I was lying anymore. Instantly, I saw the narrative shift, watched the ER nurses' expressions change from concern to something like scorn. Just another detoxing alcoholic, taking up a bed. "We'll get you some fluids and get you out of here in a jiffy," a nurse said, newly curt. As I laid there, grateful that I didn't have to do anything for at least a few hours, someone jammed a wide-gauge needle in my arm, then hooked me up to an IV that led to a yellow "banana bag" filled with vitamins and electrolytes. After an hour or so, another orderly came in, pulled the catheter from my arm, and announced, "I'll get the social worker" to no one in particular. This was the start of the weary rounds: an hour in a bed with an IV in my arm, followed by a stilted conversation with a social worker about my drinking. Yes, I've tried AA. No, I don't want to go to rehab. Yes, I have a support system at home. Now can I go?

Again, I tried to stop drinking—not through therapy, which I had dropped, nor in "the rooms" of AA, which I attended only sporadically—but on my own, white-knuckling it for a few days or weeks at a time while insisting to everyone who knew me that I wasn't drinking at all. Again, I failed. Again and again, I found myself at hospitals, where the emergency-room nurses and doctors often treated me like a malingerer, not an emergency. With all my obvious advantages—an apartment, a middle-class job, a strong personal safety net—it made no sense that I kept ending up in hospitals, tethered to an IV line. Once, I was moved to an inpatient detox after the doctors clocked my heart rate at 243. Another time, I checked in at 8:00 A.M. and checked out at 5:00, arriving back at home in time for dinner, full of electrolytes and with a fresh bottle in my backpack. The ER visits started to feel like a routine part of life—check in, get a couple bags of IV fluids, send the social worker away. People can live this way for years and years, because alcohol tends to kill you slowly rather than all at once. I lived this way for a very long time. Lots of people are living this way right now.

Two thousand ten came and went; then 2011. The medical bills piled up, unopened. Eighteen hundred dollars isn't an unthinkable amount of money to most people making a middle-class salary—a mortgage payment, or a week's vacation—but it might as well be $18 million when you're eating potatoes for lunch at the end of each pay cycle. It was easier just not to look.

Sometimes, weeks would go by when I would drink only on weekends—always in secret, the bottle stashed away in my closet or purse, comforting me with its sloshing weight—and sometimes, I could make it through for a while without drinking at all. Other times, I would steal away two, five, ten times a day, gulping room-temperature wine in the stall at work and brushing my teeth with my fingers. Over and over, I quit or slowed down, then plummeted back toward bottom. Over and over, I lost a few more things—another thousand dollars, my phone, a bit more of my dignity—then, as if it were inevitable, pulled out of the spin.

PubliCola went through a series of upheavals as we struggled to finance a site focused on local news and politics—always the hardest kind of content to sell to advertisers. Eventually, we were bought by a local glossy magazine, and suddenly we had bosses, magazine assignments with hard deadlines, and an office where we were expected to appear, more or less during normal business hours, every day. We didn't have to worry about making payroll anymore, but I was somehow more stressed out than ever. Maybe if I wasn't busy all the time, I would have time to talk to Ken, who was still, throughout all this, technically my therapist. Maybe if I wasn't drunk all the time, I'd be able to figure out why I wasn't happy.

The problem was, who would I be if I wasn't drunk all the time? The version of me that jumped naked into a hot tub at a New Year's Eve party that year was wild and uninhibited, but the "real" me was as insecure and tongue-tied as a twelve-year-old getting catcalled by a group of boys. The last thing I wanted was for anyone to meet the clenched, scared person I really was. I drank, I told myself, because I didn't know who I would be sober, because I was too shy to open up to new people without a buzz, because I didn't want anyone to see how terrified and self-loathing I really was.

But really, more and more, I drank because I had to.

Eighteen

Toxic Superpowers

I didn't admit to anyone just how out of control my life had become—of course I didn't. Instead, I told myself I was *this close* to having the situation in hand. Starting *now*, I would drink only in secret. Starting *now*, I'd drink only with people who didn't know I had a drinking problem, in bars and neighborhoods where I was unlikely to be spotted. But despite all the contortions I went through to pretend I was normal—*I'm fine, this is fine, everything's fine*—it didn't work. When I drank in secret, I always drank too much, and someone would say the dreaded words: "Have you been drinking?" And when I tried to drink "normally," around normal people, I became acutely aware of how little space alcohol occupied in other people's minds. Did you know that some people will pay for a glass of wine and then leave it half-finished on the table, or order a Coke instead of a second round? I sure didn't. Everyone else seemed to be able to regulate their drinking, just by not thinking about it, but when I didn't think about it, the first drink disappeared in one greedy gulp. I learned to monitor the level of alcohol in other people's glasses and try to slow myself down to match their pace, miming their actions like a Christmas-and-Easter churchgoer pretending to know the words to the hymns. Eventually, I figured out that the easiest way to drink "normally" was to have a little extra on the sly. Usually, I'd just keep a pint bottle of vodka in my purse, but when that wasn't feasible, I'd sidle up to the part of the bar farthest away from my companions, order a quick double bourbon, and pay with cash. Once, I excused myself from a movie, walked out of the theater, and dashed across the street for two quick shots at a dive bar called the Mecca. Five minutes later, I was back in my seat, breath freshened with two sticks of gum from my pocket. *See, this isn't so hard.*

Some alcoholics say they decided to get sober after some monumental loss—a husband, a job, children taken away by the authorities—but that wasn't my story. Quite the opposite. Once I had lost Nick, there was no reason not to drink like I wanted to—no one snooping through suitcases or checking the recycling to see if I'd shoved a bottle under the pile of soda cans and magazines. So, in that dim apartment with its sliding-glass doors that looked out to a balcony I never used, I drank. I drank to get through the weekends, napping on the couch and binging on *Big Love*, and I drank to get through the week, when I had to face Josh and his suspicious questions. I drank through high fevers and bronchitis, and I drank before and after investor meetings, when we'd try to convince rich friends to fund our struggling website. I drank through a scary bout of menorrhagia, which is when you have a period that won't stop, both before and after visits to the doctor, who thought I might need a blood transfusion. I kept drinking after I mysteriously lost my sense of smell, which my ear, nose, and throat doctor told me sometimes "just happens," and when my blood pressure started to climb, alarming my doctor, to whom I still lied about how much I drank.

I didn't drink all the time, but when I did, I drank prodigiously: two or three liters of wine a day, or a liter of wine and a pint of vodka, which is quite a day's work, and a tough secret to keep.

The National Institute on Alcohol Abuse and Alcoholism defines binge drinking as drinking enough over two hours to have a blood alcohol content of 0.08 (the legal driving limit in most states), which works out to about four drinks for women. Using standard drink sizes and a blood alcohol content calculator, I was drinking as many as seventeen drinks a day—enough to put a typical one-hundred-thirty-pound, five-foot-seven woman in a coma. And yet, I functioned. I carried on with work, wrote stories, conducted interviews—noticeably blurry at times, for sure, but never so wasted I couldn't stay vertical. Tolerance is a kind of toxic superpower—as the body and brain adjust to having alcohol around, it becomes possible to drink more and more without getting drunk, and it also becomes harder to function without a base layer of booze. After a while, the period you can go without alcohol—without going into withdrawal—becomes shorter and shorter, and eventually you're drinking all the time, the way junkies shoot up every few hours just to stay well.

The irrationality of a heavy drinker is hard to overstate. It goes with you everywhere, makes you take insane risks because you think you're invincible. At least, that's what drinking did to me. It made me jump in a car with a stranger late one night, after the bus driver had woken me up at the end of the line. The buses wouldn't start up again for three more hours, and walking home—a good four miles—wasn't an option. Neither was sleeping at the bus stop. So I walked to the street, held out my thumb, and hoped for the best. A man pulled up in an SUV, rolled down the window, and asked where

I wanted to go. "Home," I told him. "A few miles that way." He opened the door, I hopped in, and the night rolled by outside.

By accident, he was the kind stranger I was looking for. He didn't make small talk or tell me it wasn't safe to be standing out there, at the corner of Rainier and Henderson, so late at night. He didn't hit on me or flirt or offer me a cigarette. He drove me home, waited until I unlocked my door, then drove away. I should have learned that night that I'd been lucky, and that I might not be so lucky again. Instead, I learned: Don't fall asleep next time; you might miss your stop.

Most of the time, though, I wasn't hopping in cars with strange men. I was simply existing. People who aren't addicts often think addiction is a constant party. In conversation, they talk about how *they* know how to handle their liquor, and in public policy debates, they argue that we shouldn't fund services for people with addiction, because they're the ones who choose to spend their lives having fun instead of being productive citizens. What they don't realize, but I do, is that whether you're living in a tent along a greenbelt or an overpriced apartment in the city, the life of a chronic alcoholic or addict is the opposite of a party. It's *work*—a dull, tedious, endlessly repeating cycle: obsess, seek, score, consume, do it again. Periodically, this oppressive circuit (bed, liquor store, job, liquor store, bed) will be interrupted by health scares, embarrassing incidents, and altercations with people who don't understand your imperative to self-destruct. Sometimes, I got busted with a bottle in my bag. Sometimes, I woke up on a damp mattress. Sometimes, I ended up in a strange part of town, wondering how I got there and how I was going to get home.

During that blurry half-decade when I was drinking in "secret," my best days were the ones I spent quietly in my apartment, alone in my depression and anxiety and despair. The best things got was when I didn't embarrass myself, piss anybody off, or pass out somewhere other than my home. The worst things got—well, that's hard to quantify. Was it the time I woke up in the hospital after walking into the emergency room in a blackout, tubes attached to my arms and my clothes in a pile on the floor? The time I showed up at work too wasted to string together a sentence, and Josh had to glare daggers at me through the editor's office window, warding me away from a meeting where he wouldn't be able to protect me? The time I got into a fight with a ticket agent at the airport and told her belligerently, "I am GETTING on that PLANE!"? Once one of those things happens, you start running out of excuses. Once all of them do, rock bottom becomes a moving target.

There's a passage in AA's Big Book that describes a man whose "disposition while drinking resembles his normal nature but a little" and who is "always more or less insanely drunk." This guy squanders his talents in "a senseless series of sprees" and does "absurd, incredible, tragic things while drinking." I remember reading that passage (drunk, of course), and thinking, "This guy really *gets* me!" before taking another swig from the bottle at my bedside. Of *course* I was squandering my talent—I was an alcoholic! Of *course* I did absurd, incredible, tragic things—my life was absurd, incredible, and tragic! Alcoholics are self-destructive, so it makes sense that they self-destruct. My life was a tautology from which I could not escape.

And so, like Big Book author Bill Wilson himself (and countless alcoholics before and since), I soldiered on like a champ—throwing up in the office bathroom, babbling incoherently at editorial meetings, and fighting with Josh in the stairwell near our cubicle, where I'd occasionally confess to some small sliver of the truth. *Yes, I've been drinking. No, I haven't been doing it often. Yes, I'm going to a meeting right after work. Yes, I'll get my story in on time. Don't worry. Don't be mad. I promise I'll make it up to you.*

I wasn't fine. I had a fresh three-inch scar on my shin from the time I missed the bottom step while getting off a bus on the way to a meeting I was supposed to cover, and a litany of mysterious ailments as long as my arm. High blood pressure and my lost sense of smell were only the warning signs; by the time I was in my mid-thirties, my body started breaking down. Fainting spells. A chronic cough. A blown eardrum. A torn esophagus. Blurred vision. Restless leg syndrome. Constant tremors. Night sweats and terrors. Psoriasis.

A few of my physical problems could be written off as medical mysteries—to this day, I'm prone to strange maladies and Google-proof symptoms—but all of them were exacerbated by the drinking. Especially the psoriasis, an autoimmune disease that causes red, patchy scales on the skin. My dermatologist was quite clear on this point: If I stopped drinking, my symptoms would improve; if I didn't, they would get worse. I didn't stop. Over six months, exactly what she had predicted came to pass: "Oh my GOD. What happened to your arms?" people would ask me, concerned and transparently horrified. "Oh, it's not contagious, it's just psoriasis," I'd apologize, tugging on my sleeves. "It's an autoimmune disease. Nothing I can do about it."

Instead of swearing off booze, I swore off clothes that showed a single unnecessary inch of skin, and bought professional-grade body concealer—the stuff movie stars use to cover up their tattoos. Short skirts and sleeveless dresses, my uniform during Seattle's brief but glorious summers, were out; long pants and hoodies were in, even when the temperature edged above eighty. I remember covering the 2012 election in long sleeves—sweating, apologizing for sweating, hoping that no one was watching me sweat. My dermatologist ran me through the gamut of treatments: steroid creams, retinol, prescription-strength shampoo, and therapeutic tanning, but nothing helped—my tanned, moisturized, vitamin-enhanced skin still looked like the surface of Mars. On my list of reasons to get sober, "stop looking like a burn victim" was somewhere behind "keep your job" and just above "get out of debt," and all were equally unattainable.

Nineteen

Play the Tape
Forward

People love to talk about the "moment of clarity"—that fabled
instant when an addict finally makes the decision to stop drinking forever and truly means it. I've had that moment; I know it
well. Unfortunately, what I've discovered is that, like rock bottom,
moments of clarity can happen over and over, and you can keep
drinking right on through them. I had a moment of clarity when I
passed out on Josh's couch, and another when I realized I had no
desire to garden, cook, or eat—three of my favorite pastimes since
college, when I spent hours kneading flour into gluten to make vegetarian "chicken" or experimenting to see which seeds would make
the crunchiest sprouts. After each moment of clarity, I vowed to
change everything, and as soon as the moment passed, I had a drink.
Tomorrow. I'll fix it tomorrow.

But even when I couldn't stay sober for more than a day or two,

I was starting to see glimpses of a way out. I was learning what worked and what didn't—not universally, but for me. When I tried to drink moderately, I learned that I couldn't—that first drink opened up a well in my body that a thousand more couldn't fill. When I tried to get sober on my own, I discovered that I needed some kind of support. When I spent months scribbling CBT call-and-response notes in my diary—"Thought: I don't need to be at this meeting. Response: Everyone here seems happier than me so maybe they know something I don't"—I learned that I could talk back to my most insidious inner voice, the one that said, "It'll be different this time." And even AA taught me a couple of things: First, before buying that first drink or bottle, I should "play the tape forward," to the part of the story where I'm lying in bed at home, bottles shoved out of sight, with the walls closing in around me. And second, people do recover. Even hopeless drunks like me.

Today, when I tell people why I quit drinking, they often respond, "I had no idea you had a problem," or, even better, "Are you sure?" People who say this are inevitably acquaintances, never close friends; if you really knew me, it was obvious. That's why I tried not to spend too much time around people who knew me. Every relationship had an expiration date. Even the most self-absorbed guys eventually wondered why I never seemed to be able to keep a commitment, or why I was throwing up in the bathroom.

When no one else would have me, Kevin would. Since we broke up nearly a decade earlier, we'd stayed in touch—just enough for him to know about things like the trip to detox, but not enough for him to know how much worse things had gotten since then. People see what they want to see. Kevin saw the girl he knew back in Austin—a little messy, a few scars and scratches, but basically a smart, capable person who could overcome any obstacle. The kind of person who certainly wouldn't let something as common as alcohol get the best of her.

He was my island of sensibility—my one through line to the time before Seattle, when my biggest problems were insomnia, anxiety, and ennui. He was my connection to a time when things made sense. I asked him if he wanted to go out on a date. He said yes. And, just like that, we were back together—sleeping on the same old futon mattress he had hauled up from Austin, now tucked into an alcove in the finished attic of the house he moved into after the shag-carpet apartment.

Kevin didn't judge me the way my friends did—not at first. Or, if he did, he kept it to himself. Bringing up someone else's drinking, the way Josh so often did with me, can feel like an accusation, the kind of confrontation people routinely avoid because the stakes are so high. How many people want to start a conversation with, "Hey, can we talk about how out of control you were last night?" It's easier to let it go, pretend it never happened, hope the person will get help or that you're just imagining things.

Josh, of course, was the opposite—when everyone else was averting their eyes, he looked directly into mine, demanding to know whether I was drunk. I hated this directness, because it forced me to choose between honesty and unconvincing denial—between "Yes, you caught me" and "No, how dare you suggest such a thing." Josh always knew, anyway; after all the years we'd known each other, he could sense as soon as I picked up the phone when something was off—and I knew he knew. I hated lying to him. But I did. What was the alternative? At best, a profoundly uncomfortable discussion. At worst, another trip to detox, or even rehab. Either way, I'd be a disappointment and a burden, and for what? Nothing was going to make a difference anyway. I was the one who had to make the decision to quit, and I would. Soon. But not just yet.

Kevin never said I was acting weird, or questioned me when I was out of focus. Even when I slept through a full day during a trip to a nearby national park, telling him, "I'm just really exhausted," he let it pass without comment. Even when I "tripped on the sidewalk" on the walk from his house to the grocery store—explaining breezily, "I'm just not used to wearing heels!"—he accepted my excuse. In fact, it wasn't until I passed out in the upstairs bedroom after breakfast one morning at his friends' house in Portland that *he* had to admit that *I* had a problem. "I think you need to apologize to Alysse and Bryan," he said. "Also, you need a shower."

Shaky, disoriented, and disgusted with myself, I made a big show of remorse, admitting over brunch that I had a "drinking problem"— I still didn't like the term *alcoholic*—and promising to seek help. As it turned out, Bryan was an AA guy, and he invited me to join him at a meeting that very afternoon. An hour later, I found myself sitting in the back of some church meeting room, flanked by the three of them, sweating like a farmhand. The group leader, a handsome blond guy with horn-rimmed glasses that were either very expensive or very cheap, exuded an air of perfect hipster insouciance. *What makes them think they're so much better than me? What have they figured out that I can't?*

Twenty

Cindy

A gap in my own biography had started to bug me more and more, like an unraveling thread in a sweater that grows and grows until you have to cut the whole thing out. I decided it was time to contact my birth mom.

I had been thinking about Cindy superficially for many years, but there was always a period at the end of the story. Cindy was my birth mom, but she left, and no one ever heard from her again. My mom is my mom, and I don't need a new one. Cindy didn't want to see me, and now she's living her life somewhere, or not, and that's all there is to say about that. Maybe she's alive, maybe she's dead. Either way, it's none of my business.

But then, sometime after I turned thirty, I thought: Am I being immature about this? I don't know what really happened. Maybe my dad kicked *her* out. Maybe I have siblings. Maybe she was an alcoholic, too, and just couldn't handle being a mom. So I decided to ask about her.

As it turned out, Cindy had been right under my nose all along. After she left my dad, she had moved away for a while but eventually came back to Mississippi, taking a series of jobs not far from where my grandparents still lived—first selling cars, then running a forklift at a chain hardware store in Jackson—the same chain my granddad worked for in Meridian.

I found all of this out from my grandmother, who seemed oddly nonchalant about this question it had taken me more than twenty-five years to ask.

"Oh, yes, Jesse sees Cindy and her mother from time to time," Mama Opal told me on the phone. "Her family still lives right up forty-nine in Quinton. Are you just wondering, or did you want him to give her a message?"

I pictured my grandmother, standing to the side in my parents' wedding photo, lips pursed in disapproval as the teenage couple smiled nervously at the camera. "I want to talk to her," I heard myself saying. *Did I?* "Do you think he can make that happen?"

Within a week, I had an email, phone number, and an answer: Of course Cindy would love to hear from me. *Would she?* I started cautiously, with an email. "I have so much to ask you," I wrote. We made a date to talk on the phone, and then suddenly—as if there had never been any reason for this conversation not to happen—I was hearing her voice, gravelly as a chain-smoker's, on the other end of the line.

Armed with a list of questions, I settled on the floor in front of my couch and began my interrogation. Why did she leave? She was seventeen, and she wanted to be carefree. Where did she go? To Virginia Beach, to live with her mother. Did she ever try to get in touch with me? No, but she had looked me up online and knew a few basic facts about my life. Did I have any siblings? No. She felt too bad after leaving me to ever try again.

And the unanswerable question: Did she regret leaving me?

The answer was complicated. "I regret it every day," she said, but I heard a hitch in her voice. So I pressed: Wasn't she grateful for the life she was able to have without the burden of having a kid around? I know I would have been. For decades, I'd been putting myself in her shoes: If I had gotten pregnant at sixteen, in a state and an era in which abortion wasn't an option, what would I have done? Dropped out of school, stayed married, prepared for a life of drudgery? Or would I, too, have run, engaged in magical thinking, believing that my actions would never catch up with me? At sixteen, I was in an abusive relationship, looking at college catalogues, and working a part-time job at a Hallmark store. Who was I to judge anyone for the decisions they made at that age? How was I to know that I wouldn't have done the same?

Those questions are, like I said, unanswerable, because the real answers are probably: yes and no. Yes, she regretted her impulsive decision. No, she didn't regret the second chance at being a young person, doing young-person stuff like partying and hooking up and all the things motherhood strips away from girls unlucky enough to get pregnant at her age in the South. The things I got to do.

As Cindy caught me up on the past three and a half decades, part of me understood, and almost respected, her decision. But another part of me wanted her to feel the weight of everything she'd forfeited when she decided to leave—all the milestones, the arguments over boys and clothes, everything I went through to get where I was today. What it was like for me, growing up and discovering that my family was different and feeling like I had something to prove. How I admired my grandparents for taking care of me, and my dad for staying. How he had brought me up to be self-reliant, believing I could do anything I put my mind to, never treating me like I was different or frivolous or fragile because I was a girl. How do you communicate all that history in half an hour? How do you compress decades of life into a story that ends on a positive note?

"So tell me about yourself. What's your life like?" she asked.

"It's good. I live in a beautiful city. I have a boyfriend. I own my own business. I'm a journalist, just like I wanted to be when I was a kid.

"Everything's good."

When we finally met in person a few months after that first phone call, I was hungover and anxious after a night spent nursing a fifth of vodka in a New Orleans hotel. I had driven the two and a half hours from New Orleans to Jackson in a fog, washing ibuprofen down with sparkling water and swigs of warm vodka, trying not to feel as nervous as I felt. Would she see right through me? Would she be able to smell the vodka on my breath? Would we have anything in common?

Cindy lived with her husband, Bill, in a nondescript house on a nondescript street not unlike the one where I had grown up, in the same kind of anonymous suburb where my parents still live. When I pulled up in my rental car, she was already waiting outside, standing on the cracked driveway, waving me in.

"You look just like Opal!" she exclaimed as I stepped out of the car, and she was right—the older I get, the more I look like my grandmother, from my arched left eyebrow to my soft, slightly pointed chin. I scanned her face intently for signs of myself. *Maybe around the eyes?* Cindy was several inches shorter than me, a bit heavyset, with sun-browned skin, friendly eyes, and a warmth I found off-putting even with a solid base layer of vodka sloshing in my stomach. Her house was full of items she had collected at flea markets over the years—copper baking dishes above the doorway, antique duck decoys on the fireplace, and an ecumenical array of crosses spanning the full height of one twelve-foot wall. My whole apartment could have fit inside the master bedroom she shared with Bill and their little dog.

We talked for hours, looking for similarities. *You like shopping at flea markets? Oh my god, me too!* We ate lasagna; watched a reality TV show about survivalists; drove across town to meet her mom—my grandmother—at another suburban home with another wall of crucifixes. It all felt unreal, like I was playing a part written for someone else. Part of the problem was that I felt like a stranger imposing on these people's lives, asking them for time and attention I had never earned. And part of it was that I worried, at any minute, I would be exposed as a failure and a fraud. If they knew the truth, they'd kick me out. If they knew who they were welcoming into their house, they'd lock up the valuables and keep a close eye on their dog. *Don't you know I'm an alcoholic?* I wanted to scream. *Don't you know what I'm capable of?*

I stuck to my talking points for two days, avoiding the minefield of my drinking history. Cindy didn't drink anymore, but to ask her, "Why not?" was to risk having a real conversation, was to risk being honest about my drinking and all the times I had tried and failed to stop. That wasn't a conversation I was eager to have with anyone, much less this stranger I was trying to impress with how well I'd done without her.

After a night staring at the ceiling in Cindy's guest room, I was as eager to leave as I had been to make the trip. I showered, packed up, and said an awkward good-bye, hugging her too tightly and saying I couldn't wait to see her again. There was something so familiar about this rushed parting, and on the drive to Meridian, I realized that it felt like infidelity—like I was cheating on my real parents, the ones who had invested in me and stuck around even when I was writing "I HATE THEM SO MUCH" in my journal and stealing liquor from their bottles. Even speaking to her had felt like a massive betrayal. Worse, I hadn't spoken to my *real* mom since I told her I was making this trip a few weeks ago, and the last time I'd heard Dad's voice was when I'd called him on the landline before flying south—the *hey*'s and *how you doing*'s followed by awkward silences that I never quite learned to fill. Dad and I had never talked much—avoiding him was as easy as not picking up the phone—and I had been ignoring Mom's calls. I knew she would ask some version of the question I hated most, "How's it going with not drinking?" and because I knew she'd know right away that I was lying when I delivered a practiced, "Fine!" Now, after everything I had put them through—the awful scene at my aunt and uncle's in San Francisco, the alarming, out-of-nowhere call from detox—I was reaching out to someone who had never been there for me. Of course I didn't want to talk to my parents about that.

Twenty-one

A Disease of Isolation

A dozen years after I moved to Seattle, I had become a master of compartmentalization. I avoided friends who would know I had been drinking (my girlfriends Lisa and Stephanie; a new friend named Renee, whom I'd met through my reporting about a transit project in her neighborhood; and, of course, Josh) and gravitated, on the rare occasions when I felt like company, to people who didn't know my "tells"—like the way my eyes would go slightly glassy after a certain point in the evening, and some part of me would become inaccessible. Alcoholism is often described as a "disease of isolation," and that works both ways—if you're already isolated, you're more likely to become an alcoholic, and if you keep isolating yourself, you're more likely to stay one. You're also isolated in another way—even among people, your chief concern is the drink, whether that means a trip to the bar or a duck into the bathroom with your purse. In my conversations with other alcoholics, I have yet to meet a single one who didn't pull away from people or reject offers of help, sometimes explosively. Of the many ironic things about alcoholism, this is the most paradoxical: The very substance that allowed us to be sociable and uninhibited, often for the first time, eventually sends us cowering to our rooms. Alcohol started out as a shortcut to human connections and all the emotions I was afraid to express openly. But it ended up being a bypass, a short circuit that catapulted me past insight to total disinhibition.

Josh stopped answering my text messages after 7:00 P.M. or so, so I would call and call and call, and eventually he'd get fed up and turn off his phone. The morning after nights like that, I could expect to wake up to an email, equal parts concerned and annoyed. "Here's something I've noticed," one began. "Whenever you call me late at night, you don't sound like yourself. You say things that don't make sense, and repeat yourself, and you don't listen to anything I say. It makes me worried and sad for you. Frankly, you sound like you've been drinking. I say this out of concern for you as your friend. I don't want to see you throw your life away. What can we do to turn this around?" Later, his emails would get right to the point. "Again super worried and u need to get into a program immediately. What is the status of getting you into a program?" My reaction would depend on how drunk I still was, how hard the hangover was hammering my forehead. What could we do? *We* could get off my back. *We* could take me more seriously when I said I was sad instead of accusing me of being drunk. *We* could let me drink in peace.

At work, Josh would ask me questions in code—"You seem kind of blurry. What percentage are you at today?" I always lied, but here's the thing: Even saying "Eighty-five percent" meant admitting I'd been drinking. So usually, my answer was "one hundred percent"; or, more often, "Why would you even ask me that?" It's hard to sympathize with the drinker in this scenario—everything about the situation makes you want to scream, "Why didn't you quit drinking and stop putting everyone around you through hell?" But from my own admittedly myopic perspective, quitting simply wasn't an option—not now, not yet. I just needed everyone to leave me alone for a little longer, so I could figure a few things out. But Josh was always there, asking if I was drunk, asking how much of me he had today. So I drew inside myself, and I turned my rage inward, too. *Maybe if I'm the only one who knows, that will mean it isn't that bad. Maybe if I can keep Josh off my back, I can come up with a plan to pull myself out of this.* Always *pull myself out*. Never *ask someone else for help.*

My parents, as far as I could tell, had mostly given up—Mom didn't want to listen to my sobbing, incoherent calls, and Dad had run out of sympathy for my complaints about money, which seemed to flow right through my fingers. Later, I would understand that they were detaching—something support groups like Al-Anon recommend—but at the time, I just figured they were sick of hearing about it. Fine by me.

A few people knew the score. The liquor-store clerks, who saw me at my bloated, sweating Saturday-morning worst. My doctors, because every time I ended up in the hospital, it went into my medical records: chest pain, acute alcohol withdrawal, alcohol poisoning, atrial flutter. My downstairs neighbors, probably—I could hear everything they said through the floor, so it stood to reason that they could hear me retching in the toilet every morning. The cashiers at the Safeway, where I showed up, without fail, before 8:00 A.M., waiting impatiently behind the young couples in athleisure, getting a jump on the morning with my bright-yellow box of Bandit Chardonnay clutched in a shaking hand. And the tellers behind bulletproof glass at the downtown Money Mart, where I'd show up once a month or so, a week before payday, to trade $795 of my next paycheck for $700 on the spot.

Alcoholism is an expensive disease, even if you never see the inside of an emergency room, and I was pouring about $300 of every paycheck down my throat, not counting the times I'd buy a shot on the sly, or spring for a $20 bottle of wine at the convenience store by my house when I didn't feel like taking the bus to the grocery store, where a box cost $8.99. I had started going to the food bank near my house every Saturday morning, and those trips became one of the few things I looked forward to—every week, no matter what, there would be the 7:30 A.M. bus ride to the little wooden building on Rainier Avenue South, the wait in line for a number, then three hours until the place actually opened. During that time, I'd get my usual first bottle at the Safeway, then wander to my neglected community garden patch a block away, gulping from the bottle, daring early-morning joggers to judge my choices. In the garden, there were sometimes other drinkers—brazen ones, chugging Steel Reserve and littering the carefully chipped paths with chicken wings—and sometimes I was alone, sitting at the ancient picnic table with a bottle in my backpack, drinking and reading *The New Yorker* and putting my head down now and then for a little nap.

They started calling the numbers at noon. If I was lucky—if I had gotten there early enough that morning and held my ground against the tide of elderly Asian American women, all jostling to cut in line—I could be through the line and home by three, a fresh bottle of vodka from the liquor store by the bus stop tucked in my backpack for later in the afternoon. By the time I made it home, burdened with bags full of potatoes and cast-off matzo and expired prepacked salads, the first bottle of wine was gone and it was time to lie down. In the morning, I may have harbored delusions that I would wash the pile of dirty dishes, or take out the garbage that was attracting flies and giving off a sickly stench so strong that even my defective nose could sense it. By the afternoon, there was nothing to do but sink into the futon and read a few pages of the dense World War II history I'd been working on for a year, feel my head get heavy, and sleep the day away.

That was Saturday.

These food bank trips saved me a few bucks on groceries, but there was no way to balance the ledger. Making rent became an increasingly tenuous prospect. In Seattle, landlords could start eviction proceedings when your rent was just three days late, and every "three-day notice" went on your record, which could end up on your credit history. In 2014, I racked up so many three-day notices that when I showed up in person one month to pay my rent and late fees, the apartment manager pulled out a record of delinquency a half-inch thick. "Do you seriously keep all of those?" I asked her, in what I hoped sounded like indignation, not panic. "Every one," she responded, her manicured nails clacking against the green metal of the filing cabinet. *Well*, I thought, *I guess I can never move.*

There's another passage in AA's Big Book that always spoke to me, in the chapter "To Wives," which describes men at four different stages of alcoholism. The third type of husband reminded me of myself. "His friends have slipped away, his home is a near-wreck and he cannot hold a position. He admits he cannot drink like other people, but does not see why. He clings to the notion that he will yet find a way to do so. He may have come to the point where he desperately wants to stop but cannot."

By the time I became desperate enough to even show up to AA in earnest (much less to show up sober), I had made more than my share of weary rounds and lost many more things that were precious to me than I had when I checked myself into that first detox in the hospital in northwest Seattle back in 2008. I had obliterated relationships, alienated friends, and nearly torched my career more than once. I had gotten myself into a nightmarish pit of medical and drinking debt so deep I couldn't see sunlight. I had, as the Big Book also says, "all the desperation of a drowning man." So I jumped.

Twenty-two

Far from Done

Six years after my first detox, I started going back to meetings—first to get Josh off my back, then, grudgingly, to half-listen, showing up fifteen minutes late and sitting in the back. I went to meetings all over town, but felt drawn to Cherry Hall, a run-down AA fellowship hall populated by unemployed men, ex-gang members, and women who'd joined "the program" to get their kids back decades earlier and decided to stick around. For the first time in a long time—probably since before drinking stopped being fun, when being a "regular" somewhere didn't imply the sad taint of addiction—I felt like I was somewhere I belonged. Here, in this poorly lit room, with its torn secondhand chairs and fans that barely pushed the hot air around, I felt accepted even when the best I could manage was a three-days-dirty T-shirt and bleach-stained sweatpants. Half the time, I showed up drunk or well on the way—but I showed up. Years later, another member would tell me, laughing, that I had "rolled in looking like stir-fried shit," and the distance between then and now is measured by the fact that I can laugh about that now. Still I didn't get sober; still I snuck mini bottles into the bathroom and tossed the empties in the trash to be picked up by some alcoholic, ignoring the signs that clearly stated: NO ALCOHOL/NO DRUGS.

But it's hard to sit in a meeting for an hour and absorb absolutely nothing, and the stories started seeping through. AA is a deceptively simple program—you go to meetings, you listen to people talk, you do some work, and you don't drink—that works largely through repetition, something I absolutely hated when I first started going. One guy, who goes to the same lunchtime meeting every day, shared a story so similar from day to day that I can almost recite it word for word. "I started out broke down, beat up, wasn't nothing to nobody, never had a father, dropped out of school, started drinking before I learned how to read," it begins. What I started to realize around the tenth time I heard this man's story of recovery—from sneaking beers at age six to becoming a "low-down, low-bottom drunk" by the time he dropped out of high school, to finding his way to this fellowship hall fifteen years ago and sitting in the same chair ever since—was that it was my story, too. If anybody was a low-down, low-bottom drunk, I was. Like a lot of people in the room, I had done inexcusable things to the people who loved me. As it said in the first step, which we read at every meeting, I was "powerless over alcohol," and my life was unmanageable as fuck. I started to realize, dimly and with one eye sometimes literally closed, that this—for me—might be the beginning of a way out.

Here's the thing. If you're a person who needs to get sober—for health reasons or because your partner is about to leave you or because you're consumed by self-loathing and on the verge of losing everything you love—there's probably a path that will work for you, and only you will be able to figure out what it is. For a lot of people, the path might involve medication, or therapy, or religion. Mine happens to involve AA, and I have a theory about why that is. Most of the folks I know in AA are like me—Jekyll and Hyde drinkers, "always more or less insanely drunk." AA and other abstinence-based programs are for the people who end up drowning in medical debt from ER visits, the men who learned to freebase in jail, the women who abandoned their babies at the hospital. I arrived at AA at my wit's end—barely employed, living in a shitty apartment I never cleaned, and hanging on to Kevin by force of will—and everyone I know who ended up sticking around has a similar story. When you start going to meetings, they tell you all sorts of stuff that sounds like bullshit—things like, "Keep coming back," and "More shall be revealed," and "Don't leave five minutes before the miracle happens." *I know, I know.* It's cheesy and clichéd and embarrassing even to say those things out loud. But the crazy thing is, if you stick around, all the stuff that sounds like bullshit at first starts to sound like wisdom, especially when it comes from someone who's telling you about how she got her kids back after they'd spent five years in foster care, or how he finally got a housing voucher after living in a bedbug-infested shelter for seven months. "I almost gave up, but I didn't, and then something amazing happened" sounds as sincere as an infomercial when you can't get through a ninety-minute meeting without sneaking off to the bathroom or the store down the street for a nip, but something about all that relentless positivity starts seeping into your subconscious, and you begin thinking, *How do I get some of that?* Of course, my conscious mind was still able to tell me I was different—*I would never abandon my own child*, I sniffed as women told stories about doing exactly that, ignoring the fact that I had never been able to keep so much as a house-plant alive. But somewhere inside me, a seed had germinated. I saw people who loved their lives despite lacking material possessions and passport stamps, and I started to listen not for the differences but the similarities—the promises sincerely made and swiftly broken, the endless failed attempts to stop, the experience of surveying the wreckage, finding it insurmountable, but trying to surmount it anyway.

AA isn't magic, nor is it monolithic. It isn't the same everywhere, or even in every city. Some groups, and AA sponsors, require extremely rigid adherence to a specific way of doing things; others have a more laissez-faire, "take what works and ignore the rest" kind of attitude. Some meetings are dominated by guys who know what's best for everyone in the room, and some have rules about gender parity, requiring speakers to go in boy-girl-boy-girl order.

Some AA groups are superreligious; others are geared toward atheists and agnostics. Judging AA by going to one meeting or one group, historian William L. White wrote in his 1998 book *Slaying the Dragon*, is like "judging a country or city by one citizen encounter"—you have to meet lots of people, go to multiple meetings, before deciding what you think of the program as a whole.

Studies of AA, as well as other "mutual support groups" like Women for Sobriety and SMART Recovery, have largely validated its peer-counseling model. Although all studies of AA come with several obligatory caveats—it's hard to do a scientifically rigorous study of a program that has "anonymous" right in the name; AA groups are all run differently; and each study has had a different measure of "success"—there is compelling evidence that, for some people, AA works better than other common treatments. In 1997, researchers published a well-designed study called Project MATCH, which randomly assigned more than nine hundred problem drinkers to one of three groups. The first group got cognitive behavioral therapy; the second, motivational enhancement therapy; and the third received 12-step facilitation therapy, in which a counselor helps a patient work the first few steps (admitting powerlessness, belief and faith in a higher power, and writing out a moral inventory) and encourages them to attend AA meetings. Twelve-step facilitation was just as effective as both other types of therapy in the short term, and follow-up surveys found that significantly more people in the 12-step group were sober after a year than those in the other groups. Another study found that people who attended AA at least twenty-seven times during their first year of sobriety, or about once every two weeks, were twice as likely to still be sober sixteen years later. Research suggests that AA works primarily by giving people struggling with alcoholism access to people and messages that support their recovery, by strengthening their sober social networks, and by teaching them skills to deal with risky or triggering situations. It also alleviates guilt, a major cause of the stress that leads people to drink, through the eighth and ninth steps, which require members to make amends to people they've harmed.

So . . . it sounds like AA works, right? Here's the catch. *Nothing* really works all that well—not AA, not CBT, not anything. People who want to get sober (that is, people who find moderation doesn't work for them and need a program of total abstinence) have a shockingly high attrition rate. And if you're going to try AA, you have to be ready to jump into a program that requires you to believe that you're powerless over your own addiction, confess your deepest personal failings, and apologize for your behavior to everyone you've harmed, including people you have good reason to dislike (there would be more of those, plenty more, by the time I actually started down *that* road). When I started going back to meetings, during that last chaotic year before I actually quit drinking, I wasn't ready to quit. I looked at my past—a promising career sidelined by unproductive years of self-destruction—and my future, which promised more humiliation, failure, and loss, and I said: *I want more of that.* Of all the clichés you hear from people in recovery, this one, at least, is accurate: An alcoholic drinks until she's done. And I was still far from done.

Twenty-three

Last Resort

Like everything else in the American medical system, there's a class divide in addiction treatment—including, I was soon to discover, in detox. In the six years since my stay in the private hospital room in northwest Seattle, I had avoided checking myself into another detox facility, fearful of conceding defeat; instead, I detoxed in emergency rooms and ICUs. That summer, 2014, was unusually warm, and I couldn't seem to stop sweating, even with my little desk fan pointed straight in my face. At night, I would pass out around ten and wake up a few hours later, kicking restlessly until sunlight started pouring through the cheap, half-broken mini blinds above my bed around 4:00 A.M. It was after one of these restless, heart-pounding, kick-sweating nights that I decided I needed to go back to detox—needed to return, that is, to the place in northwest Seattle, where I would have room service and TV and a door that closed. This time, though, I ended up at a place called Recovery Centers of

King County, the publicly funded detox of last resort for the homeless, the indigent, and people like me who had run out of options.

Lack of access to detox is a huge barrier to treatment, and Seattle is typical in its shortage of detox options; everyplace I called told me they could put me on a waiting list or to call back in a couple of weeks. RCKC was the first place that had a bed. Could I be there in an hour? I could. I threw my ratty cloth purse over my shoulder and headed to the bus, gulping down the dregs of a few mostly empty bottles of white wine on my way out the door.

But when I got to the front desk, I almost turned around. The place was like something out of a prison movie—the scene at the beginning, when the inmates hand over their watches and shoelaces to the dead-eyed warden who seals it all up in paper bags marked "Possessions." "No makeup, shoelaces, tweezers, prescriptions, or reading material; keep your wallets at your own risk," the gruff intake counselor barked. I balked for a minute—no makeup, in a place with *guys?*—and then handed everything over. The woman showed me to my room, which already had two occupants, tossing and moaning on creaking metal beds. My bed was the one in the middle—a junkie sandwich. The room was windowless and stifling; a single overworked industrial fan roared just outside the open door, barely drowning out the shouts from the hall and the groans from inside my darkened room. After a brief intake, where I signed a sheaf of papers I didn't bother reading and couldn't have understood, a nurse handed me a cup and three pills, watched as I swallowed them, and sent me to bed, where the medication—a tranquilizer called phenobarbital and a double dose of generic Benadryl—knocked me out before I had time to look around.

A few hours later, I woke up in a sweat, sheets roped around my lower body. I was lying on a plastic-covered mattress, and under my head was the thinnest pillow I had ever seen. The room smelled sweaty, sour-sweet, and dank. A faint light filtered through the door from the hallway outside, and I could hear orderlies making the rounds down the hall, coming closer, closer, until a shadow appeared. "Vitals check!" the shadow bellowed, and I surrendered my arm to the blood-pressure cuff. Then I surrendered again to the sedatives that would keep me in a four-day haze.

There was no room-service fettucine Alfredo here, no kind-faced doctor welcoming me into his office to talk about relapse prevention plans. Instead, there were gluey burgers and spackle-textured oatmeal, provided by the same commissary that served the county jail; "outdoor time" in the tiny, smoke-choked courtyard that doubled as the center's recreational area; and numerous defectors, including one of my roommates, who went back to her abusive drug-dealer boyfriend. The men's hallway was separated from the women's by the front desk and a tiny TV room, and setting a single toe past the threshold was grounds for reprimand, as I discovered when a guy wearing an ankle bracelet offered to give me his extra pillow. "Step back from the men's hallway!" the front-desk lady barked, confiscating the pillow and ordering me to my room. "If you roll up a towel it's kind of like a second pillow," my other roommate, who had been silent until now, murmured from underneath her scratchy sheet. "You can also dip it in some water. Makes the heat a little more bearable."

I toughed it out for four days, too scared of catching something to risk the showers, before I decided I didn't belong there. I wasn't like these people. I had options. I had a job, friends who cared about me, and a family who would be horrified to see me in this place (not that I would ever tell them). I had Josh waiting for me on the outside, still hopeful that detox—not rehab—would be enough. I had seen where addiction could take me. I would never let it get this bad again. And so, on a bright Monday morning, two days before the end of my recommended stay, I signed a piece of paper, stamped "AGAINST MEDICAL ADVICE" (AMA) and walked straight to the liquor store.

I was right about two things. One, RCKC was unusually decrepit even for a public detox; it shut down, ostensibly due to unpaid wages, a few years after I stayed there. And two, I *didn't* belong there—not because I didn't need to be in detox, but because it was the only free detox in the county, meant for people with little or no insurance, and I was taking up space. In an ideal world, RCKC would have offered free, high-quality detox and treatment on demand to people who couldn't afford to pay, and I would have had multiple places to choose from; in reality, the place was a holding pen with twenty-seven beds and a high rate of recidivism, and people like me ended up there because there simply weren't enough options.

According to the Substance Abuse and Mental Health Services Administration (SAMHSA), Washington State had just twenty-two inpatient detox facilities in 2010, and nearly half a million residents with alcohol use disorder. Current law limits detox facilities to sixteen beds, and although creative medical directors have found ways to double that number, the math is irrefutable: There simply aren't enough detox beds for everyone who needs them, and until there are, people will give up or get turned away, and some number of those will die before another "window of opportunity"—the moment when an addicted person decides to seek help—opens up.

Detox isn't cheap. For alcoholics, a supervised medical detox can run between five hundred and a thousand dollars a day, which may or may not be covered by insurance. In my own experience, the cost of detoxing in emergency rooms, mental hospitals, and dedicated detox facilities ranged from about four hundred to several thousand dollars, and very little of it was covered by my health insurance; when I got sober, it was like waking up from a coma with thirty thousand dollars in medical debt.

Addiction, I was told later, is the only disease that works by convincing you that you don't have a disease, and it's hard to over-sell how convincing it can be. Denial is a feature, not a bug. Head-strong people who consider themselves independent, as I do, have a special challenge: We believe in willpower the way some people believe in angels. My parents always taught me that you can boot-strap your way to any accomplishment, if you want it hard enough, and I applied the same attitude to drinking, convincing myself for years that I could beat back addiction—I mean, *if I was even really addicted*—through sheer, bullheaded determination.

It was only in truly desperate moments, when I hadn't eaten for days and I could see my heart pounding through the skin on my chest, that I was willing to admit defeat.

And even then, I only ended up in RCKC because I got lucky—they had a bed ready during my window of opportunity. I would have sooner called Josh and told him exactly how much I had been drinking, and how powerless I was to stop, than have to wait two weeks for a detox bed to open up, when I knew it would be too late, when the window might have closed for good.

Twenty-four

A Shrinking Circle

The reality of daily life during my last several years of drinking wasn't messy—it was banal, the way a terminal disease that drags on for years can start to feel routine. I drank, I went to work (or didn't), I threw up a lot and struggled to remember to eat and drank some more until it was time to go to bed and wake up early the next morning to do it all over again. It was like I was drawing a circle around my life that, every day, became a little bit smaller, until one day, there wasn't much left outside the line that ran from my front door to the bus stop, the liquor store, the grocery store, and back. On many weekends, when I had enough alcohol in the house to last until Sunday, and the only distinction that marked the hours was waking and sleeping, that circle shrunk further, until it was barely larger than my bed and the 100 square feet of popcorn ceiling above it.

Weekdays required a bit more effort—more makeup, less napping, a deeper level of subterfuge—but the central obsession was the same. Where can I get liquor on the way to work? How can I make sure no one catches me drinking at the office? What excuse can I make to head out for more wine midafternoon? How can I get rid of Josh at the end of the day so I can grab a bottle before I get on the bus? How much do I need to force myself to eat so that I won't be as violently sick tomorrow as I was today? What stays down better—a sandwich or a salad?

If you ever hear someone accuse addicts of being lazy, please correct them: Addicts are some of the most industrious people in the world. Ginger Rogers did everything Fred Astaire did, except backward and in heels; well, we do everything normal people do, except distracted and impaired. (Oh, and worse. We do everything worse, too.) Susan Cheever, the daughter of the alcoholic author John Cheever, wrote that alcoholics' behavior is often characterized by "a pattern of self-destruction combined with compensatory brilliance," and while I was far from brilliant in those last, unsettled years of heavy drinking, I got by well enough to convince my friends not to stage an intervention and my bosses not to fire me. (Well, until they did.) I still churned out copy for PubliCola, still went through the motions of doing interviews, still turned in stories for the magazine that now owned the site. And if the person I was interviewing expressed concern for my health, or my story was riddled with typos and five days late, I could handle the criticism—all I had to do was apologize, say I was feeling under the weather, and drink until it wasn't my fault anymore.

When I look back at the two or three years I spent doing virtually nothing outside of work—seeing Kevin only when I felt well enough to leave my apartment, no writing, no hobbies or vacations or projects—I think, *How did I waste so much time?* And then I remember: I was *always* busy—busy maintaining my supply, busy coming up with lies to buy time and get myself off the hook, busy doing the emotional and mental heavy lifting it takes to be a full-time alcoholic in full-blown denial.

By the fall of 2014, though, I started to sense that a change was coming. I was sick all the time, every moment I was awake, and no one seemed particularly sympathetic. Josh was sick of pulling me out of the office to ask me if I'd been drinking. He was sick of getting calls late at night. And he was sick of telling his girlfriend he would be right back, that something had come up with Erica and he had to deal with it. At some point, I had appointed Josh as my lifeline, and I expected him to drop everything he was doing to pay attention to me, or come rescue me from whatever predicament I had gotten myself into. "My parents don't love me and they're driving me crazy and I want to shove chopsticks in my eyes!" I sobbed from my childhood bed in Mississippi. "A mugger . . . just stole . . . my computer!" I wailed, as he tiptoed out of a press conference and whispered, "Have you called the police?" For their whole relationship, his girlfriend, Heather, had known me only as a black hole of need, the person who was always in a crisis and needed constant attention. You know that friend who always turns every misunderstanding into a telenovela-level drama, to the point that you start screening her calls? Light that chick's hair on fire, throw in a fifth of vodka and a decade's worth of resentments, and that was me.

Twenty-five

Hallucinations

When I wake up one morning and see a small black spider crawling across the fleur-de-lis pattern of my purple pillowcase, I'm unfazed. I slap at the spider, and it disappears. *Huh*, I think idly, still getting used to the nausea-inducing shock of another morning. *That was weird.* I close my eyes, open them again, and the spider is back—joined by hundreds of its brethren. I lie as still as a human being can be, with one eye open, in terrified fascination. I brush my hand across the pillow—gone. Then they reappear. *Oh, I get it! This is a hallucination.* Instantly, I flash back on Augusten Burroughs's description of his own spider hallucination in his memoir about alcoholism, *Dry*, which I'd read twice as part of my own struggle to quit. *Was this what happened right before he quit?* Struggling with the sheets and a profound feeling of disequilibrium, I roll over and look at the ceiling, half-expecting a massive tarantula to descend from the light fixture. Instead, the gray space seems to fill with swirling translucent filaments, which start as two-dimensional images then spin down toward me, twisting themselves into elaborate, tightly spiraling webs. Now they're in my eyes, swallowing the bed, covering me—an opaque mass of black, swirling tentacles. I thrash around, I throw them off before they can choke me. *They aren't real. You're okay. This is all going to be okay.*

Nothing feels like it will ever be okay again.

I go in to work anyway, as always, and the hallucination follows me there. Every time the webs appear, I blink them away. *This isn't real. All will be well.* Staring at my computer seems to ward them off, but pretty soon I have another problem: A country song, one I've never heard before, is playing through the speaker of my phone. I turn off my desk fan, which I bought because I'm always sweating profusely, and listen closely, thinking the music must be coming from somewhere else in the office. But no, there's no mistaking it: The phone is somehow picking up a country radio station, and I can hear it, the fiddle and the pedal steel guitar and the singer crooning about lost love and all of it. I poke Josh, who sits in the cubicle next to me, and make him wheel his chair closer. "This is crazy—do you hear that country music?"

Josh looks at me like I'm hallucinating. And yeah, the thought occurs to me: *Maybe I'm the only one who can hear it.* But that makes no sense at all. "No. I don't hear anything," he tells me, and rolls back to his desk. "Never mind, I think it stopped just as I asked you to listen to it," I mumble and go back to staring at my computer. As soon as I'm pretty sure Josh is busy, I hustle off to the bathroom, where I've started stashing a bottle of wine under the paper towels in the waste bin in the mornings. I drink the medicine—that's all it is anymore, a remedy that tastes almost as sour going down as it does coming up—and put the carton back where it belongs, underneath the pile of wet paper towels. Back at my desk, the music has stopped.

But that afternoon, on my way back home, the spider webs return, only this time they're spinning themselves into solid objects—a boy's skateboard turns into an enormous black wolf, and another passenger's dog becomes a huge brown bear, offering me a single glistening paw. I almost laugh with relief—this is it; I'm finally cracking up. I think of Oliver Sacks's book *Hallucinations*, which I'd read almost two years earlier. In it, Sacks describes a bus ride very much like this one, when he imagined that all the people around him had "smooth white heads like giant eggs, with huge glittering eyes like the faceted compound eyes of insects." Like me, Sacks assumed he had lost his mind, but later realized he was in acute withdrawal from the sedatives he had been taking. I know the spiders and the bear and all the rest of it have something to do with my drinking, but I can't be in withdrawal—I haven't quit drinking—so what is wrong with me?

The next day, I call in sick and head to my doctor's clinic for an emergency appointment and settle into a chair in the quietest part of the waiting room. It's a big, modern office on the seventh floor of a recently built hospital, with a wall of windows that look out onto Mount Rainier on one side and a wall displaying electronic art projections on the other. The wall is new. Right now, it's running through a series of cartoon images using some kind of shape-morphing software: A bun-haired grandmother, grinning conspiratorially as she hunches over her walker, contracts and reshapes itself into an image of two babies in a stroller, which transforms seamlessly into the face of a beautiful young woman, her hair pulsating with luminous patterns. I watch the pictures for a minute, then go back to thumbing idly through an old copy of *Sunset*.

As usual, I have the jitters. I downed a liter of wine before my appointment, but my usual dosage isn't working like it used to. I look up from an article about the "Best Backyards in the West" and notice that the wall is blank.

I blink, look again. Nothing.

What I remember from that doctor's visit isn't the diagnosis—all any doctor ever told me anymore was that I needed to stop drinking—but the way the doctor regarded me, like a hopeless case. As it happens, he was the same doctor who'd sent me to the hospital with tachycardia a year or so earlier, and as he had on that occasion, he spent the entire appointment with his back to me, typing notes into his computer and occasionally grunting "Mmm-hmm" as I explained my symptoms with rising panic. "And I'm hallucinating, and I wake up every morning feeling like my heart is going to explode, and I throw up four or five times a day," I concluded.

"You need to quit drinking," he said.

I still wasn't convinced that I could die. Sure, the internet *said* I could die, but the internet says a lot of things. One of the things it told me, later that day, was that I was suffering from something called alcohol hallucinosis, a rare condition seen only in chronic, late-stage alcoholics, a category that, I had to admit, probably included me. The condition it's most frequently compared to is schizophrenia, and I guess I see why: Like schizophrenic psychosis, alcohol hallucinosis involves vivid auditory and visual hallucinations, which often include accusatory or threatening voices. (Or, apparently, country songs.) Did I close my laptop, pick up the phone, and start dialing residential rehabs right away? Of course not. I still didn't think I was *that* far gone. I told myself that now that I knew what was happening, I could deal with it, and went out and bought myself more to drink.

If you wonder why they don't give organ transplants to active alcoholics, this is why: We are some of the most stubborn people you'll ever meet, and a lot of us will keep drinking even when our bodies start shutting down. We're like the emphysema patient who keeps smoking through his trach tube, or the teenager who thinks it's safe to drive down the freeway at 120 miles an hour. *Sure, alcohol is bad for me, but I've always been so healthy. It's not like it's going to* kill *me.* I spent most of my thirties clinging to that belief. I spent months staring at hallucinations, knowing they were hallucinations, and rationalizing them to myself. Only old dudes with jaundice and rotting teeth died of alcoholism.

Not me.

If you looked at a photo of me from my final year of drinking, here's what you'd see: A pale woman, still young, with the kind of face that used to be pretty but is now swollen and splotchy, too big for her body. A bloated midsection balanced on spindly, wasted legs. A sickly, shaky figure with greasy hair, bloodshot eyes, and a trickle of sweat running down her forehead. I thought I was holding it together. But the images tell another story.

Meanwhile, I was in a full-fledged war with my downstairs neighbors. I hadn't had worse luck in neighbors since I lived in Austin and the couple who lived upstairs took revenge on me—for what, I could never imagine—by running the vacuum at three in the morning and stealing my mail. But this pair, who lived downstairs, were even worse. They stole my deliveries, reported me to my landlord for letting my friends park in the parking lot, and left a big wad of spit on the seat of my scooter when I parked it in one of the spots shared by everyone at our complex.

I wasn't an ideal neighbor: I talked loudly on the phone to my friends about my neighbors' brief but top-volume late-night sex, which happened weekly and woke me up every time. ("She needs to get better at FAKING AN ORGASM!" I'd rail to some unfortunate friend. "DO GUYS REALLY LIKE IT WHEN WOMEN

ACT LIKE PORN STARS?") I pounded on the floor a time or two when they wouldn't stop cooing at their dog, a giant gray creature that didn't belong in a 600-square-foot apartment. But that didn't give them the right to spit on my scooter. Or break into my apartment while I was at work.

The walls and the floors of that apartment were so thin, you could hear conversations without even trying, which is how I heard the guy downstairs saying my name. *Of course he knows who I am*, I thought. *My name is on all my mail.* But that night, lying with my ear to the floor of my apartment, I discovered to my horror that he knew much, much more. The fact that I laid in bed drunk all weekend. The names of the guys I'd brought home for blackout sex. Even the time I'd passed out on the phone with my friend in D.C. *Did I talk that loudly?*

Now he was going to let everybody know—starting with the people in my neighborhood. As I listened, he took a swig of Corona, walked through his sliding-glass doors onto his first-story patio, and began yelling, "Erica C. Barnett is going to lose her job! Erica C. Barnett is done!" in a menacing, singsong voice.

The taunts moved out into the street as he circled the block, yelling that I was an alcoholic, that I shoplifted, that I was going to die alone in that apartment. *How does he know all this?* I wondered, frozen to the floor. When he returned to his apartment, he told his brother, who I suddenly realized had been egging him on the whole time, about the times he'd slipped into my apartment when I was away at work, where he'd discovered a "crazy bondage dungeon" that looked "like something in *Game of Thrones*." How I had white eyelashes and worshipped the Devil.

Then he said he had killed my cat.

I didn't have a cat.

At that exact moment, I looked up and saw a large, menacing German shepherd stalking across my living room. I looked away, then back, and it was gone—out through my open sliding-glass doors and onto my balcony. I went out to investigate, and although the dog had vanished, I saw a half dozen or so teenage boys perched in the huge fir tree outside my apartment. In unison, they put their fingers to their lips and pointed to a balcony across the court-yard, where three old ladies in flowing, blue cotton nightgowns were talking about how to get control of the situation. From forty feet away, I could hear them clearly across the courtyard. "We need to get a meeting of the elders together and see what we can do to calm him down," one of them said. They went back into the apartment to con-fer. I shuddered, closed the doors, and went back into my room.

Alcoholic hallucinations come in many flavors. Many people who drink the way I did will eventually see spiders or hear voices, as their nervous system becomes dependent on alcohol to keep from going haywire. (Take away alcohol, even for a few hours, and a severe alcoholic's neurons will start firing like they've just snorted a gram of cocaine.) These hallucinations went on for months—long enough that I got used to seeing the swirling whorls of spidery black lines every time I stared at a blank surface or closed my eyes.

Further down the delusional scale is delirium tremens, a syn-drome made famous by Jack London, who wrote an autographical novel (*John Barleycorn*) describing a "gutter" drunk who, "in the extremity of his ecstasy," hallucinates "blue mice and pink elephants." What London doesn't quite explain—what no one who hasn't gone through a psychotic episode, perhaps, can fully understand—is how very real these hallucinations seem, and how different they are from the sort of thing you can brush away with a hand wave, like so many imaginary spiders. I have a cousin who suffers from schizophrenia, and he sometimes paces back and forth through the house arguing with demons no one else can see or hear. He can't turn them off, or talk himself into believing they aren't real, any more than you could convince yourself that you're just conjuring these words you're reading from thin air, or that if you jump out the window, the laws of gravity will reverse at your will. The voices—the kids swaying in the tree, the dog in my apartment—were as real as solid ground.

Back in my apartment, doors locked, blinds twisted shut, I sunk onto my creaky bed, breathing fast, and listened. A lot was going on downstairs. I heard whispered conversations about calling the police, and, when those died down, a full rebroadcast of the past year's Tony Awards, starring Neil Patrick Harris, complete with costumes, dance numbers, and songs. I heard tiptoe footfalls on the steps outside my apartment, and I heard the old ladies talking to a police officer in the parking lot as they pointed toward my building. Later, as the morning grew light, I heard my landlord approach my neighbors as they sat on the stairs outside my door and promise them he would "get her out of there" as soon as possible. I say I heard all this, but I saw it, too, from my spot on the bed—clear through the walls, through the floors, into the parking lot below my bedroom window and the courtyard on the other side of the building. I saw it all, acknowledged it, and failed to register it as a hallucination. I knew everything that I saw had happened, because if it hadn't, then I was crazy, and I wasn't crazy.

And then I got up and went to work.

Twenty-six

The Rez

That morning, things fell apart at fast-forward speed. I made my usual rounds—the trip to Safeway, the walk to the garden, the sweating, heaving bus ride downtown—and showed up half an hour late for an editorial meeting I had forgotten was happening. Everyone was laughing at something that James, the magazine's new editor, had just said. I must have looked a mess. Josh eyed me from inside the glass-walled conference room and shot me his "don't you dare come in here" look, so I slunk back to my desk, sweat soaked and gasping for air.

I couldn't seem to get any air in my lungs. I felt a dull, insistent pressure I had never experienced before—like a giant was sitting on my chest. I thought back to all the articles I'd read about women and heart attacks—how they're often misdiagnosed because the symptoms are so subtle. I got up and started waving frantically at Josh, hoping that, somehow, no one else would notice. He glared at me in exasperation. Finally, he came out.

"What is it?"

"I think I'm having a heart attack."

Josh rolled his eyes. "I have to get back into this meeting. You should go home."

"I'm serious. I'm having chest pain. I can't breathe. My heart is pounding. Feel it."

We drove to the hospital. On the way—windows down, pleasant Seattle summer breeze rustling my unwashed hair—I started to feel better. But I couldn't tell Josh it was a false alarm. I went in. Heard the familiar swoosh of the big hospital sliding doors that separate the healthy world outside from the sick world within. Lay back on the familiar gurney, let them hook me to the familiar IV, and listened as the social worker told me I needed to get to rehab, stat. And not long after that, I was standing in a daze in front of a treatment center in the suburbs, clutching a dirty duffel bag and wondering how I got there.

That's how it plays in my memory, anyway—one day I was watching imaginary dogs walk through my living room, the next I was at Residence XII, a small, private treatment center for women in a leafy suburb east of Seattle. Memory is weird that way. Some memories, like the spidery filaments that occupied every blank space in the months that led up to my first stint in rehab, are so vivid I can conjure them back to life just by closing my eyes. Others are blank spaces.

Here's what I remember: I asked James for a month off, which is the maximum amount of treatment most insurance companies cover. (Before the Affordable Care Act passed in 2010, health insurers didn't have to cover rehab at all.) The publisher, Melissa—a single mom who'd been sober for years—offered to give me some of her vacation time, so I wouldn't have to go unpaid. I came up with a cover story for people who would notice my absent byline—"personal medical condition; had to take some time off"—but ultimately, I let Josh post on Twitter that I was taking some time off to address my alcoholism. I knew, dimly, that people would mock and misread this public declaration. I didn't care. I watched him hit "tweet" and felt nothing, not even dread.

But who convinced me? How long did I go on drinking between the ER and the treatment center? What was I like for those first few days, when my body was still so toxic I could barely speak or lift my head, much less, as the counselors put it, "participate in my own recovery"? Blank as the last two-thirds of that year's diary.

I remember sitting in the big circular foyer at Rez XII, shaking with fear and withdrawal and contemplating the fact that once I signed the papers I wouldn't see this room again for another month. I remember clutching Kevin's hand in my sweaty palm. And I remember sitting through what felt like a three-hour interrogation—how much did I drink each day; had my work suffered; what was my motivation for coming to treatment—before the treatment director looked me over, sighed, and drove me to a nearby hospital to get the booze out of my system.

Most treatment centers want you to show up stone-cold sober, which is another way of saying that most treatment centers don't want to bear the cost and liability that comes with on-site detox. I showed up at Residence XII with a blood-alcohol level that would put plenty of normal people in a coma, thinking I might be able to fool them—heavy, chronic drinkers who drink like I did can register blood-alcohol levels in the usually dangerous or "fatal" range without appearing more than moderately drunk. I wasn't alone: Many of the women at Rez XII were still detoxing from something, and some of them spent most of their twenty-eight days in withdrawal. Heroin detox takes weeks, which is one reason heroin addicts tend to do even worse in conventional twenty-eight-day rehab than alcoholics; by the time their brains are capable of processing new information, they're out the door. I spent the night in rapid detox, hooked up to a banana bag and on a heavy dose of Librium, before returning to treatment the following morning. For the first time, I felt a twinge of relief. For four weeks, at least, it would be impossible to drink.

From the moment I laid my hot pink-and-white duffel bag on my floral bedspread and read the mass-produced welcome card—"Erica, Welcome to Residence XII. We are so happy to have you join us to start a new life in sobriety"—I hated the place. I hated sleeping in a room with strangers (two to a room, four to a suite), and I hated being so disconnected from the outside world. I hated that we weren't allowed to "engage in our professions," meaning that I wasn't supposed to even think about all the stories I needed to work on the minute I got out. I hated the industrial-strength soap solution they provided in the showers, which made my skin peel off in sheets, and I hated the showers themselves, which required you to punch a knob every fifteen seconds to keep the water running. I hated the fact that I couldn't read *The New Yorker* or books or anything other than AA literature, which was supposed to help me "focus on my recovery." And I hated the fact that I was gaining weight from the rich food in the dining hall, which I couldn't resist after months of subsisting on half-eaten sandwiches, pizza from the Little Caesars next to the liquor store, and whatever nutrients there are in wine.

Most of all, though, I hated the other patients. Until I entered Rez XII, I never understood what women meant when they said they "just didn't get along with other women"; once I lived with fifteen of them, I *got* it.

Everyone acted like they were the only ones who had ever had problems. Janet, a suburban mom with chunky highlights, spent her mornings doing her makeup and the rest of the day picking fights with the other women. Jenny, who talked about her bipolar diagnosis to anyone who would listen, treated group therapy like open-mic night. Monica, my sixtysomething roommate, wouldn't stop crying about her husband, who had said he would leave her if she didn't stop popping pills.

The problem wasn't me, it was that I couldn't relate to any of these women. I wasn't bipolar or worried about looking camera ready by 6:00 A.M. I didn't do hard drugs. I didn't have a husband to take care of me. Sure, I still had Kevin, but only on the thinnest of technicalities—we hadn't had sex in months, and I got the feeling that he was only sticking around because of some ground-in, fundamental Oklahoman decency. *Quit whining, lady*, I thought as I listened to Monica complain. *At least you aren't going home to an empty apartment.*

I hated the ridiculous, make-work assignments, too: vision boards illustrating what our life was like before we got to rehab (shitty) and what we hoped it would be like sober (awesome!); rosters of our "losses" and "yets" (things we had lost due to our addiction and things we might lose); letters to God ("Dear God: Even though you don't exist, I'm mad at you for letting this happen to me"); letters *from* God ("Dear Erica: Sometimes shit happens and there's no real reason, but you have to deal with it anyway"); and the "assertion script," a framework for asserting and acknowledging each other's feelings and wants.

What I wanted was for the counselors to tell me how to live without drinking, or give me honest information about my odds of staying sober. (From my notebook: "If there are no stats on relapse rate in intensive outpatient vs. nonintensive outpatient, how can you say it's 'statistically proven' that IOP prevents relapse better than non-IOP?") As a journalist, I'd been trained to scrutinize every claim, to never stop asking questions. What they were asking me to do was shut up, accept that they knew what they were doing, and follow instructions. It was almost as if questioning certain aspects of treatment—*Why* do we have to make our beds and vacuum the hallways every morning? *Why* do you let people smoke but ban caffeine and sugar when all three are stimulants?—would unleash a curse that had the power to make treatment fail. My treatment file is full of notes from counselors criticizing me for "intellectualizing" their suggestions by "asking for facts and statistics," and refusing to follow some of those recommendations. For instance, I refused to sign a letter to my doctors stating that I should never be given any kind of narcotic drug, such as painkillers, because I didn't want to make such a major decision one week after checking in to treatment. "It is a concern of this writer that patient continues to dictate her own treatment. Prognosis is guarded," my counselor wrote.

I never thought of leaving. I was determined to prove I could make it through the program, and the more I suffered, the more it would show I was serious about my recovery. So I scowled and pouted through morning "angel meditation," when we'd pick "angel cards" out of a box to inspire us throughout our day; and I gamely grimaced through lectures about my Addict and my Wise Woman, the two forces that were—per Rez XII dogma—battling for supremacy in my addicted mind.

Mostly, though, I sat and stared out the picture windows of the living area—a huge room stuffed with couches and chairs that had seen better decades—at the Douglas firs and bigleaf maples sheathed in fog and wondered whether all this nonsense about angels and wise women might be building to a larger point. Or if treatment would just be twenty-eight days of chirpy counselors telling us to rely on mythical creatures to carry us through hard times.

It wasn't all wise women and angels. One afternoon, instead of our usual lecture or group role-playing session, the counselors gathered all the women in the basement meeting room for a confrontation. This practice, which is now falling out of favor, originated at Hazelden, the famous treatment center outside Minneapolis whose "Minnesota method" is now used at most US treatment centers. Hazelden called the exercise the "hot seat," but I came to think of it as the "shame circle." Here's how it worked: One woman would sit in the middle of the room while everyone gathered around her in a circle. Then, one by one, the women would tell on the woman in the circle for things they'd witnessed her doing wrong. Pretty much anything was fair game, from drinking caffeinated coffee at outside meetings, to talking on the phone for more than the allotted ten minutes, to taking a nap during "homework" hour. "Character defects," a phrase ripped from the pages of the Big Book, were also on the table—flaws identified by our fellow patients, like selfishness, self-absorption, dishonesty, and a lack of "willingness" to give ourselves to the program.

When my turn came around, my "sisters in recovery" didn't hold back. "You think you're better than everyone else!" "You take up more than your share of time on the phone!" "You think you don't need to be here!" "You talk about people behind their back!" "You're self-willed!" By the time they got to the obligatory compliments, I was crying too hard to listen. After it was over, I ran to my room and threw myself down on my bed, wondering whether there was any point in getting sober if I was as big a piece of shit as all these women seemed to think.

Old-school treatment programs often subscribe to the notion that addicts need to be "broken down" before they can be "built back up," but there's no scientific evidence to suggest that making addicts feel worse about themselves has any therapeutic benefit. For me, it had the opposite effect: My own confidence shattered, I became a close observer of my fellow-patients, hoarding every infraction and personality defect for future use as tactical weapons against their self-esteem. We all did this, and it's obvious why: With no ability to make independent decisions about when we woke up, what we ate, or the people with whom we spent all our time, the hot seat became opportunity to unleash our stored resentments.

Not everything about treatment sucked. In the daytime, we were allowed to walk outside under supervision, although power walking was discouraged and running was forbidden for reasons that had something to do with avoiding endorphins. At night, outside volunteers would show up to lead meetings—AA, NA, and Cocaine Anonymous—and regale us with stories of their own rock bottoms, the times when they stole from the till at work, or showed up for an important meeting on the tail end of an all-night coke binge. One woman even said that when she didn't have any booze in the house, she had briefly considered drinking hair spray. For some reason, this made us laugh. *Drink hair spray? Who* thinks *like that?* I enjoyed the meetings, which gave me an opportunity to sit back and listen to other people's stories for a change, instead of participating in some activity or talking about myself. I also got into art therapy and "sober fun"—an infantilizing catchall term for everything from sugar-free ice cream socials to Pictionary—because these were the only times we got to (therapeutically) goof around. One week, we each chose a rock from a pile and painted them with our sobriety dates, sealing them with shellac to represent the fact that they would last forever. "I bet there's a whole river near here that's full of these things," I muttered to my rehab buddy Michelle, a laconic postal worker, as we painted the final coat of Modge Podge onto our rocks. Mine, which reads "August 24, 2014" in red letters on a lavender background with little yellow flowers on the border, still sits on a shelf in my bedroom.

Between all those activities, there were lectures, writing assignments, and homework—worksheets to fill out, letters to write to our Addict and our Higher Power, collages to construct.

And the biggest homework assignment of all was our first step.

If you know anything about AA at all, it's probably the first step ("We admitted we were powerless over alcohol, that our lives had become unmanageable"), often shortened in pop culture to "The first step is admitting you have a problem." This step has some basis in evidence—according to the *Handbook of Medical Psychiatry*, "denial is ubiquitous in alcoholism," so admitting to yourself that you have a problem is literally the first step to recovery. At Rez XII, taking the first step meant writing out our whole life stories, with an emphasis on how drinking or drugs made our lives fall apart, then reading it out loud to a small group and listening to their feedback.

Within days, I had written two five-page longhand drafts (there were no computers, ostensibly because writing longhand was a more "genuine" experience), making notes in the margins and on the backs of pages until I got it right. Chapter 1: A shy, sheltered only child is ripped from her idyllic Mississippi childhood and brought to the big city by her dad and a mean new stepmom she barely knows. Chapter 2: Bored at school and dying to fit in, she turns to drinking, and eventually gets in too deep to stop. Chapter 3: Trapped in an alcoholic hell, our heroine loses nearly everything. Chapter 4: Rock bottom—detox, the liquor store, the weekend binge. Chapter 5: "I woke up the morning after that binge feeling lonely, scared, tired, sick, guilty, humiliated, embarrassed, broken—and done."

I finished reading to the women who made up Small Group.

"I was done. And that's how I ended up here."

Silence fell over the room. Finally, one of the women spoke. "That was so well-written!" she said. "Wow—you really put it all out there," another gushed. "Great work. You really nailed it." That last one was my counselor. My heart grew two sizes with pride. Finally, some recognition from these people that I wasn't just a condescending brat—I could write! I was good for something! I floated down the hall on a pink cloud of acceptance. Maybe things were going to be okay.

I spent my thirty-seventh birthday in treatment, but I still had a party of sorts—my mom, who had spent years picking up my drunken Sunday-afternoon calls and locking the liquor cabinet when I came to town, flew out to visit. It was the third time she'd been to Seattle in the thirteen years I'd lived there, and the first time without my dad, whose absence was, frankly, a relief. Since high school, I had never disclosed to him anything more serious than my chronic lack of money, and I wasn't about to start now. In twenty-three years since Jennie died, neither of us had said "I love you" to the other again, and even hugging was an awkward, sideways affair. Telling him, "Dad, I'm an alcoholic and I need your help" was unthinkable. Mom and I, on the other hand, had never lost touch, even when I was avoiding her calls and telling her everything but the truth. So she was the one who made the trip.

It was the end of summer in Seattle—the perfect time for a visitor to watch the guys throwing fish at Pike Place Market, or to ride the ferry over to Bainbridge Island. Instead, Mom spent two days writing invoices and taking orders for my parents' bathroom refinishing business at the Comfort Inn in Kirkland, while I wrote a dubious "recovery plan" at my $420-a-night quarters down the street.

Mom, not surprisingly, had a few things to get off her chest. Why would I keep doing this to myself, as smart as I was, knowing everything I knew about addiction? Did I ever think of anyone but myself? Had I ever considered how my drinking affected her and the rest of our family? Didn't I know it was wrong to lie all the time?

"I just want to feel like you're being honest with me," she told me during our first family therapy session. "I don't feel like you've been honest with me for years. I want to feel like I can trust you again." In all the years I'd spent imposing my problems on my parents, especially my mom, it had never occurred to me that they might be concerned about anything other than what I was doing to myself. I hadn't thought about her—or Dad—at all. "I'm sorry," I sobbed. "I didn't know. I had no idea. I'm so sorry." Honesty—real honesty, not a slurry "I'm fine" at the end of a call that made it clear I was anything but—was a muscle I hadn't exercised in quite some time.

Would I go on to disappoint her even worse? Obviously. But at that moment, we still had hope.

My mom left me with some presents—no candy, which was verboten, but some flowers and a drugstore birthday card. "Maybe not exactly where you want to spend your birthday but what a positive way to spend your time focusing on a great future. We are very proud of you and will always love you."

For the next few nights, I dreamed about my parents, and drinking—chugging from a brown paper bag while walking down the street near my apartment, to meet them at their hotel; going to a party at their house without intending to drink but finding a beer in my purse. I woke up before my alarm went off, sweat slicking my forehead: only a dream. Things were going to be okay. Mom was proud of me. So was Dad. And so was Kevin, who sent me flowers and a birthday card of his own, which ended, "I'm prouder than ever on your birthday this year."

You know who wasn't proud of me? Josh—the person who saw me most and probably knew me best. Once I got my phone privileges (ten minutes at a time on a pay phone in the hallway, or as long as my prepaid phone card held out), I called him nearly every day, and nearly every day our calls devolved into convoluted, overlapping arguments. I was worried about whether I would lose my job at PubliCola. He was convinced I was trying to be a straight-A student instead of absorbing the lessons. I was angry that he wasn't sufficiently impressed by my progress. He thought I was being a selfish brat. After my first week of treatment, when I got off "blackout," he took two buses from Seattle to visit me. We chatted on the sun-dappled balcony outside the small dining room, which we shared with several families who were having their own tense confabs. I told Josh I was acing all my assignments, and pulled out my note-book to prove it. He told me he was worried that I wasn't taking my time in treatment seriously. I told him he needed to trust that I was doing the best I could. He wrote in my notebook, "You made your bed—please don't tell me how to support you!" After two hours, we gave each other a tepid hug good-bye. Then a counselor waved him through the sliding-glass doors and into the free world, where everybody was allowed to drink but me.

I was crushed by Josh's cool reception. But he knew something about me that I still wasn't willing to acknowledge about myself: I will turn anything into an intellectual exercise, even my own life. I learned enough about boundaries and triggers and brain physiology to get an A on the test, but I didn't think the stuff my counselors were saying about a "chronic, progressive, and fatal" disease applied to me, because I thought my intelligence and resourcefulness gave me a pass. I thought I could talk my way out of it.

A few days later, Josh sent me a letter, written in 24-point type. It began:

> I'm gravely worried about you. I'm panicking that you are on the verge of squandering this opportunity to turn this around and save your life. . . . I know you're following the rigorous program there. And I have no doubt that your 35-page paper is genius and that your hand shoots up first in every class. . . . However, my sense is that while you're killing it on paper, it's a pre-fab success story—and not sincerely about a real ground-up rebuild. . . .

"Erica, July and August"—the months when I wasn't showing up to work, or showing up drunk, or slurring my way through interviews—"were harrowing," Josh continued.

> I'm not trying to make you feel bad or guilt trip you. But my sense is that you don't fully understand how dramatic your situation was and has become. I know you're aware that you relapsed and that things were fucked up. But you need to be fully aware that your transformation into chaos was jaw dropping. I'm not judging you. But I saw it, Erica. You were going to drop off the grid and die. I say this as a true friend. This is not time for delusions. . . . You will definitely lose your job if you relapse and spin out at work again. Period. Full stop.

Everyone else, it seemed, had someone on their side who truly believed in them. All I had was Kevin, the on-again, off-again boy-friend I kept at arm's length, and Josh, the best friend who was practically setting me up to fail. I litigated my case against Josh in my journal, demolishing his argument brick by brick, with rational-ization after rationalization.

Finally, it was my last day—time for everyone to stand in a circle and sway while they sang "Stand by Me" in the morning before gathering for my "coin-out" ceremony a few hours later. Sitting in a circle, the women passed around a coin with the Rez XII logo (a single red rose on a white background) and one by one offered me a spiritual "gift." My "gifts," according to the letter someone handwrote on blush-colored Rez XII stationery, were: Sisterhood. Compassion for myself. Prosperity. Lifelong happiness. Patience.

I took my "gifts," along with my rolled-up vision board and duffel bag, and ran through an archway of clasped hands and into the waiting room.

Twenty-seven

Forgetting

Let me tell you what it's like to be sober, really sober, for the first time in years. It feels like seeing color for the first time. It feels like you've been looking at the world through someone else's glasses, and suddenly you can make out every individual blade of grass. It feels like you have a secret superpower that nobody can see—a clarity of mind that allows you to leach insights out of the most banal moments. Your body feels stronger than it's ever been. Food tastes better. Desire returns.

At the same time, everything has an intensity that scares you a little. When you feel a feeling—fuck, how am I ever going to start paying back my debts?—you just have to sit with it, figure it out, wait for it to pass. When you've dampened every experience with the white noise of alcohol for a decade or more, experiencing the world at full blast can be overwhelming. Who do I need to apologize to first? How am I ever going to make time for nine hours of outpatient treatment every week? Do I really have to go to an AA meeting every single day? Why is my boss looking at me like that—does he think I've been drinking?

It had been less than a month since I "graduated" from Residence XII, sober and hopeful and excited to get back to work. My stay there felt like a wake-up call, an important pause in a life that had been hurtling forward with no steering and faulty brakes. When I ran through that gauntlet of upraised arms, I felt the way I imagine born-again Christians feel when they emerge from the baptismal waters—not just that my life was new, but that it was finally mine.

Almost everyone had high hopes. Mom, who had been so worried when she showed up at Rez XII two weeks into my stay, told me afterward, "I'm proud of you. I know you can do this." My coworkers Melissa and Emily, both also in recovery, initiated me into their secret lunchtime ritual of driving across town to attend a noon meeting once a week, and it felt almost as good as being invited to the secret after-party. Friends asked me out for seltzer waters and coffee and sent cards telling me I was brave.

I left Rez XII fully invested in my own recovery, ready to go to AA meetings every day, work the steps, and develop healthy habits to replace the old ones that were killing me. I even got an AA sponsor, Marianne. I'd seen her speak at an AA meeting at Cherry Hall a few months back, and I liked that she didn't dwell on the positive. At the time, she was thinking about kicking her live-in boyfriend to the curb, had no income, and was facing the possibility of major surgery—and yet somehow, she hadn't had a drink in thirty years. She didn't have her shit together, but was staying sober anyway. That seemed like something even I could aspire to. I grabbed her after the meeting, sat her down on the steps outside the hall, and gave her the elevator pitch—abandoned by my friends and boy-friend, work a mess, unable to see the way forward, willing to go to any lengths. She agreed to sponsor me on the spot.

When we talk about "sobriety," or even "recovery," the words are often shorthand for "not drinking" or "not using drugs." But the really overwhelming part of staying sober isn't saying no to drinks or learning to avoid the proverbial "people, places, and situations" that induce temptation; it's figuring out how to live an unfiltered life. That's hard enough when things are going pretty much okay (How many times have you said, "I need a drink?" when what you really meant was, "This day was moderately annoying"?); it can be damn near impossible when there's wreckage stretching out to the horizon in every direction.

So, to recap: Over the past few years of drinking, I had broken my mom's heart; driven away my best friend; alienated all my other friends with my erratic behavior and constant sob stories; nearly lost my job; and accumulated tens of thousands of dollars in medical debt from emergency rooms and detoxes. I still had an apartment, but only because I was able to use paid vacation hours to go to rehab instead of taking unpaid time off; if my time or my welcome at the magazine had worn out, I could have lost my housing, too. I was ashamed to show my face at work, overwhelmed by all the amends I felt I needed to make right away, too raw to have a heartfelt conversation with either of my parents, and scared to death that Josh would continue to doubt my commitment to sobriety—or that he'd be watching over my shoulder every minute, ready to pounce on any sign that I was slacking off. I had wasted so much time. I had to fix everything right away, but I had absolutely no idea how to start.

So I froze. I withdrew to my comfort zone. I worked and went to the gym, lifted weights and worked the phones, and before long

I was too exhausted to keep going to outpatient therapy three nights a week, too exhausted to make it to AA every day, too exhausted to do anything besides trudge from work to gym to home to bed. AA meetings, which I'd attended sporadically since I walked into that lesbian meeting seven years earlier, bummed me out—everybody seemed so fucking *happy* all the time. And I found the three-hour intensive outpatient sessions that I had agreed to do as part of my postrehab treatment program repetitive and depressing: a few sad-sack losers gathered on couches in a dreary downtown office building, watching VHS videos about relapse prevention and bitching about how much sobriety sucked before blowing into their ignition-interlock devices and driving home.

Not more than a month went by before I fell back into drinking. Not jumped—fell: the way you fall into bed with an ex-lover because you don't have anything better going on. I can't pinpoint an exact turning point or moment when I said, "Screw it. This is too hard." It was more like an imperceptible slide from not-drinking to drinking—from militancy to self-pity to indifference to bottoms up. I was a non-drinker, then I was a drinker again, simple as that. I passed the liquor aisle in the grocery store, doubled back, and dropped a bottle of Smirnoff in my basket—casually, like a vegetarian tossing a tray of ground beef on top of the granola bars.

I wish I had a better story to tell you, one that made sense. Maybe if a close relative had died, or I had lost my job, or been evicted, my relapse would have been justified. Some alcoholics refer to events like this as "reservations." If my mom dies, then I'll drink. If my husband leaves me. If I get a terminal illness. But I don't have a good reason, or any reason at all. Normal people look at alcoholics who relapse the way I did and wonder: What made you take that first drink? For me, the answer was always: nothing in particular. One minute, you're a sober person in recovery; the next, you're telling yourself, *Everybody else does it—why can't I? I've learned so much. I'll manage it this time.* Maybe you don't even think about it at all. The selective amnesia of the chronic relapser is a force of nature—no matter how many bad things happen, or how many times we say "Never again," and mean it, we forget all of it the instant we happen to look up as we walk past the liquor store.

People often ask why someone would relapse after seeing how much better their life is sober. Why would anyone make the choice, after almost losing everything—their job, their apartment, their money, their friends—to risk taking that first sip? For normal people, every relapse seems like an intentional act of self-sabotage, a decision— made sober—to head back down the path of self-destruction. Surely something must have provided a push.

The truth is, for me, relapse was never a conscious decision. There was never an inner voice that said, *Fuck it, I'm going to drink.* It was more an act of not deciding—to pause, think, and play the tape to the end. If it's true, as many addiction researchers have argued, that people who suffer from addiction arrest emotionally when they first start using substances, and have trouble developing higher-order cognitive functions like impulse control and the ability to weigh actions and consequences, then I left rehab with the emotional maturity of a thirteen-year-old, and the same sense of invulnerability. It's not that I didn't remember what happened the last time I drank, or hear the words I learned to repeat in rehab: *Don't drink, no matter what, even if you want to.* I did. It's just that there was a louder voice in my head saying, *You know how to handle it. It'll be different this time.* Rehab equips you with mantras. What it can't do is force you to listen.

Relapse isn't a decision. It's a process of forgetting, of postponing vigilance for another day. When I left Rez XII, my mind was clear; my resolve was firm. Things were going to be different this time. I made a start at repairing the wreckage of my life. I paid my bills, turned in stories on time, called my mom every day. I started cooking again, cleaned the house, and began reconnecting with the friends I hurt. Anhedonia—the inability to feel pleasure, a common complaint among newly recovering addicts—began to recede. Little by little, my brain started feeling a little bit clearer. My body got stronger, and I marveled at the ability my spindly legs still had to carry me up a flight of stairs without stopping to gasp for air. For the first time in a decade, I could sleep through the night without waking up to gulp wine straight from the bottle or twisting the sheets around me in a sweat-drenched coil. Friends told me how much better I looked, and the difference was indeed remarkable—no longer bloated by alcohol, my face started to regain its structure (welcome back, cheekbones), and the clerk at my regular grocery store congratulated me on losing weight. (In truth, I had gained ten pounds.) There were so many little things I could do and enjoy again, from a clear-eyed conversation with my mom to the taste of hot strong coffee, with two Sweet'n Lows and a glug of cream.

But there was a price to pay for my new mental acuity, too. Even as I learned to take satisfaction from catching up on the news and taking out the garbage before it started to stink, I began to comprehend the enormity of the wreckage I'd created. I looked at my medical bills and wondered, *How can I possibly deal with this sober?* I started to resent the self-imposed rules that constrained my existence. I joined my friends after work for happy hour and pouted resentfully over my seltzer. I walked past an endcap of two-buck Chuck at Trader Joe's and reached reflexively for a bottle of sauvignon blanc before pulling my hand back sullenly, remembering: not for you anymore. I sat around on Friday nights and imagined all the fun everybody else was having out there without me, laughing over beers at the bars where I used to be the center of attention. I trudged to AA meetings at Cherry Hall, where they'd remind me: *It's just one day, one hour, one minute at a time. Pray, go to meetings, and don't drink in between. Poor me, poor me, pour me another drink.*

And then, over time, I started forgetting why I stopped. The memory of the last horrifying thing I'd done (nodding off at my desk; forcing Josh to drive me to the hospital for the false-alarm heart attack) began to fade, and I started to look around and think, *I'm no different from everybody else.* If anything, I was smarter, more accomplished, and more driven than most of the people around me. I thought nothing of working eighty-hour weeks if that's what it took to meet my deadlines, and I'd never failed to do anything I set out to accomplish, from talking my way into my first job to talking my way out of dodgy situations. With startling alacrity, I stopped seeing all the reasons that I shouldn't drink—reasons I'd found utterly compelling, like being told explicitly that I'd lose my job if I relapsed again—and started seeing all the reasons I should. I didn't think about what it felt like to guzzle wine from a cardboard container in a bathroom stall and hope I didn't just throw it all up again. I thought, instead, about how comforting it felt to clutch a glass of wine at parties, or to slug from a passed flask at a beach bonfire in December.

I've heard the sensation of craving described as a kind of thirst, but that's not what it's like for me. For me, craving is the intense desire for an experience: That moment when the first warm flush of alcohol hits my veins and everything feels like it will be all right. That lovely, tipsy glow. For alcoholics, it doesn't really exist—once I take the first drink, I'm compelled to have another, and another—but we're always chasing it, trying to get back to that place.

It was astonishing how quickly the compulsion returned. (In my head, the voice of someone at a meeting: "Alcoholism is cunning, baffling, powerful, and *patient*.") In the morning after buying that first, almost celebratory bottle—*Look at me, I beat this thing!*—I woke up with my hands shaking and raced for the bathroom to retch into the toilet bowl. Right away, a kind of magical thinking set in—*Whoops, looks like I overshot it. I'll taper down over the course of the week; it would be dangerous to stop drinking again all at once.* On the way to work, I grabbed another bottle—just to get rid of the tremors, I thought—and by three in the afternoon, I was peering over the edge of the same familiar pit.

In meetings, old-timers say, "You don't have to drink, even if you want to." But the fact is, most of us do. Our brains make relapse practically inevitable. Even after physical withdrawal and the fuzzy thinking of early sobriety subsided, my brain wouldn't stop whispering: *Wouldn't this be better with a drink?* Dependence doesn't just make an alcoholic person's brain less capable of experiencing pleasure, or even maintaining equilibrium, without a steady supply of spirits; it also creates long-lasting pathways between neurons that cause the brain to strongly associate certain mental states (depression, loneliness, excitement, guilt) or experiences with an overwhelming urge to drink. At the same time, long-term, heavy drinking damages the brain's prefrontal cortex, the home of higher-level thinking like impulse control.

For me, what this meant was that every time I got on the bus, I wanted a drink. Every time I saw a friend I had disappointed, I wanted a drink. Every time I walked into the grocery store, I wanted a drink. Every time I looked in my closet, at the suitcase where I had stored all my empties, I wanted a drink. Now tell me how I was supposed to resist having a drink.

Every time I relapsed and went through withdrawal, those links got stronger and stronger, making it more likely that I would relapse again.

Given the odds, then, how does anyone manage to stay sober? There isn't one way that works for everyone, but pretty much every evidence-based program for sobriety—whether it's cognitive behavioral therapy, AA, motivational interviewing, or something else—involves reprogramming your brain so that certain moods and experiences no longer make you feel compelled to drink. People who manage to avoid relapse also tend to have a few things in common. They have a high sense of self-efficacy—that is, they feel as if their actions have an impact over what happens in their lives—and well-developed coping mechanisms, which provide resiliency when they're under stress, when other people are pressuring them to drink or use drugs, or when things don't go the way they've planned. This, by the way, is kind of the whole point of the Serenity Prayer: Accept what you can't change, change what you can, and learn to tell the difference.

When I got out of Rez XII, accepting the things I couldn't change seemed almost impossible—like it or not, booze was everywhere and the wreckage I created was still right where I left it. When I got back to my apartment, the dishes were still in the sink, and the unpaid bills had kept on piling up. Life was still waiting. My problems were still my problems. Everything seemed enormous and overwhelming. Pretty soon, it became too much.

We don't talk about the high "failure" rate of residential treatments (failure, in this case, meaning that people don't stay sober after they leave). But that rate is important, and it's something people should be armed with before they decide to spend tens of thousands of dollars on what may be little more than a twenty-eight-day dry-out. So here are the numbers: Just four in six alcoholics who enter residential treatment stick it out until the end, and of those, about half will relapse within the first year of leaving treatment. Over four years, 90 percent of people who go to treatment will start drinking again, although many of them will eventually quit. Relapse, in other words, isn't just "a part of recovery," it's almost inevitable. And yet treatment centers focus heavily, almost monomaniacally, on relapse prevention, while teaching patients almost nothing about what to do about relapse when it occurs. They teach you to HALT when you feel like drinking, a mnemonic that stands for "hungry, angry, lonely, or tired," four conditions that can precede relapse. They teach you to practice DREAMS, which stands for diet, rest, exercise, acceptance, meditation, and schedule. They teach you the tools of rational-emotive therapy, or RET, which is itself a subset of CBT. (If you're having trouble keeping track of all these acronyms, imagine how hard it is for a fuzz-brained alcoholic in early sobriety; I carried a card in my wallet for months to keep them all straight.) They teach you that a craving is a craving is a craving, which is why they often ban sugar and caffeine (a controversial theory, to say the least, and one that proscribes the two primary substances consumed at AA meetings). They teach you how to respond to stressful situations without drinking, using role-playing exercises and skills training. And they teach you about triggers—identifying them, avoiding them, and learning to deal with them or ride them out. Learning about triggers is extremely important because you can't just lock yourself inside an AA meeting hall forever (eventually, even the Big Book thumpers will make you go home) and because numerous studies have shown that these contextual cues can be just as powerful as alcohol itself in making a person want to pick up a drink. My triggers, for the record, include: grocery stores, work, airports, the bus, the train, my apartment. Basically: life.

In early sobriety, your brain is still putting itself back together, during a process called post-acute withdrawal syndrome (better known by its cutesy acronym, PAWS), which can last for more than two years. In my few weeks of sobriety, when I could barely remember to brush my teeth twice a day, I pictured my brain as a soft, pliable sponge, full of holes large enough to stick a finger through.

I never found out how long it would take to get through this phase because, before I could get there, I went back through the revolving door.

Twenty-eight

Rock Bottom

What the fuck time is it?

I fumble for my phone, the sheets in a tangle around me, the mattress stripped bare. Four o'clock. Too early to get up, no stores open anyway. It's been six weeks since I "graduated" from Rez XII. I reach under the bed for the cardboard bottle of white wine, praying to the ceiling that there are a few drops left, enough to calm the twitching, make my legs stop flopping back and forth like weather vanes in a storm. I'm feverish, I'm freezing, hair sweat-pasted to my forehead, and the dizziness when I lift my head hits me like an anvil. The bottle makes a thin *swish, swish* sound when I shake it, hoping for dregs. Once again, for the millionth time, I've failed to guard against the desperation of the morning by holding back a small supply the night before.

I stumble for the wall, something to hold on to, the light. The fixture blinks on, glaring; it's too bright, so I navigate by the orange streetlights that seem at this hour to be aimed directly into my bedroom. In addition to the empty bottle under the bed, there's a suitcase full of identical empties in the closet. I can't tell you why it's there, why I can't carry my bottles down to the Dumpster in the morning, destroy the evidence like a normal person. I think back to my first year of college, when a blond bulimic down the hall saved her vomit in Ziploc bags in the bottom drawer of her dorm-room dresser. The bottles are a private history. They're the evidence I refuse to destroy.

I stagger into the kitchen, grab a glass and a pair of scissors, and grip the walls all the way to the closet, where I unzip the suitcase in the orange-gray dark. Methodically, like a lab tech conducting a delicate experiment, I cut a small slash in the corner of each box and squeeze the thick dregs at the bottom into the glass. Methodically, like a shop clerk taking inventory, I work my way through all the bottles, and by the time I'm done, there is half a cup of warm, sour white wine in the bottom of the glass. I give a little prayer of gratitude to whatever god provides resourcefulness in times of desperation. Then I gulp it down.

By the time I wake up again an hour later, the sun is streaming in through the long bank of blinds on the back wall of my bedroom and sleep is impossible. My heart is pounding so hard I'm sure that if anyone was here, they could hear it, too.

For a while, maybe a half hour, I just lie there, listening to my heart pound and flopping first onto one side, then the other, my body moving all by itself while I will it, endlessly: *Just rest. Be gentle with yourself. You'll be okay. Today will be better.*

Well, it's time to face this.

I pull myself off the bare blue mattress into a roughly vertical position. The shock of movement sends my stomach into rebellion, and I scramble the half dozen steps to the bathroom around the corner, assuming the familiar position in front of the toilet, my arms clutching its cool porcelain sides, my chest heaving in a ritual of retching.

Since there's nothing in my stomach—since, truth be told, I haven't eaten a full meal since a Reuben sandwich from the corner deli two days ago—what comes out is mostly stringy, bile-yellow spit, and a burst of involuntary tears from my bloodshot eyes. I haul myself up to the sink, drink the tiniest possible swallow of water, and go about the other rituals of my morning. I tug a pair of jeans onto my scrawny body, where they hang on to protruding hips under a booze-bloated stomach. I draw on eyeliner and sweep eyeshadow across my lids with a shaky hand, daubing myself with a tissue every few seconds to clear away the clammy sheen of sweat that keeps the makeup from adhering. I brush my teeth for a solid three seconds until the toothbrush initiates my gag reflex and I heave into the toilet one last time before pulling a headband over my greasy hair and head out the door.

Outside, even in the gray haze of a late October Seattle morning, the sun is bright, far too bright. I dig a pair of smudged, scratched-up plastic sunglasses from the depths of my backpack and plaster them on my face. The bus that stops in front of my apartment building takes far too long to arrive at this hour, but it does arrive, and I wedge myself into a row of early commuters heading to their jobs in retail or programming or finance, shrinking into my headphones and hoping to God I don't smell like booze or puke. Everyone looks so shiny, freshly scrubbed, and rested. Where do people even go this early, and what right do they have to look so cheerful? All I want is to crawl out of my skin and leave it behind me, on this bus.

Instead, I get off at the supermarket, four stops—*Angeline, Alaska, Genesee, Andover*—past my house. Stomach lurching, I shove my way out the back door and into the planting strip, over to the sidewalk that leads past the liquor store. The winos who hang out around this strip mall have started to rouse themselves, their clothes almost indistinguishable from sleeping bags, their belongings in shopping carts stored around the corner for safekeeping. I nod at them respectfully as I walk by, looking them in the eye as they share a can of Steel Reserve from hand to hand, as if to say, *I see you. We're the same, you and me.* At Rez XII, they drilled it into our heads: *Look for the similarities, not the differences.* This may not have been precisely what my counselors had in mind, but ever since I relapsed after my hopeful coin-out ceremony, I've seen nothing but similarities between myself and the homeless and marginally housed drunks who spend their days begging quarters for a can or six-pack; as far as I can figure, the only thing that separates us is that I have a family who will force me into treatment or make me move back home if I really manage to screw things up this time. Which won't happen, of course, because I have a job.

The problem is, I can't really get through my job without drinking, and drinking now starts the second I get up in the morning. Which is why, as soon as I'm done fumbling through pleasantries with the cashier—a plump, artificially redheaded lady I see more often than I see any of my friends—I erupt back out into the cold, pleasant air, wipe new sweat from my forehead, walk across the street, and crack the bottle.

The plastic teeth protecting the mouth of the Tetra Pak tear apart, and the crack-pop-crack of the lid as it releases from the bottle is the sound of comfort, sustenance, relief. I tip the box to my lips, the cool, lightly effervescent liquid pouring past my insensate tongue directly down my throat, into my raw, still-roiling stomach, which welcomes the cooling liquid, then immediately coils itself in a knot. I walk slowly, as delicately as possible, down the street toward the community garden where I've somehow managed to hold on to my weed-choked plot. I can make it, I can sit down, and I probably won't throw up again this morning.

I don't make it. I lose the wine in a ditch beside a lot overgrown with brambles, near a park where I picked blackberries just this past summer. It's a triumph that no one is around to see me retching in the bushes, and if the Spanish-speaking family who owns the cheap blue-sided house that backs up against the garden has seen me coughing violently into my scarf or passing out on the picnic table or retching into the bark behind my garden, they've never let on. It's frosty in my garden still, the weeds from last summer damp and sparkly in the rising light. I'm still sweating like a flu patient as I sit down at the familiar picnic table and chug half the bottle. This time, it stays down. The world rights itself. Despair retreats a few more feet into the distance, and I brush off my jacket, powder my nose and cheeks, and wander to the bus stop by the fish and chips stand, where I'll sit and watch a few buses go by, drinking in a manner I falsely imagine to be stealthy, before boarding the Route 7 at 8:30, heading to the back, and closing my eyes all the way to work.

In these last weeks before I checked into my second rehab, I steadied myself for work most days by drinking enough alcohol to send most people back to bed until late afternoon—half a liter of wine on an empty stomach, or a few sharp swigs of bottom-shelf vodka, straight from the bottle. Without it—a combination of intense physical discomfort and crippling dread. With it—a sense of unsteady confidence, a rickety rope bridge extending from one physical location (the bed, the toilet) to the next (the bus, the office, the press conference). Either way—everything about my body felt unsteady and alien, not really mine, and booze-scented sweat leaked unmistakably from every pore, marking me as I shed layers on the overheated bus, the only person who was red-faced and sweating and yelling "Can you turn the heat down?" in October. My thoughts were panicked and unfocused, and I kept returning to bits of songs (*Trudging slowly over wet sand / Back to the bench where your clothes were stolen*) and a new mantra that kept showing up, unbidden: I feel like the light has gone out of my eyes.

When I was sixteen, I got to play piano in a small recital among a bunch of mostly younger kids. Our piano teacher, Ted, was a jazz musician who stuck to classical teaching, so the selections were in that vein: Tchaikovsky, Dvorak, Haydn. I played the Smiths' "There Is a Light That Never Goes Out"—strings on the left hand, melody on the right. *"To die by your side / Is such a heavenly way to die."* Robert and I would read the lyrics to each other on the phone after school, collapsing into hysterics at Morrissey's melodramatic turns of phrase.

I feel like the light has gone out of my eyes.

For the next couple of weeks, I drank the way I wanted to—which is to say, constantly.

Through it all, though, I continued to work. One morning, I was running late for an interview with a city council member. I've known this guy for the last ten years, since the days when he led the local chapter of the Sierra Club in its fight against a boondoggle proposal to build a massive tunnel under Seattle's downtown waterfront, the largest and riskiest project of its kind in the world. My old acquaintance lost that battle, but it helped win him a seat on the council, where he went on to become one of the most divisive figures in the city.

As usual, I've cut it close. To make the interview, I had to haul uphill two blocks wearing too many layers—it's 40 degrees outside, pretty cold, but I'm a furnace—and my face is conspicuously red and dripping even after a quick trip to the ladies' restroom downstairs, where I splash myself with water and take a long, greedy swig of Chardonnay. Upstairs, still sweating profusely, I stumble through a terrible interview, asking long, perambulatory questions that loop around themselves and land nowhere. "Are you okay? Do you need some water?" the council member asks me, looking concerned. Did he read Josh's post about me on Twitter? Is he onto me? *No, I just need to get through this fucking interview so I can get back to the office and keep drinking myself to death.* "No, I'm fine. Sorry, just had to run up a bit of a hill to get here." We shake hands in his office—*Why does everyone keep their offices so hot?*—when it's over, his dry, confident palm clasping my damp, shaky one. I am relieved to have gotten through, and I reward myself with another trip to the restroom for a swig before tottering downhill to my office.

Back at the office, Josh eyes me warily. "Are you sure you're okay?" he says suspiciously. Every conversation these days is in code. "I'm fine," I tell him. "Just coming down with a cold." "Come with me," he says, glaring. There are cubicles all around. I roll my eyes defiantly, like the fourteen-year-old girl I sometimes still feel like on the inside, and follow him reluctantly to the stairwell. This is where he takes me to dress me down, out of sight of the people who could fire me. "You've been drinking," he states flatly, for the millionth time. "Look at me and tell me you haven't been drinking."

This is a ritual. I play my part. "I have *not*," I lie, as usual, steadying myself against the wall with my left hand as I gesticulate with my right. "I don't know where you get off making accusations like this. You're supposed to be supportive." Josh shoots me a disgusted look and slams his hand into the wall. "You're going to get fired," he says, "and I'm not going to be able to protect you. You have to get your shit together. You cannot keep doing this shit!" I glare at him like I glared at my mom when she caught me with a pack of cigarettes. *How dare he catch me red-handed.*

Finally, the usual conversation ender: "Do you want to just go home? I don't know if I feel comfortable having you here." I insist on staying, because that seems like what an innocent person would do. I stumble through a phone interview with a political consultant with Josh in earshot, and after I'm off the phone, he hisses, "What the fuck was that? Your questions didn't even make any sense! Just— don't do any more interviews today." Thus unburdened from the responsibility of human interaction, I go about the day's remaining tasks: acting normal while maintaining a buzz, heading to the nearby deli for a sandwich that I will barely nibble and two $2.99 mini bottles of Gallo (a store up the street sells them for a dollar less, but Josh will get suspicious if I'm gone too long), and getting through the day with minimal eye contact and even less conversation.

On our way up the outdoor stairs to catch our respective buses that evening, Josh stands behind me and observes that I'm stagger-ing. "No, I'm not," I tell him; this feeble response is the best I can do. I could probably tell what's in his eyes if I was able to focus, but I already know—it's a mixture of frustration, betrayal, sadness, and anger, same as ever. He won't wait for the bus with me this time. That's fine by me. As soon as I see him round the corner toward his bus stop, I take off like a shot for the downtown grocery store.

I don't show up to work for days. I'm supposed to turn in my story about the council member on Monday, but I can't focus enough to turn on my computer, and I can't face what I know will be an in-box of accusatory emails from Josh and James. The truth is, I can barely stand up. I've been spending most of my time lying in bed, staring at the shifting, colorless patterns on the ceiling—spiders, cobwebs, and whirlwind scribbles—in between sips from the bottle by the bed.

When I do return to work, I can't focus. I can't remember what I'm doing from moment to moment. At some point, I shuffle off to the bathroom to get my head straight, which means sitting in the stall and drinking until I feel steady enough to work.

That's where Emily finds me: passed out on the bathroom floor, my liter box of white wine carefully tucked away in my messenger bag. Calmly, but with a sick-of-this-shit tone, she coaxes me out of the stall and back to my cubicle before handing me off to Josh. "She can't be here," she says. Josh, glaring, marches me downstairs, where he furiously calls an Uber, then a cab. (The Uber has trouble finding us. "WE! ARE! IN THE ALLEY! RIGHT BEHIND WESTERN AVENUE!" I hear him shout.) He can barely look at me. "You are going to lose your job," he growls. I stare at him, insensible, and fumble for my keys, which are suddenly too slippery for my fingers to handle. In the course of this struggle, my bag tips over and the box of wine falls out, splashing on the sidewalk. Panicked, I lunge for it, but Josh gets there first, and dumps out the remaining precious few ounces in a nearby trash can. "Jesus Christ, Erica." That old refrain. We wait in silence. The cab arrives. Josh tells him where to go—my apartment, no stops on the way—and hands him fifty dollars, telling him to keep all of it. As we pull away, I watched Josh walk back into the building, shoulders hunched in the manner of a man with too many burdens. Time skips forward, and I wake up in my bed the next morning, dirty sheets tangled around me like a rope.

And then, as if trying to erase and rerecord the actions of the previous day, I raise my throbbing head, toss on the same clothes

I'd worn a day earlier, and head back to the office, where the same nightmare scenario plays out again, identical in nearly every detail. This time, someone else finds me—a salesperson, heading to the bathroom for a morning pee, only to find an editor passed out on the floor.

This, finally, is where drinking took me—to the dirty floor of an office bathroom in downtown Seattle, passed out cold at 11:00 A.M., not once, but twice in two days' time. Of many rock bottoms I'd hit, this one is, if not the lowest, the most brutally humiliating. Emily and Josh hustle me out of the building and across the street. It's important, Josh insists, that I get away from magazine "property," because James is threatening to call the cops, and Josh thinks I can't be arrested if I'm on public property.

Time passes. Hours, maybe a day. I drink. I sleep. And when I wake up, I know, without hesitation, that if I don't make some kind of decision I will meet my end here, in this rancid apartment, alone. This, I think, is what they call a moment of truth. Or a rock bottom. Whatever.

I pick up the phone, pause for a few ragged breaths, and call Melissa.

Twenty-nine

Collapse

H ello?"

"Um . . . hi, is this Melissa?"

"Yes?"

"Hi, it's Erica. Um. Ineedtogotodetoxcanyoutakeme?"

The words poured out in a jumble. "Slow down. Slow down. What are you asking?"

I was crying now—hysterically crying, river-of-snot crying, unintelligibly crying—but also trying not to throw up while I was on the phone with the publisher of the magazine that, for the moment, still employed me. "I'm at home, and I feel like I'm dying, and I relapsed, and I need to go to detox. But I owe James a story, and I don't want to get fired, and I don't know what to do, and I'm wondering if you can help me. Can you help me find a detox? Can you take me? I don't know where else to turn."

And, as an afterthought: "Please."

Melissa was calm, but her voice was clipped. "I'll call you back."

I collapsed back onto the bed, every bit of my energy expended in dialing the ten digits, putting my problems in someone else's hands. I stared at the ceiling, willing the familiar patterns to go away. A minute, or an hour, later, the phone rang.

"It's Melissa. I got you a bed at Fairfax." Fairfax was a mental hospital in the nearby suburb of Kirkland, the same suburb where Residence XII was located—the kind of place where my childhood friend Jennie's parents locked her up when her depression became too much to handle. They also had a small detox wing. "Emily and I will be there in an hour. Get dressed and try to have something to eat."

Eating was unthinkable. I hadn't been hungry in weeks—my stomach, by now, was swollen and hollowed out, a poisoned sac sloshing bile. There was still time to walk across the street to the Busy Bee convenience store, where I knew I could buy a couple of mini bottles of Gallo or a half-liter box of Chardonnay, before Melissa and Emily arrived. So instead of eating (the food in the fridge mostly rotten anyway, vegetables liquefying in their bags, half-burned attempts at curries molding in their Tupperware), I pulled on a T-shirt, jeans, and a hoodie and walked to the store in the cool, early-autumn air. The wine, cold and acid going down, restored me enough to run a comb through my hair, scrub under my arms, and fill a stained white canvas bag with the clothes that seemed cleanest—T-shirts, pajama bottoms, sweats, and a few thongs from the dregs of my underwear drawer. I struggled down the stairs and waited. The alcohol had softened the edges of my resolve, but it was too late to reverse what I'd set in motion. Melissa and Emily would pull up in my parking lot, I would get in the car, and they would drive me to Fairfax. I would walk through the sliding doors. I would do what they told me to do. Once I was admitted, someone else would take over—someone in a white jacket, with drugs that would knock back the shakes and make the hallucinations recede. I didn't know if my insurance would cover any of this (and, ultimately, they didn't). I didn't care.

Melissa squealed into my parking lot in her big, champagne-colored SUV. I was the reason she, Emily, and I were in this car together, but they acted like I wasn't there. After a few perfunctory questions about how I was feeling and a stop at Starbucks for a breakfast sandwich I could barely stand to look at, I stared out the open window and sobbed self-pityingly, trying to hold down a single bite of egg and English muffin while Melissa and Emily chattered amiably about the work day they had ahead, after they finished dealing with this distasteful errand. "I don't know how we're going to close on this issue on time if Amy doesn't nail down the ad copy for the rest of the bridal section." "Yeah, what is up with her? Do you think she's looking for another job or something?" Why don't they seem more concerned about me? I wondered, sulking into my sandwich. So this is what it's come to—the only people left to take me to detox are two yammering women from work who cared more about the stupid magazine than they did about me, the human being sitting next to them in agony. "Do you think I'm going to lose my job?" I blurt. Melissa gave me a chilly glance. Paused. "Let's just worry about getting you better."

The lobby at Fairfax was designed to project a sense of order and calm. Even as orderlies rushed through pushing a stretcher to which a large, screaming teenage boy had been strapped, there was a hush about the place, decorated in placid blond wood and taupe plastic benches and soothing shades of yellow and mauve. Just get through the next five minutes, I told myself, my sweaty arms adhering to the faux-leather bench. Just get through the next thirty seconds. Finally, an officious-looking man in a white coat and wire-rimmed glasses called me back to give me a Breathalyzer test. "Have you done one of these before?" he asked. "No," I said. (This was true. Despite all the times I'd driven drunk, I'd never been pulled over, and the only alcohol tester I had ever seen up close was attached to the ignition of a car belonging to a guy I met in outpatient treatment and convinced to drive my drunk ass home.) "Just blow in the tube as hard as you can until I say stop." I did as he said.

"Okay . . . 0.242," he said. I pictured the signs you see on the side of the road, the ones that say: ALCOHOL LIMIT .08. Technically speaking, I was three times over the limit. According to studies on the effects of alcohol intoxication, a blood alcohol level between 0.21 and 0.29 is characterized by stupor, loss of consciousness, black-out, and severe motor impairment. And yet here I was, walking upright and carrying on polite if stilted conversations, with a level of alcohol in my system that would put a normal person on a stretcher. There was a part of me that felt a little proud. *Holy shit, look at what your body can handle!* But I didn't say that part out loud. Instead, I asked, "Do you think you can admit me soon?" My BAC may have suggested otherwise, but the wine was wearing off, and my body was starting to shudder into a familiar state of hyperarousal.

If the northwest Seattle hospital where I'd detoxed six years earlier was the Four Seasons, and Recovery Centers of King County, where I'd been earlier that same year, was a fleabag SRO in the seediest part of town, Fairfax was a roadside motel where twenty-nine dollars would get you a mattress with busted springs, sheets of dubious cleanliness, and triple locks on the door. Except, of course, that there were no locks on the doors—nor, effectively, doors at all, since the rules stipulated that they could never be closed. As at RCKC, tweezers, shoelaces, and pens were viewed as potential suicide implements. The funhouse mirror in my room was familiar from the county detox, too—mental institution standard issue, made of warped, unbreakable metal. Each room was spare, with three plastic-covered beds, austere nightstands, and a small cubby for hanging clothes.

With nothing to do until the nurse came back to do my intake, I introduced myself to my roommates—Sara, a stringy-haired heroin and pill addict whose mom brought her to Fairfax and stood in the lobby so she couldn't leave, and Hannah, a go-getter, type A alcoholic who spent her free time walking up and down the ward's single hallway, counting steps. "I love to walk!" she told me cheerfully as she made a U-turn at the end of the hall. "Three thousand seven hundred seventy-four, three thousand seven hundred seventy-five . . ." After two days, Sara would go AMA and get into her junkie boyfriend's car. One day later, Hannah would finish her term and bounce out the doors, reunited with her Fitbit.

I started pacing up and down the long hallway, peeking inside people's rooms. The place appeared to be packed to the rafters with junkies, degenerates, and drunks like me—the puffy-faced lady in sweatpants and a stained T-shirt, clutching the walls and itching for a handful of Librium. I noticed a woman with scraggly gray hair perched on a folding chair outside the nurses' station, waving some kind of scribbled manifesto. "Why won't they let me out of here?" she wanted to know. "I'm not supposed to be here! Can you tell them I'm not supposed to be here?" Involuntary commitment cases like hers were fairly unusual. While Fairfax was a lockdown facility—once you were in, you couldn't just walk out the door—most of the people on the detox wing had walked in under their own power, and many went AMA once they started feeling better, or wheedled their way out early, like me.

Fairfax didn't hide the fact that it was a mental hospital—my stay there began with a full strip and cavity search, and people were always coming and going between the mental and detox wards. The impression was enhanced by the fact that most patients on the detox ward spent their days doing what was universally called the "Librium shuffle," a slow, sedated walk that looked like you were sweeping the floor with your shoes. Everything seemed designed to hold patients in a state of stupefied dependency. The refrigerator was stocked with an endless supply of apple sauce, milk, and those foil-covered orange and apple juice containers you get in middle school. When I wasn't shotgunning those, I spent most of my time in the TV room, watching *Xtreme Off-Road*, *Bar Rescue*, and *Auction Hunters*, and waiting for everyone to leave for meals so I could switch the channel to the Food Network. (Men outnumbered women at Fairfax three to one when I was there, which helped explain why the TV was always tuned to Spike TV.) When I wasn't vegging on the couch or dodging the attention of one of the many predatory guys on the ward—truly, there isn't a single place in the world where men won't try to get in women's pants—I was worrying about my overdue story, calling James, and leaving messages for Marianne, my nominal AA sponsor.

Marianne and I had left things on pretty shaky terms. Since that first meeting outside Cherry Hall six weeks earlier, she had had me create daily gratitude lists and mail them to her every day, which I did—sporadically. "Today I am grateful for: The changing of the seasons. The fact that I made rent. No arguments with Josh. Sunshine." She asked me to call her every day, which I did—sort of. Once I started drinking again, I responded to her voice mails with texts. "I can't sponsor you by text," she protested. So I called her, drunk, trying to hide my condition by speaking slowly and E-Nun-Ci-A-Ting every syllable. "Recite the ninth step promises," she demanded one night. "If we are painstaking about this phase of our development, we will be amazed before we are halfway through," I slurred. "We are going to know a new freedom and a new happiness. We will lose interest in ourselves . . . and gain interest in . . . others?" Why hadn't I just looked up the fucking thing? "You aren't serious about this," Marianne said. Then the line went dead.

After that, we kind of fell out of touch. But now, I needed her. Panicked at the idea of leaving Fairfax without a sponsor, I left messages for her at Cherry Hall. But when she didn't call me back at the hospital, I wrote her off. *Fuck that bitch. Some sponsor* she *is.*

Thirty

Fired

Fairfax let me leave after just four days—less than the five-to-seven-day recommended stay, but enough to pronounce me "stabilized" and free up a bed for the next quavering addict. Kevin picked me up, or maybe I took the bus; that day, or the ones that followed, have been ripped from my mental calendar.

How fast did I start drinking again after leaving? Was it right away? After I saw how hopeless things were at work? Or was it not until the day of my big meeting with James, the Monday after I left the hospital, and four days before I fell on my face, in the rain, after taking the train to the office to pick up the stuff I hadn't been allowed to carry with me out the door?

Let's say it was that Monday, and I came in to work after drinking a half liter of wine—just enough to take the edge off what I knew was going to be a tough meeting with James. At 10:00 sharp, James summoned me into his new corner office and sat down behind the swimming-pool expanse of his enormous glass desk. Ariella, the managing editor, was already waiting. "Sit down," she said, and pointed to a chair.

Rattled by her official-seeming presence, I launched into my speech. "I know I haven't been present at work, and I truly apologize. I've outlined some steps that I plan to take in the future to ensure that nothing like this ever—"

Ariella cut me off.

"Given your performance over the last few months, and the fact that we did give you every opportunity to deal with your issues by taking some time off a month ago"—my stay at Rez XII—"we believe we have no other alternative at this point than to terminate your employment, effective immediately. We need you to take your bag and leave the building."

I had never been fired before. I had known this was a possibility, but at the moment, my brain couldn't process what was happening. I did the only thing I could think of: I tried to argue my way out of it.

"Wait—wait. How about if you put me on probation for six months? Or let me take some time off to get my shit together? Unpaid, even. I would be willing to do that. This takes time. What about if—"

"No. We're not putting you on probation. You're fired."

"Fired?"

"Yes," she said, her patience clearly wearing thin. "Fired."

"But—I started this company with Josh. PubliCola is my company. It's the most important thing in the world to me. How can you just fire me?"

Finally, James spoke. "Please collect your things," he said. "You need to leave immediately. Who would you like to have escort you out of the building?"

Time stood still. I stopped protesting. This was real. This was really happening.

"Josh."

I left James's office, feeling certain my knees would buckle underneath me. I caught Josh's eye above our shared cubicle wall and drew my finger in a slashing motion across my neck. *Fired. Dead.* What was the difference? I saw his face fall—*so he hadn't known!* I shuffled over to my cubicle, gulped back the scream that was rising in my chest, and motioned to Josh to walk me out of the building. We took the elevator down in silence.

And then, the second we got outside, I erupted. Screaming, inconsolable, monstrous sobs. A howl that could surely be heard on the seventh floor, where the magazine's staffers sat in their cubicles, tap-tap-tapping away on the latest listicle—"Seattle's Best Happy Hours" or "Killer Weekend Getaways" or "The City's Best Cosmetic Dentists." I didn't care who heard. I sobbed like I hadn't sobbed since Jennie died. For me—and I know this sounds histrionic—that's kind of how it felt, like I had lost something that I could have saved, if only I had tried a little harder, been less selfish. Finally, I managed to choke out a few words.

"What am I going to *do?*"

Josh put his arm around me, but he didn't say much—what are you supposed to say when your friend is not only well on her way to killing herself, but has just put the business you started together in existential jeopardy? "I don't know. Don't go home. Go to a meeting. Let's get you into treatment again. A different one. The first one obviously didn't work." I nodded, suddenly overcome with the skin-crawling need for a drink. "I'll go to a meeting." "You promise?" "I promise." "Okay, I've got to go back to work." We hugged, and, uncharacteristically, I did what I had promised. I went to a meeting.

And then I drank for the next seven days.

I mean, I didn't *just* drink. I drank, I went to the store, I drunk-dialed friends and barely friends, and I drank some more. After several days of this, I decided it was time to sober up. The way I should sober up, I decided, was by moving back to Mississippi for a while—a terrible idea for many reasons, the biggest of which was that my grandparents were not remotely prepared to deal with me, but the best plan I could come up with at the time. Fortunately, fate intervened in the form of a ticket mix-up, a bout of sudden-onset mental paralysis, and a pair of TSA agents who called the ambulance that brought me to a suburban hospital near the airport.

You already heard the first part of that story.

What happened next was, for me, fairly unremarkable. First, I was sent into triage, where the front-desk nurses saw I was in bad enough shape that they sent me straight to the ICU. I spent the night, and part of the next day, in a large curtained-off area directly across from the nurses' station, which buzzed all night with activity. At some point in the night, I got up and clattered with my IV stand over to the restroom, walking past patients in much worse shape than I was, including an elderly man with bluish-gray skin so mottled and translucent I was sure he was dead. This was when I decided that I didn't really need to be there. After submitting to a few more hours of vitals checks and four bags of fluids, I was on my way. On the cab ride home, I pulled the spare bottle of vodka out of my suitcase and took a long, sneaky slug. I watched the lights illuminating I-5 streak overhead as the car sped toward downtown, waiting for the vodka to drown out the critical voices that were screaming in my head; grateful, at least, that the night hadn't cost me anything more than money.

I needed to go back to treatment. *Duh*, you say, and that's right—but, insensate as I was, it was just as likely that I would drink myself to death. Toss of a coin. I started calling treatment centers the following morning.

Most people who get to the point where the options are treatment and death, as I did, don't have the time or capacity for a long, thoughtful period of research and reflection. Instead, we tend to settle wherever we're hurled—by our finances and insurance plans, by parents if we have them and if they're willing to intervene, or by happenstance and opportunity. That's how I ended up at Lakeside-Milam—a treatment center located, as it happened, right next door to Fairfax Hospital in Kirkland. Previously, I had rejected Lakeside, as it was known, because all the online reviews made it sound like an overcrowded dump. But my standards had changed. The only thing that mattered was that they could get me in right away.

"I mean, like, today. Now, if possible."

"We can get you in. But it may be tomorrow. Can you pack a bag and wait by the phone?"

"Yes, absolutely! Thank you so much. You don't know how important this is."

I made an emergency appointment with my doctor for a taper dose of Ativan (another benzo often used for "ambulatory," or outpatient, withdrawal), called Kevin, and clutched my phone in a sweaty palm.

Kevin, who told me a few months back, "I can't be with an alcoholic," was still willing to show up for me. It's kind of inexplicable. Maybe, being older, he had more perspective on the kind of experiences people have to go through before life clicks into place. Maybe he knew that without him, I probably wouldn't make it all the way to Kirkland. Maybe he just had a lot more faith in me than I had in myself.

Technically, we were still sort of together, if you can call occasionally passing out in the same bed as someone being "with" them—but we weren't using the labels boyfriend and girlfriend anymore. I had a primary partner. It was alcohol. Everyone and everything else was secondary.

Around 4:00 P.M., Lakeside called. Kevin and I were sitting, appropriately enough, in a pub. I was feeling a little steadier—the Ativan, which I'd swallowed dry right in the Safeway as soon as the pharmacist handed over the bottle, was kicking in—and I looked at Kevin over my half-eaten veggie burger and root beer and told him the news. "They have a bed for me tonight. I got in."

Thirty-one

Consequences

This time, there was no tearful visit from Mom.

No angry letters from Josh warning me in capital letters: "YOU WILL LOSE YOUR JOB." I'd already lost it.

There was no AA sponsor for me to call listlessly every day or two so the counselors would get off my case—I left a message at the hall for Marianne, but she wasn't calling back. There were no deadlines to miss. There wasn't even a rent check to worry about: Mom and Dad, who had always insisted that I deal with my financial problems on my own, had taken care of that. I had asked them for loans, casually, a couple of times in my adult life—the answer was always no—but this was the first time I had been truly desperate. When I asked for the thousand dollars, Mom said through tears, "Is that all you want from us? Money? Fine! I'll pay your rent. But that's it." I don't know if she knew how much I hated to ask.

There was time—twenty-eight days, more or less, to figure out how I landed in rehab again and how I was going to start to pick up the pieces now that I'd lost my job—which is to say, everything. There were copies of *The New Yorker*, smuggled in by Josh the first time he visited. (The act of compassion, from someone who had all but given up on me, made me collapse in tears the minute the big wooden doors swooshed shut and he disappeared in the crack of light between them.) There were people of every imaginable background and with every conceivable reason for being here, people who'd been through things I thought only happened to late-stage street alcoholics who'd been drinking for forty years—things like multiple organ failure and cirrhosis and a condition called ascites, a fluid buildup in the abdominal cavity that can make a skinny man look pregnant. There was a guy who walked in under his own power—so yellow with jaundice I thought I was seeing things again—and left in a wheelchair two days later, headed for intensive care. There was a homeless dude who seemed to have just wandered in off the street, with no appointment or anything, and who ended up crashing on the couch in the lounge area for a few days while they waited for a bed to open up. There was a former rock star and a guy who claimed he just left prison on rape charges and a long-haired, bearded guy with a predatory vibe whom I immediately dubbed Creepy Jesus. There was, I guess, hope. At least I didn't have jaundice. At least my organs hadn't failed me yet. At least I had a home. At least I was still alive.

Lakeside-Milam was where I learned that people don't always make it, and where I realized that "rock bottom" was the most dangerous phrase in the recovery lexicon. People believe in rock bottom because they don't want to imagine anything worse happening to them, or because it's comforting to believe the lies the recovery industry—AA and treatment and all of it—tells everyone about how recovery works, that it's either rock bottom to redemption or "jails, institutions, and death." There are those things, of course—death is the real rock bottom—but there are also the years and years you can go on living, and that many of us do go on living, that are just one rock bottom after another after another. The most common advice people get about how to deal with a loved one who suffers from addiction is to let them hit rock bottom; it's also the very worst advice, because who are they to judge, and what happens when their addict hits rock bottom and then falls further still? I used to believe in a theoretical rock bottom, knowing from school and my own reading on addiction that everyone has one and everyone's is different (in the recovery world, some people are said to have "low" or "high" bottoms that they hit before they quit), but I learned, during my second stint in treatment, that there are places addiction can take you that you never thought to think about. Lakeside-Milam was the place where my sense of personal invincibility evaporated, where I stopped saying, "At least I'm not as bad as that person," and started thinking, "That's where I'm going next."

I still have a copy of my intake photo from the night I showed up for treatment, a night when, I remember, I was shaky, unwashed, and desperate for sleep. Kevin walked me in, steadying me with his arm, and sat beside me on the dumpy couch in the front lobby, watching the bright-yellow tropical fish swim around and around in an incongruously cheerful tank until the night nurse came to take me inside. ("Erica admitted yesterday with a BAC of 0.192. She has a gash on her lip and an aged black eye that she reports to have received during a fall when intoxicated.") I've never shown this photo to anyone (including my current boyfriend, who met me nine months after that photo was taken and has never seen me take a drink), but I pull it out from time to time when I'm alone in my apartment, just to remind me of what it felt like to sit in that blinding intake room. My hair is stringy, plastered to my head by sweat and a black cloth headband, and my eyes are droopy, vacant, and disinterested. My split lip is visible even in the low-resolution black-and-white printout, and my gray hooded sweatshirt is slouched toward my left shoulder, like I didn't quite finish getting dressed. Everything about the image says, "I give up."

My intake records indicate that I was in pretty lousy shape—in addition to my fucked-up face, the counselor noted "spasms, shaky, tremors, high BP" and "clouded sensorium (confuses/confabulates)," but I don't remember any of that. What I do remember is asking—begging, actually—for Librium, and being ushered to a darkened room on the detox wing, where I mumbled a perfunctory "hello" to my roommate—a brusque but sweet Romanian woman who was just about to graduate to the regular rehab wing—and passed out for twelve hours straight.

The first few nights were like every detox I'd been through—tossing and turning on a thin plastic mattress and a plastic pillow barely thicker than a rolled-up T-shirt—except that, starting on day one, we were expected to attend group and lectures and movies. And so, on November 7, 2014, I dragged myself out of bed and down the hall to Brown Group, where a half dozen women who already knew each other were waiting to make my acquaintance.

"So, for introductions, we're all going to go around and share our names, what got us here, our treatment tips, and a fun fact about ourselves!" the counselor, Jeannette, was explaining, as I tried to hold up my pounding head and keep from drooling on Kevin's University of Tulsa sweatshirt. My fun facts? "My first concert was the Monkees, with my dad." *So fun!* Did my voice sound as shaky as I felt? Everything seemed unreal, like I was watching it from behind a screen. I pulled my skinned-up knees under the oversized sweatshirt and tried to get a bead on the other women. There was Kristi, a rough-looking biker chick with dyed black hair who, ten days earlier, had been slamming eighteen PBRs a day; Vanessa, a stunning community college student who had landed at Lakeside after overdosing on Oxycontin, but said her main problem was depression, not drugs; Hayley, a waiflike benzo freak who had stolen her dad's car and sold it for pills; Anika, an Inuit from Alaska who said she drank a handle of vodka a day; and Jeannette, our counselor, who had just stopped smoking meth four years earlier and told us her proudest day was when she finally got new teeth.

Brown Group (every group got a color, and we got the worst) started every morning with a special rendition of the Serenity Prayer—special in that instead of reciting it quietly, we joined arms in a circle and screamed it like maniacs, so loud the guys' group next door would often scream, "SHUT UP!" at us through the wall. "GOD!" we bellowed. "GRANT ME THE SERENITY! TO ACCEPT THE THINGS I CANNOT CHANGE! THE COURAGE TO CHANGE THE THINGS I CAN! AND THE WISDOM! TO KNOOOOOOOOOOOW THE DIFFERENCE!!!"

Group happened twice a day—once in the morning, once in the afternoon. The main activities during group were sharing and offering feedback—listening to someone read her first step out loud (a process that usually took up at least an hour) and saying things like, "It seems like you aren't ready to take responsibility for your actions" or "I still hear a lot of defensiveness in your description of your husband's response when you didn't come home at night." Other times, group activities revolved around walking a group member through some problem she was having in treatment—like the time when the rest of the group tried to talk me down because I was furious that another patient had been caught drinking and hadn't been immediately kicked out. "I just don't understand why she's allowed to stay here when we're the ones trying to actually *focus* on our *recovery* and they are letting toxic people get in the way!" I blubbered. (I learned later that this was a common problem at Lakeside, which was right down the street from a 7-Eleven.) "Why don't you try focusing on yourself and your own recovery instead of worrying about hers?" someone suggested. I glared at her. "Do you understand that I am trying to take my recovery seriously this time?" I asked. "If there are no standards at all, I might as well just be trying to get sober on the outside, and not paying thousands of dollars to be in here where there are *no rules anyway!*" Another time, everyone tried to intervene to keep Vanessa from walking out of treatment after just twelve days; she was fed up because her insurance company was only approving a day or two of treatment at a time, so she never knew when they might decide her time was up. "You can't do anything about the insurance company, so you just have to trust that it'll work out and focus on what you can do in here today," someone said. "If you leave, you know what will end up happening," another offered. "You'll go back to that guy, and then go back to using, and you'll be dead before Christmas." She went AMA three days later.

One of our activities at Lakeside involved completing a "Ladder of Consequences"—an informal version of the questionnaire I had been given during my intake interview. On it was a checklist of bad things that can happen to people because of their drinking, arranged down a page from northeast to southwest in order of escalation: From "sneaks drinks/drugs" all the way down to "insanity and/or death." I marked each one that applied to me with an "X." The result looked like a diagonal line of cross-stitch running down the page, with only "insanity and/or death" unchecked.

Thanksgiving rolled around somewhere between my second first step (cribbed heavily from the one I'd written at Residence XII) and the second and third screenings of a taped lecture from the 1980s by a Catholic priest who had once been affiliated with the treatment center. Lakeside-Milam leaned heavily on these ancient VHS tapes to pass the days, but they had plenty of in-person lectures, too. We heard from a scion of a prominent local family—a philanthropist, developer, and owner of a profitable racetrack who nearly died from addiction—and we heard from a guy whose lungs were calcified by decades of pot smoking, and who apologized for chewing gum ("I know you guys aren't allowed sugar, so this is kind of a dick move on my part") by explaining that his body no longer produced saliva. We also heard from the counselors themselves. For the most part, the staffers stuck to pedagogy—in general, drug treatment counselors are cautioned to set clear boundaries between themselves and patients—but even before I knew the statistics, I gathered that they didn't just stumble into this line of work. No one ends up working in a windowless office at a twenty-four-hour treatment center for low pay and minimal gratitude without a good reason.

I scribbled notes frantically, jotting a star beside anything that rang particularly true. "Every time we drank, we didn't get in trouble, but every time we got in trouble, we'd been drinking." "We all started drinking for different reasons, but we all kept drinking for the same reason." "Alcohol doesn't make us do things better; it makes us care less about doing things badly." I was a dutiful student, as I had been at Rez XII, but it was more than that. I had a sense this time that I was in treatment to save my life, especially now that my job was gone and my life, it seemed, was all I had.

After my first couple of weeks, Josh took the long bus ride across Lake Washington to visit—the same bus ride he had taken just two months earlier, when I was down the street at Residence XII. It was a brisk Sunday afternoon, cold and clear after days of driving rain, and we decided to head outside.

Unlike Residence XII, where visitors were restricted to two highly supervised areas, Lakeside-Milam let visitors roam freely around the grounds. On visiting days, most people congregated in the central meeting area, a cold concrete room where, on Wednesdays, we'd line up for "bank" to withdraw up to five dollars in quarters from our accounts; or near the smoking area, where little kids could kick a ball around or shoot hoops in the tiny, fenced-in court while their parents cried and puffed. Josh and I took our time wandering around and around along the quarter-mile path, and as we passed through the ring of smokers a second time, he told me gently that I should start envisioning a life after PubliCola.

"They told me in their letter that I could interview again in six months," I said, my voice rising an octave. "Do you not think they meant it?"

"I'm not saying it's impossible—who knows what could happen in a year or two—but I don't think that's where you should be putting your energy," he replied. We crunched through the leaves and brushed past the salal bushes that lined the little creek that ran through the property. I changed the subject. "See these bushes? The assistant counselors sweep through here every night to make sure no one has dropped any drugs or booze in the bushes. Can you believe that?" Josh ignored me. "They're pretty mad at you," he continued. "James in particular. They feel like they've already given you every chance already. I don't think they're going to hire you back."

I knew he was right. Had I tried to push them on the six-month offer, they'd bring up everything that made me such an obvious liability. All James would have to do is remind the higher-ups at the magazine about the time he almost called the police to come get me, or the *two* times I passed out in the bathroom, and any case I could make for myself would crumble. I sighed, stopped to perch a foot briefly on a wooden bench puddled with rain, and cried for a minute. Finally, in a small voice, I said, "I know."

We walked on. The conversation turned to FDR, who we both agreed was the best president of the last century (if only I could remember the details of all the World War II books I'd read that year), and where I would live after I left Lakeside-Milam. The counselors were putting the screws on me to consider moving to sober living in an Oxford House, where I'd have to share space and household chores with eight or more women and take random drug and alcohol tests every couple of days. I found the idea of living with strangers in the real world intolerable—exactly the kind of thing that would drive me to drink.

I kept that to myself, though. No reason to invite one of Josh's lectures about how I wasn't taking this seriously. Instead, I protested on the basis of geography. "I think the only Oxford Houses for women are in, like, Lynnwood," a suburb an hour north of Seattle, "and Edmonds," even further away. How was I going to get a job and rebuild my life if I was living in the middle of nowhere, miles away from my support system? Josh shook his head and gave me a sharp look. "You can't go back to that apartment. That place is poison." It was true—besides my hated downstairs neighbors, I hadn't bothered to clean the place in months, and even taciturn Kevin, who went over to throw away the rotting food in the fridge and empty the fly-infested garbage, said he'd found my living conditions "scary."

For twenty-eight days, I worked hard. I wrote "YOU ARE NOT YOUR JOB" over and over in my notebook. I dug deep, admitting to my worst thoughts and listening to feedback I didn't want to hear, like the time the group agreed that I was being narcissistic and blaming external forces (James, the HR lady, Melissa and Emily) for my problems. I spent my ten daily minutes on the phone talking to friends—Stephanie, Lisa, Renee, and others I'd more or less ditched in favor of my best friend, booze—and told them where I was, and that I was sorry for what I'd put them through. It was the first step—I hoped—in repairing friendships with the people who'd stuck by me all these years. Old Me would have continued to complain that Josh wasn't being a good-enough friend. New-ish Me did have to admit that he had not only put up with more than any other friend but had tried to save me from myself, even warning me that I was about to lose my job when I was too arrogant to listen.

I didn't change overnight. I got into a huge fight with one of my two roommates, Tina, because she led the counselor-wardens to my contraband cookie stash after I kept her up with my snoring one too many times. ("You're doing it ON PURPOSE!" she screamed one morning, before demanding reassignment to a different room.) On visiting day, when I noticed her talking about me to her husband and pointing in my direction, I screamed, "You should be in a mental institution, you fucking freak!" But, as they say in AA: progress, not perfection. I was trying to have humility, accept what I couldn't change, and stop questioning every goddamn thing I was told. I kept my lips sealed through an hour-long lecture in which a nutritionist gave us batshit diet tips for recovery, recording them dutifully in my notebook: "Body doesn't know difference between sugar and drugs; eating sugar will create craving for cocaine etc."; "Eat turkey at night—tryptophan triggers sleep"; "Don't eat too much fish in early recovery—triggers overthinking."

I knew, on some level, that a lot of the stuff they were teaching us was bullshit, handed down through generations from a time when scientists really did believe that women were just less likely, or Native Americans more likely, to be alcoholics. (These pseudoscientific theories were among the central themes of a book by Lakeside co-founder James R. Milam called *Under the Influence*, which is sold in many AA bookstores and which we read out loud to one another in lieu of class or counseling on understaffed Saturdays.) I tried to absorb it anyway.

But as hard as I tried to "take the cotton out of my ears and put it in my mouth," as some of the counselors were fond of saying, my notebooks quickly overflowed with the same old questions. How does Lakeside-Milam know how many of its former patients stayed sober? Why can't I call my landlord to make sure I haven't been evicted? If I go to intensive outpatient treatment like they're insist-ing, how often will they make me take a pee test? They keep telling me that sober-living group homes are one of the best ways to stay sober after treatment, but is that true for introverted only children who have lived alone for most of their lives?

Then there were the lists: phone numbers (some written down from memory, some scribbled on scratch paper when I managed to manipulate a counselor into letting me check my phone bill online), people I needed to call during my five minutes on the pay phone in order of priority, people to whom I owed money and apologies.

Despite all my efforts (the sincere ones as well as the ones that were just for show—like reconstructing my second first step on the scaffolding of the first one), my counselors regarded me as manipu-lative, narcissistic, and at "high risk for relapse." (I found all this out after the fact, when I requested my treatment notes—at Lakeside, as at Rez XII, everyone stuck to the party line that if you went through their full course of treatment, including intensive outpatient and aftercare, you were unlikely to drink again.) I couldn't stop questioning everything. After a bunch of the young guys who were bunked in trailers across the grounds from the main building got busted for having a late-night "party" with heroin and beer, I asked the group rhetorically, "Why should I have to follow stupid rules like 'lights out at eleven' when apparently you can just *snort heroin* and get welcomed back here with open arms?" I had more to say on that topic, but Jeannette interrupted. "Intellectualizing! Stacy, do you have anything to share with the group?"

"Intellectualizing" was a catchall term that meant, essentially, "You are refusing to surrender to the program," and it came up all the time—when I questioned the efficacy of prayer, or objected to the concept of "powerlessness," which I found particularly noxious.

"As women, we've all been conditioned to believe that we shouldn't seek power. Are we supposed to just accept whatever happens to us, even when we're being manipulated or abused? Shouldn't we have agency?"

"You're intellectualizing," Jeannette would respond.

"Why should I have to go to intensive outpatient at Lakeside-Milam? Is all the material the same as it is here? Can't I just get on the phone with some other treatment providers?"

"Intellectualizing!"

Finally, I just started writing down my list of objections, along with Jeannette's actual or imagined answers.

No one in my family is an alcoholic.

There probably are alcoholics in your family; you just don't know about them.

Maybe I'm depressed.

Alcoholism is a primary disease; you have to deal with the addiction before tackling other mental health disorders.

But alcoholism isn't *an allergy.* (This was based on a chapter in the Big Book, "The Doctor's Opinion," which suggested that alcoholics have an "allergy" that makes them especially sensitive to alcohol.)

Maybe it's a *metaphorical* allergy—something that's bad for you in quantities that aren't bad for other people.

There were signs that I was making progress. I stopped dominating meetings like a tenth-grade theater kid, and managed to keep my cool when a guy in his midfifties, still detoxing from Suboxone (a heroin replacement drug that can also be abused), called me "a fucking bitch just like my wife" after I criticized him for talking over women in the group. Afterward, Jeannette told me that Suboxone was one of the hardest drugs to detox from; a few weeks earlier, she had seen a guy lay down right in the detox wing's communal bathroom, his face pressed up against the base of the toilet, because "it was the coolest surface he could find."

By the end of week one, I had settled into the comforting predictability of institutional life, with its 3:00 P.M. towel handouts, 10:00 A.M. and 9:00 P.M pill queues, and jarring 7:00 A.M. wake-up calls. "Good morning, Lakeside-Milam patients!" the speaker over our beds would announce. "Breakfast is in thirty minutes!" By week two, I had started walking, then running, out on the path, belting out Stars' "Your Ex-Lover Is Dead" and Lucinda Williams's "Crescent City" as I dodged raindrops and watched the last leaves fall into puddles on the path. And by week three, I was shuffling gratefully from one scheduled moment to the next—breakfast followed by group followed by lecture followed by lunch followed by me and my imaginary playlist on the path. I forced myself to open up to the women of the Brown Group, even when that meant recounting my most humiliating moments—the emergency-room wake-ups, passing out in the bathroom, going home with guys who figured I knew they were married and didn't care.

Every day, when I arrived at the trailer for morning Brown Group, using my thin polyester coverlet as a coat (as usual, I had packed randomly and inappropriately), I gamely picked up a dry-erase marker and wrote my intention for the day on the whiteboard: "Today, I will focus my energy on letting go." When the rest of the group wrote down the personality traits that were holding back my recovery, I barely flinched, even when Jeannette added "feminist" to a list that already included "argumentative," "intellectualizes," and "superiority." I wrote daily gratitude lists, sticking to the basics—*Today, I am grateful that I was able to take a hot shower and brush my teeth*—without noting that that shower wasn't really hot, or that my gums still bled every time I tried to brush.

When anything bad happened, I tried to view it as a learning opportunity—*Mom wasn't around when I called, which is good, because we probably would have fought about where I'm going to live when I get out of here*—and when anything good happened, I tried to edit God, or at least a cosmic sense of order and justice, into the story. *Today I am grateful that I got a new roommate so I don't have to live with that bitch Victoria anymore. Today I am grateful that I didn't make the list to go to an outside meeting*—a coveted position, since it was the only time we got to leave the facility—*because I got to lead a meeting. Today I am grateful for the blanket that arrived in the box along with my new contacts, with a note from some anonymous call center worker wishing me well on my recovery.*

Greg, *The Big Book*-thumping old-timer who worked the front-desk night shift, called the blanket a "God shot"—a stroke of luck too remarkable to be a coincidence. "Everything happens for a reason," he told me. "God is looking out for you." Unlike Greg, I don't think everything happens for a reason or that God has much interest in whether I'm cold or hot, but I could work with this. *Maybe this is the* universe *letting me know that there will always be people to help me, even if they aren't the people I expected.*

When you start looking for signs, you start seeing them everywhere. The time that a nonverbal patient pulled the fire alarm in the middle of the night, forcing everyone to stand outside as the first frost of the year crackled in the grass. A dream in which I kept shushing a girl named Perfect who was talking over a lecture I was trying to hear. The fact that I had spent my birthday, then Thanksgiving, in institutions rather than God knows where. What I read into all these "signs" isn't really important—most of my epiphanies were thuddingly obvious—but they all pointed me toward a new appreciation of life in all its fragility and imperfection.

The other patients, though they didn't know it, were signs, too. At Rez XII, a hothouse stuffed to the rafters with damaged women whose every personality defect was amplified and subjected to cross-examination, it was easy to convince myself that I had little in common with the gap-toothed meth addict who was about to lose her job stocking groceries, or the glamorous junkie who could barely crawl out of bed the first two weeks she was there. I knew what my problem was—I needed to stop drinking. The women at Rez XII seemed to have much steeper hills to climb, hills with names like schizoaffective disorder and childhood trauma and bipolar type 2. I felt for them, but I didn't consider myself one of them.

At Lakeside-Milam, paradoxically, living among a much larger and more diverse crowd of fellow fuckups seemed to jar something awake in me. Some small voice that said, "Yes, you too." An extremely overweight young woman, maybe twenty-six, told me she had just gotten out of the hospital after being treated for multiple organ failure and was in treatment for the fourth and likely final time, and I didn't think: *Well, sure, but she's so overweight. Not like me.* I thought: *I'm ten years older than her. I can't beat the odds forever.* When a woman in rehab for the eighteenth time told me she considered treatment a chance to catch some "me time" before going back to the party, I didn't cluck to myself, *She must not be working her program.* I thought, *This must be a lot harder than I realized.* And when the rumor went around that the young woman who had been caught using heroin on campus, bright with promise when she graduated treatment one week earlier, had turned up dead, I didn't think, *Well, that's why I never got into heroin.* I thought: *How many times did I just miss driving off the road, or getting hit by a bus, or falling asleep somewhere I shouldn't have been?*

Don't get me wrong: I still hated most of the staff—the way they woke us up in the middle of the night for blood draws, the way they watched over our shoulders like they were just hoping we'd break one of their 40 million rules. But something broke in me at Lakeside that stayed broken even after I got out, relapsed, and quit drinking again. I could have died, but I didn't, and even if there are no miracles, that was close enough for me.

I graduated Lakeside-Milam on a blustery morning in early December and there was no one, not even Kevin, to pick me up. I cadged a ride from a staffer who was driving some patients to an outside meeting—it was me, ten women, and another treatment orphan—and got off at the park-and-ride to wait for the bus that would take me back across the lake to Seattle. The other guy got off with me, crossed the pavement with purpose, and swung his suitcase into the trunk of a waiting car. I sat down, brimming with nervous optimism, and waited. The sunlight and the sight of the freeway stretching off toward downtown made my nerves raw and jangly. The bus arrived. I boarded, set down my bag, and made my way to Cherry Hall. I arrived just as people were announcing their "proud time."

"My name is Erica, I'm an alcoholic, and I've been sober for twenty-eight days today." The hugs and applause carried me through almost three weeks.

Thirty-two

Not Quite Yet

Every time I relapsed was the same old story. I had every intention of staying sober. I went to a bunch of meetings—usually one, but sometimes more, every day. I reconnected with Marianne. I dutifully attended Lakeside-Milam's intensive outpatient treatment, even though I resented the fact that our workbooks were full of the same old assignments I had already completed in inpatient. I wrote gratitude lists every day and sent them to Marianne in the mail—one envelope, one stamp, every day. "But why do I have to mail them to you?" I wanted to know. "Can't I just send them by email?" When Marianne asked me if I was "willing to go to any length," I said, "Of course I am" to get her off my back. And at some point—maybe after a frustrating night at intensive outpatient treatment, or a job interview that didn't go the way I'd hoped, or maybe for no reason at all—I got discouraged, or gave up trying, or decided I could drink just a little. One day I wasn't drinking; the next it was like I'd never stopped.

By the time I started drinking again in earnest this time, my whole family was there to watch me fall apart.

It was shortly before Christmas, and I was at the airport, drinking Bloody Marys for my "nerves." I was flying from Seattle to New Orleans, where I had plans to meet up with Cindy before driving on to my grandparents' house in Meridian the following day. On the plane, more "nerves," and more curative Bloody Marys—doubles, since the airline mini bottles hardly count as shots at all. I took a mental inventory of my supply: Still almost a gallon of vodka in my suitcase, more than enough to last through my five-day trip. Worst-case scenario: I had a rental car. I could make some excuse to go to the liquor store. Maybe, I thought, I could say I'm going to a meeting.

Cindy and I met at the hotel where we were sharing a double room, embraced, and had an awkward conversation about how the rest of my family was doing and how much time we had lost. There was just something so presumptuous about her familiarity, I thought—so much intimacy from this woman who had given birth to me thirty-seven years earlier and left me behind not much more than a year after that. Family, I thought then, is a status that's earned—you don't get to call yourself family just because you finally show up. *Okay, fuck this,* I thought, and excused myself to get ready for dinner. *Click.* Behind the hotel-room bathroom door, I powdered my face between gulps of vodka—Gordon's—straight from the gallon-size plastic bottle I'd snuck into the giant orange backpack I used only for airport trips. "You ready in there?" I heard from the bedroom. "One second!" I shouted back, freshening my goth-red lipstick and filling up a plastic water bottle with vodka for the long night ahead.

Outside, the sky was crisp and clear, and if I stumbled in my low-heeled shoes, I could blame the cobblestoned streets outside our French Quarter hotel. We walked to Galatoire's, one of the grandes dames of New Orleans fine dining, for oysters en brochette, shrimp etouffée, and what I can only imagine was a muddled, confusing conversation. (I have to imagine it, because I blacked out during dinner.) We returned to our hotel and Cindy discovered the gallon of Gordon's I'd hidden in my suitcase. I needed her to give it back to me, more than anything I'd ever needed in my life. This is when my memory, punishingly, clicks back on—right as I was trying to wrench the bottle out of her hands.

Cindy looked horrified, like someone playing with a docile lapdog that had suddenly turned into a wolf. My birth mother knew basically nothing about the last few years—the trips to detox, the rehabs, the emergency room visits—because I had given her only the barest outline: I drank too much, I struggled a little with quitting, and then I quit. The comforting narrative had become the only story I knew how to tell, now that I had tried so many times and failed: I had a drinking problem, but it's under control now. I was crazy for a while, but now I'm dependable, trustworthy, and sane. I struggled, but I made it. I did just fine without you in my life.

"What is *wrong* with you?"

What's wrong with me? What's wrong with *her*, disappearing from my life for three decades and then thinking she can hold on to the vodka that I paid for with *my* money, like she's some kind of authority figure all of a sudden?

"Give it back!" I screamed, no longer caring that, earlier in the evening, I'd been trying to convince her I was doing better than fine. "If you don't give it back to me, I may go into withdrawal and die, and that's going to be *your* fault!"

Cindy disappeared with the bottle, and I spent the rest of the night plotting to get away from her so I could replace it with another.

When I woke up the next day, Cindy was already awake, showered, and ready to go. I didn't feel sorry. I felt humiliated. How could I have let this happen? I wondered, for what must have been the millionth time, why I didn't just stop after *just enough*—just enough to be calm, just enough to make the night bearable. Why, once I started a bottle, did I feel compelled to finish it? If the bottle had held two gallons of vodka, or three, would I have kept drinking it until I died?

Drinking was the thing I did to avoid thinking about such questions. And speaking of which: I had to go. (I had plans to see her again, anyway, in Meridian.) I apologized, showered quickly, and hurried to my rental car, where I plugged in my phone and typed "liquor store" into the mapping app.

Two hours later, guided down the slow back roads by GPS, I landed in Meridian, Morrissey blaring, windows down despite the 35-degree chill. As soon as I arrived, after hugging Mama Opal and Papa Jesse, I pulled the bottle of vodka from my suitcase and hid it in the big double closet, the one that had once held my train sets and Lincoln Logs. My parents hadn't told them much about my situation, and I'd seen no reason to fill in the gaps, so they didn't know about the trips to detox, or the hospital visits, or precisely why I'd lost my job. My family built firewalls around unpleasant information. What was I going to do, call my elderly grandparents and announce that I'd been fired for passing out in the bathroom, then add the punch line: "Twice"?

For the first day, I snuck to my room every half hour, gulping from the bottle, trying to ration out the precious drops. As always, the vodka ran out much sooner than I had planned. By the end of the second day, after my grandparents had gone to sleep, I crept out of my room and started scouring the house for alcohol. This was no small feat in a house of Southern Baptists who hadn't had a drop in fifty years, but I knew that they kept a stash of bottles gifted to them over the years in the cabinet to the left of the kitchen sink. In thirty years, just about the only thing that had changed in that kitchen was the appliances. Everything else—the ruffled curtain over the sink; the honey-oak cabinets; the drawer full of hand-quilted, casserole-stained potholders—was exactly as it was when I lived there as a kid. I grabbed the bottles and snuck back to my room to see what I'd scored. One bottle of cooking wine, half used. A bottle of white wine, opened long ago, almost full. A heavy, rose-colored glass decanter, filled with something murky. *Score.*

I stashed them in my suitcase, threw back the thin covers, and turned on the fan. When I woke up, it was well before dawn, and I could hear my grandmother moving quietly through the house. As silently as possible, I unzipped my suitcase and glugged down the foul contents of one of the bottles. Then another. By the time I had finished off all but one of the bottles, sleep felt possible. I closed the suitcase, climbed back under the covers, and sank into oblivion.

When I woke up later that morning, the bottles had disappeared, and I could hear Mama Opal and Papa Jesse talking in hushed tones in their room down the hall.

"I don't know how long that stuff has been in there!"

"Well, I don't know, but it's all gone now."

"I've locked up all the bottles in here—pretty sure that's all there was in the house. What do we do now?"

"I guess we need to call Paul and Jonee."

Oh shit.

Paul and Jonee—Dad and Mom—were arriving at the Meridian airport later that afternoon, my dad's four-seat Cessna loaded with brightly wrapped Christmas and Hanukkah gifts. They didn't know about my relapse, but they were about to find out. Unless I could somehow convince my grandparents that everything was fine.

"End-stage addiction," David Carr wrote, "is mostly about waiting for the police, or someone, to come and bury you in your shame." I was waiting for my parents to come and—what? Kick me out of the family? Force me to confess everything, then die of humiliation? Lock me up in an institution until I learned my lesson?

I leaped from the bed and strode into my grandparents' bedroom.

"Hey."

"How you feeling?"

"Fine, I guess." Defensive. Like if I pretended everything was fine—*just fine*—they wouldn't ask me any questions, and I could go to the liquor store like always, and all this unpleasantness would just go away. *If I could just get everyone off my back, just for one goddamned minute . . .*

"Do you want to have something to eat?"

"Um . . . I'm okay."

I went to the living room and sat down on the sagging sofa. When I was five, I'd jumped from this same couch onto a cylindrical stool turned on its side, hoping to run across the room with it under my feet like I'd seen in the Hanna-Barbera cartoons. Instead, I flew across the room and landed hard on my left arm, and I'm told I didn't stop screaming until we got to the hospital where Mama Opal worked. "It's bwoken! It's bwoken!" Mama Opal recalled me squealing, mimicking me, not unkindly, in a child's high-pitched voice. "And then the nurse said, 'Okay, can you move this finger?' And you said, 'Yes.' And then she said, 'Can you move your hand?' 'Yes.' 'Can you move your arm'? 'Yes.' 'Can you wave bye-bye to me and say bye-bye?' 'Bye-bye!'" The moral of the story, I think, is that I always had a theatrical streak. Or maybe that I was always a pain in the ass.

Papa Jesse sat down in his rocking chair and pulled it so close our knees almost touched. This was not in itself unusual—for as long as I'd known him, my grandfather had been nearly deaf, the result of his service in the engine room of a Navy ship in Korea, so he tended to be a close talker—but his next words were. "Erica, you know, I had a cousin who had your same problem, and we didn't know what to do with him. He ended up blowing his head off"—here he mimed the gun in the mouth, pulling the trigger, his head jerking back—"just like that." This was the first time I had ever heard this story, and in that moment, I knew exactly how his cousin had felt.

In treatment, you learn a lot about letting go of guilt and shame, and it's often phrased just like that: "Guiltandshame." But the difference between the two emotions is that guilt is directed outward, whereas shame is internal; it's the feeling not that "I did something bad," but "I *am* bad." Guilt is what leads newly sober people to call their exes and apologize for their past behavior. Shame is what causes grown men to put a gun to their temples and blow their brains out.

Papa Jesse was still talking.

He was saying, "Erica, if you let this kill you, I will cry every single day until the day I die."

I flashed back to the time when Papa Jesse wouldn't let me ride my bike outside our driveway, for fear I'd get hit by one of the few slow-moving cars that rolled infrequently down the barely two-lane road in front of our house. The times when he'd walked down the road as our car pulled away on its way back to Houston, looking forlorn and waving good-bye. He once told me he cried for a whole month after I moved away to Houston, and for once, Mama Opal didn't contradict him.

I knew what he was saying was true. And I knew I couldn't do that to him.

That's guilt.

"I'm not going to let this kill me," I told him. "I'm going to beat it. I promise."

Of all the promises I'd made to everyone I'd disappointed over the many years of my addiction, this was one I was going to keep.

But not just yet.

While my grandparents were in the living room, watching Fox and making arrangements to pick up my parents, I went into their bathroom, ostensibly to use the shower. The door to their walk-in closet, where I'd seen the bottles piled up earlier that morning, was locked, and I sat down queasily on the blue shag carpet, trying to figure out what to do. I thought back to the woman who led that meeting at Rez XII—the one whose insane impulse to drink hair spray made me laugh and think, *At least I'm not that bad*—and I wondered if my grandmother had any hair spray.

I opened the cabinet underneath the sink. My eyes skipped over the rubbing alcohol, then remembered it was poisonous—like, kill-you-dead-after-a-few-ounces poisonous—and moved along. Finally, I saw the quarter-full bottle of Listerine—the amber, old-school, mouthwash-flavored kind—in the back. *Don't drunks and high-school kids sometimes drink mouthwash when they can't get anything else? I think I remember reading that somewhere.* Good enough for gutter drunks, good enough for me. I chugged the foul, nasty-tasting liquid and replaced the empty bottle in the cupboard. *Ah. That's better.*

If I had harbored any hope that my grandparents hadn't told Mom and Dad what was going on, my first look at my mom as she climbed out of Dad's Cessna and onto the tarmac at the Meridian Regional Airport disabused me of that hope. I could tell she'd been crying, and when I went to embrace her, she hugged me back half-heartedly, like she was already letting me go.

"Why are you so upset?"

She paused. "Let's go inside."

My stomach churned as we walked toward the pilots' lounge. I felt like I was twelve again, sitting sullenly in the passenger seat of Mom's Plymouth while "Everybody Wants to Rule the World" played on KRBE. I looked back at Dad, who was transferring piles of cheerfully wrapped packages to the trunk of my grandmother's Honda. I sighed dramatically—still determined to spin this the best way I could—and followed her inside, where we sat down on two leather chairs, separated by a scraggly potted palm.

"I'm sor—"

"Just—don't."

"I'm going to get better, I swear. I know you don't believe me. I—"

"Erica, do you have any idea how much you've upset your grand-parents?"

"Yes, of course I do. Do you think I don't know that?"

"They had no idea that any of this was going on. The extent of it. And for you to just come in here and scare them like this—they're *old people*, Erica. They don't need a shock like this. I am so disap-pointed in you."

Like I needed her to tell me.

Days crawled past—the day before Christmas Eve, Christmas Eve, Christmas Day. No one let me out of their sight. "Taking a drive" was off the table. Finally, the day after Christmas, Cindy picked me up to take me to her mom's house in the woods just out-side Meridian. I asked if we could stop by the drugstore.

"What do you need?" she asked.

"Mouthwash."

Drinking mouthwash isn't the worst thing, I told myself, setting aside memories of the time I was affronted when Josh thought I'd been doing exactly that. *At least I'm not as bad as that woman who talked in a meeting about drinking hand sanitizer mixed with Diet Coke. At least I can prove to everyone that I can make it through the rest of this trip without drinking. At least I can go home in two days and this nightmare will be over.*

I made it through Christmas, fidgeting on the couch in my grandparents' overheated living room. I said good-bye to Cindy, avoiding the subject of New Orleans, building my own firewall against that ugly memory. I avoided Mom and Dad's suspicious stares and hardened myself against my grandparents' overbearing concern. *I just need to get back to Seattle*, I thought, *and things will go back to normal. I just need a few more weeks and then I'll really quit. I just need everyone to leave me alone.*

Back in Seattle, free from the heavy air and freighted conversations in Mississippi, I got back to drinking—less than I had during my trip, but more than enough for Josh to notice. "You haven't been yourself for a few days," he texted. I ignored him. For the first time, I canceled our traditional Hanukkah gift exchange, telling him I had relapsed. "Thank you for letting me know," he said, or some version of that. Our friendship, these days, was full of dead ends and blind corners— places we knew better than to go, because we knew what traps were waiting there. "Go to a meeting." And I did. I started showing my face at Cherry Hall again—sober, drunk, half-sober; properly dressed or in stained leggings and a sweatshirt, I went. I sat in the back, on the yellow upholstered bench unofficially reserved for newcomers who wanted to sneak out unnoticed, and wondered what all these sober alcoholics had that I didn't. *What quality did I lack?*

I started going back to outpatient treatment, too—occasionally sober, more often half-sloshed, sometimes badly enough for the treatment staff to notice. "We think it would be best for the other group members' recovery if you came back when you don't smell like alcohol," the counselor who pulled me out of group told me. I figured I must be the only asshole in history to show up at *treatment* drunk. But I did go back. I drank less, drank more again, got stronger breath mints.

New Year's Eve came and went like any other day—passed out at 9:00, up at 2:00, back to bed at 4:00 to sleep until 7:00, when I could head to the store and do it all over again. I faced 2015 with a dull determination to just get through until something changed. I didn't know what, exactly, but I'd know it when it happened.

What happened was that I ended up in the hospital again. An acquaintance had given me a temporary job in his office—nothing too heavy, just a little writing and comms work while I got back on my feet. It took me less than a week to blow it. Zonked on alcohol and Ativan—I had started taking an old prescription, hoping that by self-medicating I could wean myself off booze—I passed out at my desk, and came to as the EMS guys were lifting me to my feet and toward the stretcher. "No, no, there's no need for any of this," I told them groggily, but if you have any experience dealing with ambulance crews, you know that they don't take no from a semiconscious patient for an answer. Instead of leaving quietly the way they'd come, they strapped me to the gurney, hiked me into the rolling position, and pushed me (slowly, far too slowly) past a dozen gawkers, their eyes wide with curiosity at the unprecedented sight of a stretcher pushing a strange woman through their office.

By now, you know the drill as well as I did—hospital, overnight detox, then back to the grind. Another day in the glamorous life of a late-stage alcoholic. I didn't bother calling Josh to meet me; I didn't call anyone, because what was the point? "Hi, I relapsed again, just getting out of the hospital, wanted to let you know, bye"? No one needs to hear that for the seventh or four-hundredth time.

This time, though, something *was* different. Over the past few months, it was as if something physical had been breaking down inside me—some structural element that had been propping up the beams while everything else, from the façade to the foundation, crumbled. It had started to bend while I was sitting on the couch in Mississippi, listening to Papa Jesse as he told me he would cry every day until he died if I let alcoholism kill me, and it hadn't stopped bending since.

And then it snapped.

It was like the time, in ninth grade, when I finally figured out how chemical formulas worked—one minute, I was sitting across from my science teacher, nearly sobbing with frustration; and then the very next instant, I just *got* it. More than that, I got how that knowledge opened the door to understanding every chemical reaction in the universe. Is that what counts as a revelation? I knew what I had to do, and I did it. Isn't that how most so-called miracles work?

Thirty-three

What Works

So here's the formula, my foolproof formula, for getting sober after you've failed over and over again. Have a revelation—or, if you prefer, a mental breakdown. (I can't tell you how to do this, but trust me, when it happens, you'll know.) Don't tell anyone about it—who the hell would believe you anyway? Consider rehab. Reject the idea. You've learned everything they're going to teach you. Instead, call up a mental hospital and ask for a detox bed. As soon as you hear the voice on the other end of the line say, "We'll see you soon," call a cab. (Taking three buses across the city might make you lose your nerve.) Stroll down to the nearest convenience store and buy one last bottle of red wine, for the road. Drink half the bottle, then puke it up all over the floor. Mop the floor with bleach while you drink the rest, more slowly this time because you know this—*this*—is the last drink you will ever have. Run downstairs, forgetting to lock the door, and tell the cabbie the address of the mental hospital where you're going for detox, this one last time. Realize that your account has a negative balance, then guilt the cabbie into letting you pay the $98 fare with a $150 check, dated for two days in the future, when the latest severance check should hit your bank account. Step out into the damp February air. Hear the whoosh as the automatic doors close behind you. Say hello, without hesitation, to the counselor who recognizes you from the last time you were in detox here at Fairfax, just three months ago. Listen hard in counseling and get the number of a counselor who seems to actually believe you can do it this time, just in case you need it on the outside. Pay attention when they tell you that it's going to take work, that you'll have to be the one who does the work, that it's going to be hard and you can't do it alone. Stay five full days—longer than you have to; as long as they'll let you—until you believe in your bones that this time, you'll be the one in nine who actually makes it.

Breathe, it will seem, for the first time in years.

That's how I did it.

"So how did you do it?"

"One day at a time!"

That's the call-and-response you'll hear at AA meetings, when someone, usually an old-timer, is celebrating their recovery "birthday." And it's true: You do it, literally, one day at a time. But you also do it figuratively: By not thinking too much about a week from now or a year from now or twenty long, alcohol-free years down the line. Of all the clichés they teach you in AA, this is the most useful and universally applicable: Whatever your goal, whether it's losing forty pounds or not drinking for the next forty years, there's no way to tackle it all at once. If you look at recovery as "never drinking again for the rest of my life," it can feel like you're being asked to bail out the ocean with a teaspoon, but if you look at it as something you need to do for just twenty-four more hours, it feels more like setting aside a few dollars a week in a savings account: Before you know it, you've accumulated twenty thousand dollars, or five years clean.

But what do I know? Not a lot. I nearly tore my guts up and lost what was left of my mind before it finally dawned on me that I didn't want to die. Some people get sober and decide they're going to spend the rest of their lives going to AA meetings every day. Some never go to any support group or therapy at all. Some get new addictions—sugar, food, yoga, religion, men. Some decide they can't go to bars ever again.

I didn't gain a hundred pounds and I don't live at the local AA hall. I didn't depend on Josh to keep me accountable, or Kevin, though we stayed friends. I go to bars. What I don't do is wall myself off from other people. Drinking gave me an excuse to cut myself off from the world, to hole up on weekends and eat shitty pizza and pass out on the couch until it was dark, or maybe the next day, and go out for another bottle. When I stopped drinking, my first goal was to make up for lost time—to pick up with friends who'd written me off for dead, and find out what the hell they'd been up to for the last ten years. So I did that. Yeah, I went to meetings too—and therapy, and sometimes yoga. I don't think you have to do all those things, or any of them, to stay sober. It's just what worked for me.

Eight months after I quit drinking, I was at the Comet, a former dive bar refurbished for hipsters around the corner from *The Stranger* office, watching the first 2016 Democratic debate with Josh. We were cracking up about something on my computer—probably somebody making a joke about Bernie Sanders, who had a cultlike following in Seattle—when my phone buzzed. It was a message from Marianne, who was nominally still my AA sponsor. "I see you're really working on your step work," she said. "Don't call me again." Attached was a photo of me and Josh, taken from the sidewalk just outside. We looked happy. But all Marianne could see was an alcoholic sitting in a bar.

I didn't call her again.

Instead, I got a new sponsor—Dallana, a five-foot-two drill sergeant from Boston by way of Puerto Rico—and started doing what she told me (which, notably, did not include getting a new set of friends or avoiding places where alcohol was served). I also called the counselor who had helped me during my second stay at Fairfax, the only person there who had taken me seriously when I told her I was really ready to quit this time, and asked her if she knew of any female therapists who specialized in recovery. I didn't really know what to ask for—I just knew that I didn't want another Ken, someone who would tell me to just keep doing my best. I needed someone who knew how a person's brain was affected by addiction, how we shame and second-guess ourselves and convince ourselves that maybe there was nothing wrong with us in the first place, not because of some inborn character defect but because we have a disease that tells us we don't have a disease. She gave me the name of a woman across town named Timi, who specialized in something called "trauma-informed addiction counseling." I figured any trauma I had was self-inflicted, but I was intrigued by what the counselor said next. "She's been in recovery a long time. And she doesn't think AA is the only answer."

I knew I would keep going to AA, that AA would be part of whatever solution saved my life. But I also knew that I had a lot of shit to deal with that I couldn't talk about in meetings. (Meetings are about sharing your "experience, strength, and hope," and what I had was a lot of inexperience, weakness, and despair.) So I went to Timi, too. And I discovered that for some reason, unlike every other therapist I'd had in Seattle, I could tell Timi the truth. We talked about how I spent my whole life resenting Cindy for leaving when I was too young to get to know her; how certain I was that no one would ever forgive me; my feeling that because I'd had a lot of good luck in life, I had no right to complain about how anyone else had fallen short. I couldn't tell people in meetings that I didn't think I deserved to survive when so many others hadn't. But I could tell Timi, and she helped me work through it.

I showed up in therapy, and back in AA, with the idea that I needed to fix everything, right away, this minute, *now*. Get a job, get out of debt, get my friends back, get my parents to trust me again, get over even the *idea* of drinking, starting with the cravings that still asserted themselves when I least expected. Imagine that you've been in a coma for ten years, and you wake up, and there are your friends and family, maybe your husband or girlfriend or partner, and they've gone on living for the past ten years while you've been in suspended animation. All you want to do is catch up, so that things can be normal again, the way they were. But nothing's normal, not from your perspective—the technology is all different, and your partner remarried, and your parents are suddenly so much older, or dead. The career path you chose for yourself in college may not *exist* anymore, or may not be open to old drunks who have burned through every chance. All you want is to have those ten years back, but that's the one thing that's impossible. The years are gone. All you can do is start living now—relearning how to exist in a world that may feel sharp edged and unrecognizable. But how can you even figure out where to start?

I started with gratitude lists—literally writing down everything for which I was grateful every single day, like I had with Marianne but for real this time, and for myself. A few themes emerged. The first is that I was grateful, sublimely grateful, not to wake up every morning with a hangover. The old routine—running to the bathroom, vomiting, dabbing the cold sweat from my forehead, putting on makeup with shaky hands—was gone. The second was relief that I didn't have to start lying the moment I got out of bed anymore. Drinking, especially drinking when you're not "supposed" to, casts a pall of uneasiness over every encounter—Did I talk too much? Too fast? Are my eyes bloodshot? Am I walking straight? *Can everybody tell?* When you stop drinking, the secret burden of holding it together is lifted.

But the biggest theme that emerges from these early lists is how grateful I was for the chance to see the world every day with new eyes. I don't mean to say that I was awed by every blade of grass. I mean that all the old, familiar places—the Safeway where I used to buy wine every morning, the community garden where I'd vomited in the dirt, the back seat of the bus where I would sneak sips when I thought no one was looking—looked almost like alien landscapes, places I'd need to learn how to navigate without a bag of rocks on my back. How do you check out in a grocery store if you aren't trying to buy your wine as quickly as possible and leave before you run into anyone you know? Where do you sit on the bus if you're not trying to sneak sips from a bottle in your backpack, and how many layers do you wear in the winter when you don't have to worry about sweating through your clothes? How assertive can you be with the landlord when he refuses to fix the dishwasher, knowing that he's disliked you, with some justification, for most of the six and a half years you've lived in the place, but that you're also well within your right to complain? How mad are you allowed to get at your best friend when he accuses you—incorrectly, for maybe the first time ever—of seeming "off," because you're acting a bit too giddy? A normal amount? Just a little? Not at all?

No one told me, when I first got sober, that I would need a whole new map to navigate the world, my city, my neighborhood, even my apartment. AA, treatment, books on staying sober—they all tell you how to avoid and manage "triggers," but they don't tell you that you'll need to learn a whole new geography. Unemployed, with nothing but hours stretching out before me, I walked through a city littered with secret landmarks and tried to build new memories. On my way to the library, to fill out job applications and work on the blog I started, and abandoned, before I stopped drinking. The apartment where I spent countless hours passed out and throwing up and forgetting food on the stove and drunk-dialing my friends and drinking and drinking and drinking. The convenience store where I bought minis when I couldn't make it to the Safeway, sometimes leaving Kevin back at my apartment while I "went out for the mail." City Hall, where I sweated and bumbled my way through interviews, drunk or hung-over or both. Alleys I'd ducked into to drink from a bottle in broad daylight or vomit behind Dumpsters. Everything had to be made new, by experiencing it with sober eyes.

After a month or so, I decided it was time to start looking for a job—and, as it turned out, it took only a few weeks. I realize, oh, do I realize, that this is not the circumstance in which most alcoholics who throw away their careers find themselves. But this is how it actually happened: I put out the call, and right away I was inundated by calls and texts and emails from politically connected women offering to help me out. I started another consulting gig, with a friend of a friend who needed some help researching a local zoning issue. I started picking up a little bit of campaign writing work. And then a local consultant friend told me about a job I was perfect for— running the communications shop at the state chapter of NARAL, the pro-choice advocacy group—and promised to put in a word with the executive director, who happened to be her very close friend. I'd like to pretend that everything in the world happens on merit alone, but we all know that's not true. Every workplace I've ever been in had a group of managers (men, usually) who rose through the ranks largely because of who they knew. I was no different, except that my helpers were women. Anyway, why am I apologizing? In April 2015 I got a promotion from "unemployed alcoholic" to "sober person with a full-time job." It felt like a miracle.

I moved into a new apartment. If there's one truly ridiculous thing I believe in without reservation, it's bad vibes, and the place where I had made some of my worst memories was full of them. AA people call this "doing a geographical"—trying to solve your problems with a new environment—but I didn't go far, just a few miles up the street, to an apartment in an old Victorian house where the floors slanted and the walls were crooked and the shelves in the freezer were made of wood. The place was off-kilter and a bit precarious, much like me. It was perfect.

I still had a lot of work to do. One of the first things Dallana made me do, besides calling her every single day, was to carry a notebook with me and make a note of every time I encountered alcohol in the wild—not the thing itself, necessarily, but objects or people or encounters that made me think about it. This was my first step, a real one this time—realizing, and spelling out, the ways in which I was powerless over alcohol in the most literal possible sense. It turns out the entire world is an advertising platform for this amazing activity called getting drunk. (Or, as I used to joke to Josh, pushing a vodka soda or a whiskey across the table after a rough day at work: "Here, try this. It's a magical drink made of alcohol!")

My notebook—a black-and-white paisley Vera Bradley number, given to me by my birth grandmother, Charlene, when I first met her and set aside on a shelf ever since—quickly filled with examples: "An ex texted me this weekend from a party, obviously drunk, wanting to hook up." "Was looking at an apartment and the rental agent showed me the terrace, which he described as 'a great place to have a glass of wine.'" "A recipe called for a half cup of white wine." (Imagine, if you will, the impossible alchemy required for a sober alcoholic to conjure up a half cup of wine.)

Then there was my internal landscape, with its unceasing monologue: "No one sat next to me at the show and I figured it was probably because everyone there had seen me drunk." "My office is full of booze donations for the auction and I think everyone worries I'll steal something." "Karaoke last night—sang the first song and made a joke about being sober, which I worried made people uncomfortable." You can, as a newly sober person, decide to believe that your inner critic is simply wrong—of course no one's looking at you weird; of course no one thinks you'll guzzle the uncorked bottle in the fridge the second everyone's backs are turned—or you can just decide it doesn't matter. The truth is, people *do* treat you differently when they know you used to drink and don't anymore. They try too hard in one direction or another—either self-consciously ordering water or nonalcoholic beer (something no one has ever done casually, ever) or taking pains to tell you about their cousin or high-school friend or work acquaintance who had their own struggle with addiction, as if we do that with any other disease. It's normal, I suppose, for people to treat a newly sober alcoholic, especially one they've seen drunk a dozen or a thousand times, with some trepidation, but all I wanted in those first months of sobriety was for my friends, family members, guys I was dating who had never seen me drink a drop, to treat me like a normal person.

But I'm not normal. I have this thing hanging over my head—not a guillotine, exactly, but a lead weight that could drop at any moment and render me as useless, worse than useless, as I was four years ago, when the friends who still thought of me often worried (they told me later) that I wouldn't live through the year.

Another thing you learn when you stop drinking is that not everybody drinks all the time, and it's not just because they had to stop like you did. Alcoholics, especially those of us in professions (journalism, politics, law, medicine, maybe all of them) where heavy drinking is the norm, tend to surround ourselves with other drinkers and assume that just because everyone in the bar is drinking, that must mean that everybody drinks.

For years, I didn't date a single person who didn't like to get shit-faced, at least on occasion—not one. Nondrinkers (not that I knew any) struck me as insufferable bores, the kind of people who get up at five in the morning to go to the gym and come home twelve hours later to make poached salmon and steamed broccoli for their husband and two kids. Turns out I was wrong. Nondrinkers are also people like me, the kind who stay up until two in the morning and sleep until nine and still hang out in bars because it's where our people are. I didn't think this at first, but I've met enough of them now that I'm forced to acknowledge I'm not as unique as I thought.

After I did my first step, I decided to keep on going. (Whether you're doing the 12 steps or not, most recovery programs start with recognizing that you have a problem that you haven't been able to solve on your own, proceed through actions to help you address the problem, and conclude with a program for maintaining your recovery, however that term is defined.) The fourth step involved writing down every single person or institution I resented, from the QFC that banned me for a year after I got caught shoplifting to "James, the asshole who fired me," then write down what I had contributed to that conflict.

This is the step where a lot of people say "I'm out" and tell AA to fuck off forever. I don't blame people who don't or can't dredge up every horrible memory from their past. People have different experiences of trauma, and confronting everything at once isn't always healing; there's a good chance it will only induce more shame. But for many people (myself included), there's another element at play: Resentment serves a valuable, even protective, purpose. When I was drinking my guts rotten, I didn't want to think about the damage I was doing to other people with my behavior.

People always say drinking helps you ignore the consequences of your behavior, and that is absolutely true. That may be alcoholism's number one selling point. The problem is that when you quit, it's not like anyone throws you a fucking parade. The best you can hope for is that they'll forgive you eventually. But for a while, you really do just have to do the work and wait. At sixty days sober, I was like a burn victim walking around in brand-new skin—a falling leaf, or a suspicious glance from Josh, could have crushed me. Six months in, facing some of that stuff felt . . . well, not good, exactly, but like pouring peroxide onto a wound. It hurts, you marvel at the bubbles, you bandage it up and wait for it to heal.

It took a full day to read all my lists out loud and discuss them with Dallana (step 5) and an evening to carry the inch-thick pile of papers to the beach, where she planned to have me burn them (step 6). We drove in a blinding late-fall downpour to Alki Beach in West Seattle—a sandy stretch of shore that, on an ordinary night, looks out across Elliott Bay at the postcard skyline of Seattle. Tonight, though, the view was obscured by driving rain, and as we staggered out onto the wet sand, the raindrops battered the hood of my black L.L.Bean windbreaker like a jackhammer. We scanned the long expanse of the beach, searching for anything that looked like shelter. "There!" I shouted. "Look! Is that a bonfire?" Improbably, it was—a mile, it seemed, down the barren beach, in the middle of a deluge.

We ran back to the broad sidewalk that runs along the beach and started hurrying toward the flicker, and by the time we got there, we were soaked to our socks. I hung back, a little embarrassed. "Hey, excuse me, do you mind if my friend and I use your bonfire for just a second? We need to burn something," Dallana said, addressing a group of people gathered around a cooler under a rickety awning. It took a minute to get their attention. "Oh my god, yes, totally!" the lone woman in the bunch finally exclaimed, staggering our way. "Would you like a beer?" "No thanks, we're good, we just need to borrow your fire," Dallana responded. "We were surprised to see someone out here with a bonfire on a night like this!" I added.

"Oh, yeah, me and these guys, we do this every single Wednesday, no matter what!" the woman slurred, beer sloshing over the rim of her Solo cup. Her companions, all guys, nodded, looking bored. "Come sit down on my lap, Stephanie," one of them cajoled. Stephanie grabbed another beer and flopped down next to him. "You guys should join us!" she said. "Thanks, maybe we will," Dallana replied. We threw the papers in the bonfire, where they turned into ash almost instantly.

Thirty-four

Clearing the
Wreckage

The steps are not a requirement for getting sober. But going through the steps was important for me—if I was going to try AA, which seemed like a pretty good idea since nothing else had worked, I had to try it with my whole heart. So I embraced the stuff that made intuitive sense to me—cataloguing the "wreckage of my past," as the Big Book puts it, and letting it go—and when something annoyed me or felt ridiculous, I just rolled with it. I knew there was no magic to any of this, but I did it because it couldn't possibly hurt. Left to my own devices, I would be passed out on top of a bottle somewhere, or in another hospital emergency room with an IV taped to my arm. *Fuck it*, I thought. *I'll memorize another goddamn prayer if it keeps me from that.*

I don't believe in the power of prayer to change anything material in your life. I don't even know if I believe in God—certainly not a God so small and petty as to care whether I, Erica C. Barnett of

Seattle, get the job I want or get sober or continue to exist. What I eventually came to believe is that there is a power in the universe beyond my understanding, and that when my own life becomes too large for me, I feel better if I give some of those things up to whatever's out there. I just say, "Here you go. I can't take these. You hang on to them for a while." Or I focus on someone else, especially when I don't want to. I find that praying for people—something as simple as, "I'm sending good energy out into the world for this person"—makes my own life easier to bear. Usually, by the time I've spent a few minutes thinking about other people and letting go of my problems, I find that I'm ready to face them. I don't know why it works. It just does.

If you think AA made me get religion or turn all pious, let me disabuse you: AA, at least at the meetings I go to in this godless corner of the country, is about the least pious place I've ever been, and talk of Jesus (or any specific religion) is strictly discouraged. When I talk about prayer, I really do mean: Talk to whatever you believe in, even if it's your friends who've supported you or the mystery of the universe or the power of science to solve all the remaining mysteries. Here's my favorite, which Dallana taught me when I told her how angry I still was at James: *Hey, God. You know that motherfucker? I'm praying for him.* And goddamned if it didn't make me feel better—just praying for that fucker, whoever he or she happened to be. I may not believe in a God who cares about every grain of sand and blade of grass, but I do believe that it's free will that gives us the ability to let something bear down on us our whole lives or let it go. *Hey, God? That fucker? Praying for him.* Willpower alone won't get anyone sober, but it can keep you from getting maudlin about all the work you have cut out for you once you are. "Think of how much work you did every day to stay drunk all the time, and put just as much effort into doing this work," Dallana told me, and, to the best of my ability, I did.

And then I started making amends. This, if you're following along in your books, is the dreaded ninth step, the one they tell you not to worry about until you get to it, at which point you will worry about it a *lot*. Maybe you've been the bewildered recipient of a call from someone you haven't heard from in years, nervously asking you to meet for coffee because they have something they need to tell you in person. "No, I know, but it's really important." "Okay, what is it?" "Well . . . I'll tell you when we meet."

To get started, Dallana had me divide my list of everyone and everything I resented into three columns: The people to whom I would definitely make amends; the people to whom I might make amends; and the people to whom I would definitely never make amends. When I was finished, there were more than fifty names. "Okay. You're gonna make amends to all of these people." At this, I barked a laugh. Make amends to my birth mom, whom I was ready to never see again if it meant avoiding the shame of acknowledging what had happened between us over the holidays? "But not yet. For now, we're going to start with this list." Phew. At least I wouldn't have to start with "randos from Linda's," the bar where I used to pick up guys at 2:00 A.M.; that amend was in the future, in the "maybe" pile. She handed me the page on which I'd written the "easy" ones—Sandeep, who'd loaned me $6,300 to pay off a debt collector; my parents; my friends Josh and Lisa and Stephanie and my new friend, Renee, who'd shown up at my apartment with soup shortly before I went back to Fairfax—and told me to close my eyes and put my finger on the page.

"Really? I have to start with John?"

"Good a place as any."

John was a tough one. For one thing, I was still pissed at him. And rightly so! *That fucker*—I thought to myself—*never loved me, never had any intention of leaving his wife, manipulated me into abandoning relationships that had real potential.* . . . And then I stopped. Making amends is supposed to be about the other person, not my ego, right? What better place to start, then, than with someone who would be a real challenge? I wrote out what I was going to say in the form of a letter. My first draft began:

> Dear John,
>
> I think you're pretty familiar with how these things work, but if you aren't, here's the deal: Leaving aside any wrongs I think you did to me, I'm telling you what I feel I need to own up to on my part from the time before, during, and after we were seeing each other, before and after everything fell apart.
>
> First, I think I need to address the fact that I was drinking during a significant portion of the time we were seeing each other, after the point at which I said I had stopped. This probably won't surprise you, but I had a lot of relapses in the years after 2008, when I first tried to quit drinking, and I deceived you by not telling you what was going on. There were times when I wasn't really present for you like I should have been, both when we were together and when we were apart and arguing or doing things to make each other jealous or having innocuous conversations in which I wasn't, if I'm honest, 100% there.

It went on like that for several pages.

I showed the letter to Dallana and she just laughed and laughed. "This is all about you! You need to make it about him. I want you to rewrite this and take out everything that's about what he did to you, and just talk about what you did, and say you want to make amends, and end by asking him how you can make things right."

So I did. I apologized for being drunk all the time, and for flaunting the fact that I was having sex with other people, and for a dozen more things I had done, unintentionally and on purpose, to make him miserable. And I got through it. Sitting stiffly across from him at my kitchen table in the new apartment—paper shaking, rushing through it, barely able to look him in the eye—I read the letter, asked him what I could do to make it right, and burst into tears. I can't tell you I remember what he said—probably something about not lying to him in the future, and just staying sober. "Well, I should go," he probably said, and I probably said, "Okay," and he probably opened the door, his mop of hair, now turning silvery, grazing the frame as he turned toward the stairs. What did I want in that moment? An acknowledgment? An apology? For him to say, "I really did love you" in a way that seemed either totally convincing or satisfyingly fake? Whatever it was, I didn't get it. Instead, I was left with a feeling that I had done the hardest possible thing, and that I'd have to do it another twenty, forty, fifty times before this voice— the one that told me I had done things that were simply unforgivable— would quiet down.

But I was wrong.

It only took another three weeks before I started to understand why making amends to people was worth it. (I get why apologizing is important—I'm not a monster—but the systematic process of making things right was just a completely new concept for someone who once started writing a life-skills book called *Half-Assing It*. You can probably guess what happened to that one.) Operating from the same instinct that used to get me out of bed at six to hit the gym before work, I had decided to get the hardest calls out of the way first. That meant my dad was next—Dad with whom I never shared a personal detail, Dad to whom I had once blurted drunkenly, "It just seems like you don't even love me!" Dad who is the most rational, least squidgy person I know.

"Hi, Dad?"

"Hang on, let me put in my Bluetooth. . . . I'm just out here at this hotel we're working on, and you would think that someone would have communicated to them that they needed to move everybody out of here before we came in to refinish all the bathrooms, but there are people just *living* here, and we're not gonna be the ones to give them the eviction notice—"

"Dad!"

"Yup?"

"I'm calling for a kind of serious reason. Do you have a minute to talk?" (Thinking: *I bet he thinks I'm calling to ask for money. Again.*)

"Sure, lemme just go in this other room where I can talk. . . . What's up?"

"So, I want to make amends to you for the way I've treated you over the years, including when I was drinking but also before that, when I just wasn't grateful enough to you for all you did."

"Okay."

We've all been there, right? That moment when you start confessing to something and you realize you can't turn back—the second after you say, "We need to talk," or "I have to tell you something," and the other person sits there waiting in anticipation, not knowing if the next words out of your mouth will be "I'm cheating on you" or "We have to break up" or "I'm pregnant"? I don't know what my dad expected me to say in that moment, but I know what I did say, because I had it written down in front of me, and I tried to make it sound natural as I read it to him over the lousy cell-phone connection. I told him I was sorry for all the times I had showed up drunk and lied about it, or forced him to reason with me on the phone when I was hysterical, or pretended everything was okay except when I needed something from him. I told him I was sorry that I hadn't ever tried to have much more than a superficial relationship with him. I told him . . . well, it just kind of all poured out, four or five handwritten pages of everything I was really far too scared to say to him. I couldn't possibly do it. So I just kept talking until the words were gone. "I'm sorry for being distant from you over the years, and for failing to do my part to let you know that I love you and that I care about what's going on in your life, too," I read. "I'm really grateful to you for teaching me to be independent and self-sufficient, and I'm sorry I haven't expressed that to you more often." I ended by telling him I was sorry that I had failed to accept him for who he is and for trying to force him to be someone he wasn't—someone more like me, every nerve ending right there on the surface. Then I was quiet for a second. "So, I guess the last thing is, um, what can I do to make things right?"

A long pause. Was he . . . sniffling?

"Well, dang it, Erica, you didn't tell me you were going to make me cry."

I was crying, too. "Ha," I sniffled. "Gotcha."

"I guess what I want is . . . well, could you maybe call me more often? Just to let me know how you're doing and what's going on with you?"

I don't know what I had expected—maybe something more along the lines of, "Pay back the thousand dollars you owe us and don't call again until you do"—but it took a minute to process what he was asking for. That's it? Call him more? Don't I owe him . . . like . . . a lot more than that?

"Of course."

"I love you, too, you know."

Not all of them went like that. Mom was gracious but a little stiff—understandable, given the fact that she'd been the target of so much of my emotional vomit for so many years—and she thought it was weird that I thought she might feel insulted or displaced when I got back in touch with Cindy. (Turns out the massive cyclone of guilt I had whipped up about "cheating" on her by talking to my birth mom was all in my mind.) James, my old boss, told me he'd think about tossing me some freelance work, asked me for advice about someone in his life who was struggling with addiction, and then never contacted me again. My friend Renee, who is the kind of person who sends Christmas cards to acquaintances from thirty years ago and would offer near strangers her whole apartment if they happen to be passing through London, where she used to live, wanted to know what *she* could do for *me*. Nick, to whom I made an unplanned amend when I spotted him in the beer line at a conference we were both attending, was warm but awkward, understandably so.

And I still have a long way to go. Lots of friends are still on my "definitely" list, but I've been putting it off, probably because things are so much better between us now. I haven't totally paid back the

QFC, but I'm getting close. Tristan and Tiffany, two people I still haven't seen my way to forgiving, remain on my "never" list, but I'll get to them.

But all of them ended up being worth it, not because I can say, sanctimoniously, "I did it," but because I really did start letting go of the guilt.

Not all of it, though.

Thirty-five

Just What Is

In a dream, I'm heading to an important conference in another city, where I have to give a presentation that will make or break the organization I'm working for. I start drinking on the plane—a little red wine, something sophisticated, just to calm my nerves. The next thing I know, it's two days later and I'm coming out of a blackout on a hotel bed, an empty bottle of vodka on the night table beside me. I've blown the presentation, lost my job, and have no idea how I'm going to get back home. I'm out of booze and there's nothing in my bank account. Then it hits me: The hotel room is paid for. I clutch the sides of the bed and make my way toward the minibar.

Another dream: Josh has agreed, reluctantly, to meet me for coffee, but I decide to start drinking again a couple of hours before our date. By the time I show up, I'm a wreck—my shirt's all twisted around my body, I can't figure out how to pay for my scone, and Josh glowers at me from a table across the room while the cashier helps me count out 98 cents in pennies.

Drinking dreams are the price I pay for the years that I drank and prayed that no one around me noticed. These half memories, half nightmares, which still come three or four nights a week, are a form of penance that force me to relive my worst moments in slow motion, only underwater and upside down. The guilt I feel in those sheet-twisting hours stays with me during the day, and I have to open and close my eyes hard sometimes, to convince myself I didn't relapse after all, and that no one is mad at me today, at least not for drinking, that everything's okay. This feeling sometimes lasts throughout the morning, and I have to pinch myself. *It was only a dream. It wasn't real. Your sobriety is.*

When I was drinking, I didn't dream. Sleep wasn't sleep—it was obliteration. Pass out, wake up, drink more, pass out again. Now, it's like my subconscious is speeding through a ten-year backlog, and despite all the treatment and therapy and AA meetings I've been through in the last five years, I still feel like this nightly reliving is something I must deserve.

Addicts have a hard time being happy with just what is. We're always chasing what's just around the corner—the next drink, the next hookup, the next get-rich-quick, big-money scheme. The notion that someone can be content with what's right in front of them— like, say, a tumbler of whiskey they've been nursing all night—strikes us as almost literally insane. It took me nearly three years—years spent frantically making amends, digging out of debt, getting a job and then starting a website and then working impossible hours to prove to everyone that I was back—to realize that not everyone has this force pushing them from behind. Not everyone who binge-watches Netflix shows is an addict, but I'm willing to bet—based on no scientific evidence, just my own observation—that people who can turn off the TV on a cliffhanger are less likely to feel the need to drink an entire bottle of whiskey. I'll probably never enjoy that lack of turmoil I imagine normal people feel when they walk away from a half-empty glass, or turn off the TV because it's their bedtime, but I'm learning that there's more than one way to be. I can even fake it when I need to.

The weirdest thing about not drinking, when drinking has been your primary occupation for nearly a decade, is how many things feel like you're doing them for the first time. First kiss. First job interview. First time around people who are smoking pot. First move into a new apartment. First furniture not purchased on a drunken impulse or dragged in from the street. First time quitting a job. First sex. First unrequited crush. First boyfriend who has never seen you with a drink in your hand. First time actually paying off a debt, then another, then another, then all of it. First trip through airport security. First international flight. First time being stopped by security in another country because of a mysterious shape in the lining of your suitcase, which you cut out to find an ancient Jack Daniel's bottle. First time finding that sort of thing remotely funny.

There are lots of things you give up when you stop drinking, too. When my phone flashes with a text at six in the morning, I don't have to worry that I said something stupid the night before, or that it's Josh asking if I'm going to be able to make it in to work today. When I get a letter in the mail from my health insurance company, I don't throw it in the trash because I know it's just another bill I can't pay. When I fuck something up, I don't think, "There goes my last chance," or "They know I've been drinking," or "I guess I need to blow my brains out." I think, "Whoops," or maybe, "I'll have to make up for that and make sure it doesn't happen again." Sobriety makes you think boring shit like that. It also makes you realize that if you got through all *that*, you can get through anything.

I see this all the time. Someone I know who had been sober about three years told a room full of women that she still had one "reservation"—one reason to drink that she held in reserve. "If my mom dies," she said, "I don't know what I'll do." Two years later, she was in a meeting when she got the call. I saw her the following week. She didn't drink. I'll confess I haven't been through anything like that yet. But I have been cheated on, lied to, and rejected. I've lost work because of my reputation as an unreliable lush, and I've been told to come back in a couple of years, once I've proved myself a little more. I've been the target of a couple of intense online harassment campaigns, and had my share of scary run-ins with people who think they have the right to grab me, or back me into corners, or scream in my face because they disagree with my opinions. I've been excluded from events because nondrinkers make a surprising number of people uncomfortable, and I've lost touch with people I thought were friends. None of that stuff is easy, drunk or sober. The difference when you're sober is that you actually deal with it, instead of adopting a false bravado and figuring out who else to blame.

If you want to, you can also start looking for things to be grateful for—not as difficult as you might imagine, especially if you spent your last few years passing out at bus stops and waking up in emergency rooms. Depending on your baseline, just waking up in your own bed with dry sheets might be a triumph. Or check this out: If I hadn't lost my job, I probably wouldn't have stopped drinking when I did. (I'm not talking about rock bottom. I'm talking about my external motivation not to go to treatment: How could the magazine possibly function without me, the least functional person who had ever darkened their doorstep?) If I hadn't had a few months of unemployment to force me to come up with some structure for my days (including those early, blind-mouse days, when I would write "brush teeth, shower, go to noon meeting" in a notebook and cross them out), I wouldn't have had time to shake my brain cells back into their places and figure out what I wanted to do next. If I hadn't gotten a job that took up only thirty hours or so a week, I wouldn't have been able to start my blog. If I hadn't gotten two years sober, I wouldn't have had the guts to quit that job and strike out on my own. Best-case scenario, I would have gone back to PubliCola, groveled at James's feet for a couple of years, then quit after realizing he'd never trust me, no matter what I did. Do I know that any of those things would have happened? No, but finding serendipity in events you can't control is a choice. Sometimes that means cutting your losses and moving on, and sometimes it means jumping off a ledge even when you don't know what's down there.

My life today doesn't have the kind of drama I once craved. I have a boyfriend who isn't a musician or married or an alcoholic. He isn't unstable or erratic, and he doesn't manipulate me into feeling like I can't live without him, or vice versa. I work at home, on my own terms, and have more freedom than I ever imagined would be possible when I was struggling to show up at my office job and praying no one would notice I was drunk. I travel constantly, trying to make up for all the time when I thought travel was for people who had their shit together. I don't worry unreasonably about going broke, or ending up homeless, or any of the things that I used to avoid thinking about by drinking. I pay my bills, don't have debt, and try to avoid extravagant purchases. I show up for friends now and try to make up for all the years when I didn't. It sounds like my life is boring, but it really isn't. What was boring was the years I spent watching my world get smaller and smaller, until I barely existed.

Recently, I had an opportunity to revisit the old Recovery Centers of King County building where I went to detox back in 2014—the detox center of last resort, where the orderlies barked instructions like prison wardens and my roommate taught me to make a pillow out of towels. The occasion was the grand opening of a new detox and treatment center in the same building, and I was there, this time, as press. I made it all the way inside and to my chair before I realized I had been there before. Everything looked different—everything, that is, except the tiny, fenced-in yard where the patients had been allowed to go once an hour to smoke. Looking out at the courtyard from a room that had once been the center's cafeteria, but was now swarming with elected officials, medical professionals, and other members of the press, I had a sense memory so strong it took my breath away, of the first time I stood out in that courtyard and tried to fill my lungs with oxygen through all the smoke. A young woman with elaborate eye makeup was talking about her plans to go back home to her drug-dealer boyfriend as soon as she got out. A guy was complaining about getting robbed the night before. I was standing on the outside of the circle of smokers, hoping someone would come over and talk to me.

I never felt like I fit in at RCKC, with all the homeless people and junkies and kids with ankle bracelets who were only there because they had to be, but of course I did. I knew it then, when I lined up for vitals check at the single metal chair by the entrance, where the nurse yelled at me for leaning into the men's quarters to grab a pillow, and I knew it now, looking down the once damp, dripping hallway at a set of brightly lit new rooms with wood-grained vinyl floors, all ready for the first crop of addicts and drunks to stagger to their metal beds with their thin plastic mattresses. During a quiet moment on the press tour, I snuck into one of the empty detox rooms—I knew, as the rest of the press didn't, that there were no locks on the doors—and poked my head into the bathroom. I wanted to see if they still had the shitty, unbreakable metal mirrors. The mirrors had gotten an upgrade—no more distortion—but they were still unbreakable, and I looked at my reflection and gave myself a thumbs-up. It isn't often that you get to visit a dreadful moment in your past, walk right on the site of events you never want to live through again, and see how everything has changed, and how much you've changed. I walked back to the old nurses' station, where the new treatment director was taking questions. I raised my hand.

"What did this place used to be like?"

After Rock Bottom

Why me?

That's the question most alcoholics ask themselves, once they've gotten past denial and acknowledge to themselves that they don't process booze like other people.

Prior to the mid-twentieth century, when the American Medical Association first defined alcoholism as a disease, doctors and theorists of all stripes offered a wide array of explanations for why some people became alcoholics (or dipsomaniacs, a fun nineteenth-century word that would also be a great name for a punk band) and others didn't. Doctors seeking a medical explanation believed that alcohol poisoned human cells in a way that produced dependence. Others, including religious leaders, believed that alcoholism was caused by a genetic moral deficiency that could only be addressed through eugenics—that is, denying treatment to alcoholics as a way of weeding them more quickly from the gene pool. And proponents of psychological theories, like Sigmund Freud, believed that alcoholism could be blamed on bad mothers; one Freud follower, Ernst Simmel, suggested that drug use was "an effort to resolve castration anxiety," by symbolically poisoning the source of that anxiety, the alcoholic's mom.

Alcoholics Anonymous came on the scene in 1939 as a progressive alternative to quack remedies and loopy Freudian theories. It was written primarily by Bill Wilson, a self-sabotaging stock speculator who was hospitalized four times for alcoholism before stumbling on the idea that peer support could help chronic alcoholics recover. (Later still, he became an advocate for LSD as a treatment for addiction, an idea that is gaining mainstream acceptance today.) Beginning with a letter from the doctor who had met Wilson at Towns Hospital in New York City and judged him untreatable, Dr. William Silkworth, the book establishes that alcoholism is a disease that is chronic, progressive, and fatal: chronic, because no "real alcoholic" can ever go back to being a normal drinker; progressive, because it only gets "worse, never better," even during periods of abstinence; and fatal, because untreated, it will lead to an untimely death.

Modern definitions of alcoholism are not all that different from the one AA came up with in 1939. The National Institute on Drug Abuse describes addiction succinctly as "a chronic, relapsing brain disease that is characterized by compulsive [substance] seeking and use, despite harmful consequences." The first part is key: Alcoholism causes physical changes to the brain's structure and how it works— not only reducing the amount of mood-balancing chemicals the brain naturally produces (substances like dopamine and serotonin, which help prevent mood swings and provide mental energy and stress relief), but also changing the structure of the brain's reward system so that those chemicals, known as neurotransmitters, no longer reach their target receptors, making it harder and harder for a person to feel pleasure without the addictive substance—and, eventually, making it extraordinarily painful, psychologically as well as physically, to function without it.

Under the Influence, a primary text in the 12-step world, maintains that alcoholism is, "in the main, hereditary," and that genetic factors are "a primary determiner of who becomes alcoholic." The 1981 book, which was based on research its author, James Milam, self-published in 1970, goes on to argue that alcoholism is caused by an enzyme imbalance in the livers of people with a genetic predisposition to alcoholism. Consider it a hearty grain of salt that *Under the Influence* also argues that racial susceptibility to alcoholism is based on how long a culture has been exposed to alcohol, a theory that has been widely discredited.

Today, the National Institute on Alcohol Abuse and Alcoholism estimates that genetic predisposition accounts for between 40 and 60 percent of the risk of alcoholism; the rest is the result of environmental factors, such as the age a person starts drinking, family dynamics and trauma, cultural norms, exposure to stress, and access to social and community support. "Age of first use," according to a 2012 study by the National Center on Addiction and Substance Abuse at Columbia University, is "particularly predictive" of who becomes an alcoholic; 96.5 percent of people who develop alcohol use disorders started drinking before they were twenty-one, an age when the brain is still developing and more susceptible to addictive substances. Drinking at a young age can create a kind of positive feedback loop by slowing the development of the prefrontal cortex— the impulse-controlling, decision-making part of the brain. Compounding this problem, brain scans suggest that many alcoholics and addicts may have smaller prefrontal cortices to begin with, which translates to sensation-seeking behavior and problems with impulse control.

The association between trauma in childhood and later addiction has also been well documented. If you experienced physical or mental abuse as a child, you're more likely to develop a substance-use disorder such as alcoholism; you're also more likely to develop a drinking problem if you were uprooted a lot as a kid, making it hard to form lasting friendships and connections to a community. Gabor Maté, the Canadian physician and addiction expert, believes that all addiction is caused by childhood trauma, and while this view is pretty controversial in the addiction and recovery field (critics call it reductive and fatalistic), a major study of seventeen thousand middle-class Americans (the Adverse Childhood Experience, or ACE, study) concluded that addiction is an adaptation to childhood traumatic experiences, and that "unrecognized adverse childhood experiences are a major, if not the major, determinant of who turns to psychoactive materials and becomes 'addicted.'" People who experienced trauma as kids, in other words, are more likely to turn to substances for relief, usually when they're in their teens, and addiction isn't so much a brain disease or a mechanistic interaction between neurotransmitters and substances as "a readily understandable although largely unconscious attempt to gain relief from well-concealed prior life traumas by using psychoactive materials."

But what about people like me—people who drank as teenagers or preteens, stopped drinking, and then picked up again as adults? Researchers have found that "late-onset" alcoholics—those who abstain or drink normally for many years before tipping over the edge into alcoholism, like I did—generally become alcoholics not as the result of genetic predisposition, but because of some circumstance or event in their life (divorce, job loss, major physical or psychological dislocation) that throws them off balance and leads them to drink more and more, until they become addicted. Women are also more likely to become alcoholics later in life; in one study, the average age when women became "problem" drinkers was forty-six, compared to twenty-seven for men.

Statistically speaking, women are still less likely to develop alcohol use disorders than men, and more likely to suffer serious health consequences, like nerve damage and cirrhosis, when we do—the result of social conditioning in the first instance (historically, drinking to excess wasn't considered "ladylike") and biology in the second (our bodies are smaller and contain less water than men's bodies, so alcohol affects us more, and we progress from heavy drinking to addiction more quickly than men do, a still-mysterious phenomenon known as telescoping). We can't do much about our biology, but we can decide whether, and how much, to drink, and we are choosing to do so more and more. In a massive 2016 analysis of international studies on drinking, researchers concluded that women born after 1991 are almost as likely to drink, and to drink problematically, as men born during the same period. That's a remarkable transformation from the situation one hundred years earlier, when men were more than twice as likely as women to drink alcohol, and three times as likely to have a drinking problem.

Perhaps because medical practice is slow to catch up with epidemiological trends, women's alcoholism still is frequently misdiagnosed by family doctors and therapists, who often point to depression or anxiety, rather than substance abuse, as the source of women's problems. My own primary care doctor, a woman, never thought to question my self-reported drinking—"about two drinks a day"—even when I showed up in her office with an endless series of mystery ailments that could all be explained by the gallons of wine and vodka I was pouring down my throat. Women—already judged more harshly than men for engaging in risky sexual behavior (*Slut!*) and failing to conform to traditional gender roles (*She's going to regret not having kids!*)—also suffer disproportionately from the stigma that clings to all alcoholics. The stereotypical male alcoholic is a tragic figure, driven to drink by a terrible childhood or a bad home life or genetic factors beyond his control. At best, he is a creative genius; at worst, an abusive boor. But what is the stereotypical female alcoholic? A crazy bitch. A hot mess. A train wreck. A *bad mother.* Pregnant alcoholics, in particular, face such intense stigma that they often hide their drinking or decline to seek treatment, leading doctors to misdiagnose pregnant alcoholics and contributing to some forty-two thousand cases of fetal alcohol syndrome a year.

We know a lot more about alcoholism than we did in the age of Freudian theories and racist speculation (seriously, rehabs should stop using that book). But we shouldn't be too smug. Despite overwhelming scientific evidence that addiction is not a disease of choice, nor a purely psychological problem addicts should be able to conquer through force of will, our public policies toward addiction are based on false assumptions about what causes addiction. We still pretend alcohol and drug addiction are moral choices, to insulate ourselves from the possibility that it might happen to us, or someone we love. We still delude ourselves with myths about the "type" of people who become addicted, believing the reassuring lie that education, money, upbringing, or love can inoculate our families from a disease that strikes almost indiscriminately. We still tell ourselves that since we can stop drinking after one or two, everyone else should be able to do the same.

So where should people turn if they want help with their drinking? The years I spent cycling through the treatment industry have led me to a few conclusions. First, the treatment industry helps no one by pretending that treatment just "works," and that if it doesn't, it's the alcoholic or addict who's the problem. When I relapsed after leaving Residence XII, I felt like I had failed treatment, not the other way around, and many of the narratives I learned in treatment reinforced that belief. I hadn't "stuck with the program" or been "willing to go to any lengths." I forgot that "meeting makers make it" to long-term sobriety.

And what was the solution the treatment industry presented me with when I wondered how to get sober again? I had to start all over at square one, by going—where else?—back to treatment. I met people in rehab who were there for the sixth, twelfth, or nineteenth time. That's a lot of twelve-thousand-dollar checks. (And the treatment centers I went to were among the most affordable ones in my area. Treatment can easily cost twenty, thirty, even fifty thousand dollars.) I don't mean to be cynical about the people who dedicate their lives and careers to helping people suffering from addiction, but research backs me up here. The problem with most treatment programs isn't that the people who are in them are lazy or don't want to get better; the problem is that their methods aren't evidence based, and that twenty-eight days is barely long enough to start sifting through the damage, much less to acquire a whole new set of coping mechanisms to deal with life on the outside.

The stigma associated with "failing" at treatment extends beyond the inpatient treatment world, of course; it's prevalent in recovery circles, too. Although AA officially welcomes people back from relapse with open arms, the recitation of sobriety dates ("I'm Erica, I'm an alcoholic, and my sobriety date is August 24, 2014") and comments like "I don't have another drunk in me" can alienate people who are "starting over" after "going back out." Many recovery groups and aftercare programs look askance at medication-assisted treatment (MAT) with drugs like naltrexone (which reduces the pleasurable effects of alcohol and helps heavy drinkers drink less) and acamprosate (which reduces cravings), because they see those drugs as a chemical crutch—much the same way groups like Narcotics Anonymous may consider heroin addicts who take methadone or suboxone to be active users.

Fortunately, some treatment centers (and many AA groups) are coming around. Hazelden, the largest residential treatment company in the United States, started offering medication-assisted treatment in 2012. (Gabapentin, a neurological drug I took to stave off cravings during my first six months of sobriety, is itself a kind of MAT.) Still, the stigma against chemically enhanced recovery is strong enough that fewer than one in ten alcoholics who get formal treatment use any kind of medication to help them stay sober.

What would actually help people avoid relapse, or bounce back from a "slip" without ending up far worse off than they were before? First, treatment programs need to start being honest with patients about the likelihood that they'll relapse, and stop treating relapse like it's an all-or-nothing proposition. Treatment taught me a single slip is the same thing as total failure (another AA maxim: "One drink, one drunk"), and as a result, I was so profoundly ashamed when I relapsed after spending so much time and money getting "fixed" that I told no one, lying about my drinking until it was obvious to everyone.

Second, they need to start teaching people how to deal with slips—not by treating them like catastrophic tragedies and running straight back to the cocoon of residential rehab but by taking immediate responsibility; reaching out to their support network, therapist, or sponsor; and making a new plan to address whatever caused them to relapse in the first place—right away, before they have an excuse to say "fuck it" and wreak more havoc.

Third, the treatment industry has to be more transparent about its methods. Most people choose a treatment center in roughly the same condition I did—desperate, terrified they'll lose their resolve, utterly uninterested in details like what kind of program the treatment center offers, the credentials of its staff, or whether most of the patients are there involuntarily or by choice. The second time I went to treatment, the hundred-plus other patients included a large number of young men on temporary leave from jail or prison, a cliquish group of young heroin addicts who scored every chance they got, and a high percentage of people who were there against their will. This is the kind of thing that might have concerned me if I was a sober person looking for a treatment center for someone else, but I was desperate, so I didn't care. Nor was I particularly bothered by the high number of people who had tried rehab over and over and still weren't "cured." Any one of those factors might be a red flag for a person who was seeking treatment in a rational manner, the way people choose schools or day cares or laundry detergents. But few people choose a treatment center in a rational manner. They do it hastily, whenever the elusive window of opportunity opens up.

Treatment centers take advantage of this desperation. You go in, you sit down, and they give you an assessment—a long list of questions that you're supposed to answer to the best of your ability. Has your performance at school, work, or home been affected by your alcohol consumption? Have you ever gotten into trouble at work because of drinking? Have you ever been hospitalized because of drinking? The treatment provider takes in all this information and tells you the best course of action for your individual case—which, surprise, surprise, typically ends up being a twenty-eight-day stay in their facility. (This is why it's important to know that you really do want to go to residential treatment before you start calling around. Outpatient treatment may be a better fit.)

The pressure doesn't let up when you hand over your insurance card. Starting about a week before you "graduate," the treatment provider will begin urging you to sign up to extend your time in their program through intensive outpatient treatment—by definition, a minimum of three three-hour sessions a week—followed by weekly outpatient treatment, group therapy, counseling, and follow-up visits. There are exceptions, of course—people with less severe addiction may be referred directly to intensive or regular outpatient care, and patients with severe mental disorders may be referred to dual-diagnosis programs that can address both issues simultaneously—but for the most part, treatment centers provide one-stop shopping—assessment, diagnosis, and long-term treatment, all under the same roof. When I was a patient at Residence XII, I had to take extraordinary steps to sign up for outpatient treatment with a private clinic outside the Residence XII system; my counselor warned me repeatedly against going outside the program, even though the private program I picked had meetings after hours and was in my city. Staying with Rez XII would have meant a long bus commute to the suburbs three times a week, when there were plenty of other programs less than a mile from my apartment. The upshot is that the relationship between a patient and a provider may last for two years or longer—from that first desperate, shaky phone call to the end of long-term aftercare, all billable to the same private company or nonprofit organization. It's a closed system that leaves little room for desperate people to argue or assess other options, especially if their insurance company will only pay for one chemical-dependency assessment.

Contrary to what you might believe, there are no nationwide

standards, and few formal education or training requirements, for addiction counselors. Most states do not require addiction counselors, who make up the overwhelming majority of staff at treatment centers, to have so much as a bachelor's degree, and fourteen states require addiction counselors to have only a high-school diploma. In my state, a chemical dependency certificate requires only a two-year associate's degree in "human services or a related field," or sixty semester hours of college credits from an approved school. (People who lack those credentials can acquire them while working as trainees; at Lakeside, ACs, or assistant counselors, outnumbered fully licensed counselors by a substantial margin.) One nationally representative survey found that only two of the programs surveyed were directed by a medical doctor, less than 15 percent had a single nurse on staff, and most did not employ even one psychologist or social worker. Another nationwide study found that half of all treatment centers had at least some full-time counselors on staff who had no degree; 59 percent had at least one counselor with a bachelor's degree; 62 percent had a master's-level counselor; and just 12 percent had a doctorate-level counselor.

In lieu of formal education, addiction counselors tend to have life experience: About half of all addiction counselors are in recovery themselves. They are, in effect, peer counselors with a couple of years of extra formal training. I don't mean to imply that people without college degrees can't or don't make excellent counselors—as former alcoholics and drug addicts who managed to turn their lives around, their life experience is, one might argue, a highly relevant qualification—but it's worth knowing what you're paying for. Few staffers at treatment centers have the kind of medical knowledge that you might expect when you check into what looks like a hospital.

Perhaps more concerning is the fact that many treatment centers engage in practices that have been shown to be ineffective—such as requiring people whose brains are still incapable of thinking in compound sentences to take in hours of films and lectures—or counterproductive, like pitting patients against each other, teaching them that it's their fault if they relapse, and treating a return to drinking or using drugs as a personal failure rather than the near inevitability it is. The 2012 CASA study concluded that the level of care at typical US treatment centers was so low it might constitute "a form of medical malpractice." According to the CASA report, "Much of what passes for 'treatment' of addiction bears little resemblance to the treatment of other health conditions," which typically involve testing, evidence, and proof. Imagine treating cancer, for example, with a combination of support groups and behavior modification techniques but no medication, long-term medical monitoring, or intensive follow-up. If we believe that addiction is a brain disease— and the American medical establishment does believe this—then it makes little sense that treatment centers aren't required to follow standard protocols for treating diseases.

Both times I went to treatment, I stayed in low- to midrange facilities—several notches above your typical government-funded treatment centers for the indigent, but several worlds away from the kind of places that get covered in the tabloids when a celebrity goes off to rehab. You may think that rich people are buying better treatment, but money buys amenities, not quality care. The main difference between a rehab that costs a hundred thousand dollars (like Passages Malibu) and one that costs eleven thousand (the average of the two programs I attended) is that the former will offer equine therapy, drum circles, and coffee, while the latter will take away your cell phone and *The New Yorker* and force you to quit drinking coffee and eating sugar.

So what do good treatment programs have in common? The biggest common denominator is that they include a truly personalized treatment plan—one that considers a patient's history of trauma, past experiences in treatment, goals, risk factors, cultural background, and individual strengths and needs. A treatment plan should also take into account potential challenges—like a partner with a substance-use disorder, a stressful work environment, or a lack of transportation to get to follow-up appointments. The plan might also include help accessing services such as childcare, welfare, and sober housing. If a person isn't religious, a good treatment center won't shame them for not believing in God, or push them to change their beliefs; if they've been a victim of gender-based violence, a good treatment center won't force them to reveal their history of trauma to a mixed-gender group (as I was at Lakeside-Milam, when one counselor didn't show up for work and we combined two ordinarily gender-segregated groups). A good treatment center will also, in my opinion, include programs for people with co-occurring mental disorders, like anorexia, depression, and bipolar disorder—not just a single group session once a week, but one-on-one counseling to identify underlying problems and come up with a posttreatment plan to tackle them.

Treatment centers too often deliver one-size-fits-all solutions to patients whose problems *are* distinct and diverse—go to meetings, learn to cope with triggers, don't isolate, call your sponsor if you want to drink. People who raise questions about one or more elements of the standard protocol, as I did, are told they suffer from "terminal uniqueness"—the (apparently fatal) flaw of thinking you're different from everyone else. It's a harsh and humiliating indictment—who wants to be the person who thinks she's more special than everyone else?—and it has the effect of shutting down discussions of *any* differences, as if someone with bipolar disorder who drinks alone in her apartment has the exact same issues as a person who copes with abuse at home by blacking out in public every night. I don't want to blame my treatment center, or the treatment system, for my failure to remain sober after I left, but the prevalence of relapse suggests that the problem extends beyond the patient and his or her "terminal uniqueness" to the inadequate tools we are given for surviving in the outside world. Most of what I learned at Lakeside-Milam happened between lectures and movies and writing assignments, when I was simply talking with other patients. I don't remember my treatment plan and I certainly didn't follow it—reading it now, I see it includes steps such as "get a job unrelated to journalism, with less stress/hours"—but I do remember talking to my roommate, Nancy, whose husband was about to leave her, about what it was like to feel isolated even when you're surrounded by people.

Good treatment lasts as long as a person needs it. There's little evidence that twenty-eight days is long enough for people to prepare themselves for living without alcohol or drugs in the outside world, and in fact, the twenty-eight-day limit seems to have its origins in historical accident: When the US military began sending soldiers to residential addiction treatment, four weeks was the longest they could stay away without being reassigned. Insurance companies adopted the twenty-eight-day standard, and since then, that (more or less—some insurers will only approve residential treatment in seven-day increments) has been the standard. The result is that residential treatment is essentially acute care—long enough to get a person stabilized and aware of the need to make big changes, but poorly prepared to deal with all the temptation and problems waiting for her outside the treatment center grounds. Fixing the patchwork, insurance-dictated treatment system in the United States is a trickier, longer-term project still. But as my own experience proves, even imperfect treatment can help.

For me, what "worked" to keep me sober, which was my goal, was a combination of medication, AA, cognitive behavioral therapy, self-forgiveness, and the rational-emotive tools I learned in rehab. Others might need group counseling, life-skills training, and a long-term intensive outpatient program. The point is to keep trying things until something clicks. If treatment "fails," it isn't because you failed the system, or even that the system failed you (although it can and, far too often, it does). You just haven't found what works yet. Relapse isn't failure. Dropping out of treatment isn't failure. The only failure is not trying again.

Acknowledgments

I started writing this book in my head about a year after my final stay in a detox center, in the winter of 2015, and began putting a rough outline on paper, titled "secret project," later that year. Eventually, I wrote a fifty-page outline in a single feverish weekend, and that's probably where it would have ended if not for the capable red pen of my agent, Daniel Greenberg, who helped me immensely throughout the writing process and talked me down from many ledges.

Josh, my bestie, was my constant through all the events of this book and remains so to this day. I'm grateful every day that he didn't give up on me. His unconditional enthusiasm and support for this project helped me through all the days of second-guessing and self-doubt.

I'm endlessly grateful to all the friends who put up with me through the worst parts, as well as those who got fed up but never gave up hope: Lisa, Stephanie, Renee, Mark, and especially Kevin. Thanks also to my friend Sandeep, who was generous enough to let me use his home on the island as a personal writing retreat whenever I got stuck.

To my boyfriend, Daniel, thank you for your love, forbearance, and encouragement. I'm so lucky to have you in my corner.

My family—in particular, Mom, Dad, my grandparents, and Cindy—supported me when I was struggling and have been my champions during the writing of this book. I hope they read it despite all the swears.

I'm grateful to Allison Lorentzen, my editor at Viking, for whipping this memoir into shape. She saw the big picture when I could not, and challenged me to rewrite, rethink, and reimagine this book. I am so grateful to her for pushing me to open myself up and for helping me tell my story with clarity and integrity.

This book would have been impossible without my sobriety, and my sobriety would be impossible without sober sisters who showed me that it was possible to live without drinking, especially Dallana. Thanks for helping me stay on the beam.

Author's Note

This book is a memoir, consisting of my recollections of my own experiences. While writing this book, I had frequent conversations with close friends and family members about how they remembered the events I describe, and I relied on my own contemporaneous journals, emails, and letters to bolster my memories. Much of the verbal dialogue has been recreated from memory, often with the help of these additional resources.

I obtained my treatment files from the Residence XII (inpatient) and Lakeside-Milam (inpatient and outpatient) treatment centers as part of my research. I also relied on files from Fairfax Behavioral Health that I obtained upon my discharges from that facility as well as workbooks and materials I received during my stays in treatment and detox.

The names of some people in this book have been changed, and a few identifying details have been obscured.